11 Words
for
Winning

Finding Certain Success
In an Uncertain World

Tom Ruddell

Capstar Corporation
Dothan, Alabama

Printed in the United States of America

ISBN 0-9649284-5-0 (hard cover)
       0-9649284-6-9 (soft cover)

Library of Congress Catalog Card Number: 99-094719

Cover and internal graphics designed by Bryant Graphics, Inc.

*Dedicated to all those people
who still believe that love of
God, country, and family
is the foundation of
true success*

Thank You!

There's no such thing as a self-made book. Any such effort requires many hands, many minds, and many thanks from a grateful author.

For me, the first three thank-yous are reflected in this book's dedication — thanks to God for allowing the words to come, thanks to my country for the freedom that allows the words to be published, and thanks to members of my family whose loving support endured all the outbursts of joy and frustration, not to mention wastebaskets overflowing with defective drafts.

Special thanks to Nancy, my partner in life for more than 36 years. We were a newsroom romance and I was her editor. Now it's her turn to be the editor, and she does a great job.

Our daughter, Jennifer Crowe, also wielded a mighty blue pencil in the course of all this, catching a slew of things that zipped by *both* her parents.

Also, I'd like to thank Cecil R. Price of Christian Information Ministries International in Dallas for his research on what bad or questionble choices are costing us as a nation each year, along with his most-helpful comments on the manuscript.

Linda Bryant of Bryant Graphics in Tampa has worked with me on a half dozen book and book-related projects in recent years and her superb design skills are reflected on the covers and all the graphics in between. Once again, thanks Linda!

And there is a wonderfully diverse group of folks who reviewed and commented on the manuscript, among them: D. Wendal Attig, Fred and Dr. Laurel Blackwell, Dr. Sandra Jones Campbell, Joe Ford, Bob Harris, Dr. J. Walter Jacobs, Rod Jurado, Carol Maier, John Powell, Rev. Dr. Michael K. Mitchell, Dr. Dan Mullett, Jim Orchard, Cecil Price, Dr. V. Chan Roark, and Barbara Winter.

Many thanks, everyone!

Contents

Introduction

What Was Isn't, What Is Won't Be

For starters:

Life today can spin so fast, switch directions so often, and have so many ups and downs that it can make you as confused as a termite in a yo-yo.

I wrote this book for you, for me, and for anyone else who wants to win certain success in a world that's *certainly uncertain* — a world that's complicated, chaotic, creative, competitive, compelling, certifiably crazy, and rapidly changing, changing, changing.

If you're confused about life, you need this book!

If you think you've got life all figured out, you need this book!

If you want to improve your life and win, you need this book!

If you believe you *can't* improve, you *really* need this book!

Now that you know you *need* this book, be prepared to embrace two very simple realities as you *read* this book:

1. What Was Isn't

If life doesn't have you joyfully pinging off the walls, take my word for it — you're wasting some or much time and mental energy focusing on past mistakes, mishaps, miseries, or magnificences.

You'll get a lot more out of this book if, between now and the page after next, you become willing to get over what *was* and get on with what *is*. Learn from the past? Yes! Keep looking back? No!

It reminds me of a scene from an old comedy flick. A has-been movie mogul is turned away at the gate of the studio where he once reigned supreme. Indignantly, he bellows at the guard: *"Do you realize who I used to be?"* Bottom line: Who cares? Move on!

2. What Is Won't Be

Life on this earth is temporary and so is every aspect of it. I don't agree with those who urge us to live life only in and for the present and let the future take care of itself.

You need *a plan* if you want to get the most out of life, and I hope this book will serve as a good guide. Live in the present, but *plan* for the future — and *plan to win!*

Even the sage advice to "live each day as though it will be your last" is rooted in planning for the *ultimate* future — Judgment Day. Between now and then, take advantage of what you learn from this book. Plan *well*!

Life in Context

In my view, the *best* context for living is a spiritual one as spelled out in great religious scriptures — principles and standards for successful living that apply as much now as they did in the days of the prophets and Gospel writers.

There's another context, though. It's the often mind-boggling *circumstances* we face in our daily lives.

I believe you'll discover, as I have, that the more you develop a strong and unchanging *spiritual* context for your life, the better you'll handle the ever-changing circumstances that surround you.

What to Look For

You'll find in *11 Words for Winning* a spiritual dimension that should be "common ground" for people of most religious faiths. You'll also find tongue-in-cheek humor that I hope will make the book as *enjoyable* as it is *enriching*.

Most quotations are set apart in the text, and are in a different type style. If a quote is not attributed to someone, the words are either mine or from a source I was unable to identify. My apologies for not giving credit anywhere it was due.

Chapters 1-4 deal with the *context* for your life's journey.

Armed with a stronger context, the rest of the book gives you an effective *process* — presented as five questions. While coming up with your own best answers, you'll discover five of the 11 words that I call your imperatives for *certain* success in anything.

What's that, you ask? What do I mean by *certain* success?

Do I mean certain *kinds* of success or do I mean success that will be a *certainty*? Well, my answer is...

Yes.

Applying the techniques and principles found in this book can help you find success in certain areas of your life. Adopting the winning *attitudes* found in this book is *certain* to bring you success in life overall, not just certain areas.

Like life, this book is a journey. It begins at the top of the next page. Get started and *gain much* every step of the way to winning — and to *Finding Certain Success in an Uncertain World*.

Learn from the book, have fun with it, and keep in mind that:

The only sure thing in life is uncertainty, maybe.

4

Part 1

The Context

- The 3 Accountability Words
- Circumstances in Perspective

You don't live life in a vacuum, you live it in the *context* of the people, places, things, and events which are all around you and which affect you.

In Part 1, you will gain a deeper understanding of the *context* for your life.

You will set the stage for certain success by harnessing the life-changing power of *personal accountability* through which you become a victor over — not a victim of — your circumstances.

---

11 Words for Winning

Chapter 1

The Power of Personal Choices

- **Choices / Circumstances / Outcomes**
- **Want / Way / Work**
- **5 Imperatives for Success in Anything**

Consider this:

Life is a series of *choices*, made under the *circumstances* that surround you, leading to *outcomes*, in keeping with the will of God.

Think about it.

You and I and everyone have the power to make *choices* for our lives. That power has been handed down to us for thousands of years, ever since Adam and Eve stood in the garden pondering the *circumstances* of having it all — except for that *forbidden fruit*.

"Hmmm. Should we or shouldn't we?" they probably pondered before making their *choices* and experiencing the *outcomes*.

What does God's will have to do with it? God lovingly gives us the power to make *choices*. He allows us *circumstances* in which to make them. And He watches over us in the *outcomes* that result.

You Are Making at Least One Choice Now

In fact, may I suggest that you are making at least one of those God-given *choices* right now. It's your choice to believe or not to believe that *life is a series of personal choices*!

You've just discovered the first three of the *11 Words for Winning* and making life even better. Why do I say *even* better? Because I believe that, whatever the *circumstances*, life is good!

Maybe you don't agree with that. Maybe you think life is the pits. If so, I'm counting on you to change your mind — to *choose* a different view of life by the time you've finished reading this book.

Yes, life is a series of *choices* — but....

It's the _circumstances_ that so often dominate the personal _choices_ we make, resulting in _outcomes_ that can _ruin_ our lives or _redeem_ our lives or _relegate_ our lives to ongoing mediocrity.

Circumstances are both the all-time No. 1 _excuse_ for making bad personal _choices_ and the all-time No. 1 _reason_ for making good personal _choices_.

Life is full of good or bad _choices_, good or bad _circumstances_ and good or bad _outcomes_. That's a statement on which you and I and everyone would agree — right?

But here's the huge, defining question:

Are the good or bad _outcomes_ you experience mainly due to the _choices_ you make or to the _circumstances_ you face?

It's the Choices!

I strongly believe — and I hope you do, too — that, in the long run, nearly _all_ the _outcomes_ in life are due to personal _choices_ and _not_ due to _circumstances_.

Take, for example, the splendidly symbolic story of identical twins. It's hard to imagine two boys growing up under worse _circumstances_.

Their father drank heavily, was on drugs, and flew into violent rages in which he beat the boys and their mother, too. Late one night, the father was killed in a shoot-out during a drug deal that went awry.

Their mother also was on drugs, turning to prostitution to support her habit. Now and again, she served time in jail. She died of a venereal disease before the boys were 12 years old.

The twins were homeless for a time, living on the streets. They were raised through the intervention of various government agencies and private charities, living in a series of foster homes — some of them pretty bad.

Each Interviewed By a Reporter

Years went by. The twins grew up. At different times, each was interviewed by a newspaper reporter.

One of the twins worked his way through college, became president of a very successful company, and was well-known in the community for helping disadvantaged kids.

A reporter interviewed him in the executive suite of his company.

The other twin got on crack cocaine. He murdered two people in a botched attempt to rob a convenience store. He was arrested and convicted on two counts of murder in the first degree.

A reporter interviewed him on Death Row.

The reporter who interviewed the first twin asked how he had become so successful that he ended up in an executive suite.

"I had such a lousy childhood," the twin laughed, "that I couldn't help but end up here."

The reporter who interviewed the other twin asked how he had gotten into so much trouble that he ended up on Death Row.

"I had such a lousy childhood," the twin said bitterly, "that I couldn't help but end up here."

Same question, same answer, same *circumstances*. But much different *outcomes*. Why? Much different personal *choices*.

Better Circumstances Than Ever

Today, you and I and everyone have a greater-than-ever range of good *choices* to make and better-than-ever *circumstances* in which to make them.

If you doubt that, take a hard look at how technology and a worldwide unraveling of government oppression and regulation are opening up more opportunities than ever.

Take a hard look at history, too.

When I was a kid (I'll be *dating* myself here) everyone was scared of polio. Public swimming pools were closed out of fear that swimmers might catch the deadly disease. I remember being told to stay away from other children, not share food with anyone, etc. Still, no one knew who was going to be struck down next — to die or be crippled for life, no matter *what* precautions were chosen.

Polio was an epidemic of *circumstances* far more than an epidemic of *choices*. The epidemic was eliminated by vaccines, and now many people don't even know what polio was.

An Epidemic of Bad Choices

AIDS stands out as a most-feared epidemic today. Unlike polio, AIDS cannot be acquired by the *circumstances* of casual contact. AIDS is sweeping populations of people who *choose* to engage in illicit sex, needle-sharing drug use, and the like.

The *outcomes*? Millions of people dying of AIDS and associated illnesses as a result of personal *choices*, not *circumstances*.

Are there innocent victims of AIDS? Yes, including the real *heroes* of the AIDS epidemic — the health care workers who risk their lives daily caring for AIDS patients.

Babies infected by their mothers, and adults infected by promiscuous spouses are two more examples of people whose life *outcomes* are forever altered by *someone else's* bad personal *choices*. But the number of such cases, relatively speaking, is very small.

Polio was eliminated as a major health threat with vaccines that protect people from bad *outcomes* no matter how *good* their *choices* might be. While important and needed, AIDS vaccines would serve mostly to protect people from bad *outcomes* no matter how *bad* their personal *choices* might be.

I share with many people, however, the view that *virtues* not *vaccines* best can bring a speedy end to the AIDS epidemic. It's a remedy, I might add, that's scoffed at by what I call "the anti-accountability crowd."

It's a remedy that's *undermined* by free needle exchanges for drug addicts. It's also undermined when one arm of government *hires* people to hand out free condoms in public schools while another arm of government *arrests* people for handing out free literature calling for people to live according to God's laws.

To set the record straight, it's the *Ten Commandments*, not the *Ten Suggestions*.

More Freedom, More Choices

If you still have an inclination toward blaming bad <u>circumstances</u> for whatever bad <u>outcomes</u> you may experience in your life, take a look at history — at the <u>circumstances</u> surrounding people who live where you live.

Go back 50 or 60 years and you'll find a world ravaged by the most devastating war in history. Compared to now, people who lived and died then were very short on good <u>choices</u> and very long on bad <u>circumstances</u>.

And what if you were born in the 1800s or earlier, anywhere in the world? The far-and-away odds are you would have been a peasant, serf, or slave, living under <u>circumstances</u> that offered such crushing <u>choices</u> as "work in the fields today or get flogged!"

And even if you were one of the few *lucky* ones born into the role of "flog*ger*" rather than "flog*gee*", imagine how "fulfilling" life would be working six days a week in the hot sun beating people!

Okay, you say, that was *then* and this is *now*. Aren't the <u>circumstances</u> today still pretty bad, even in prosperous countries? What about all the people being fired from their jobs? What about people working themselves to death just to make a decent living?

If those are questions rolling around in your mind right now, I'm sorry — but it still comes down to <u>choices</u>, not <u>circumstances</u>.

Why do I say that? Personal experience.

'You're Fired!'

I've always been a goal-oriented kind of guy and for *years* I pursued the goal of becoming vice president of a large company with responsibility for my field of expertise. It took 16 *years* to win the position, and less than 16 *seconds* to lose it.

"That's *outrageous!*" you'd probably exclaim if I shared *all* the details of how, back in early 1990, I was summarily fired for no apparent reason right after (1) getting the biggest bonus of my life for outstanding performance, and (2) being told I was to receive my professional association's highest international honor for my work — much of it for the company that fired me.

Or, you might say: "You think *that's* bad, Tom, listen to what happened to *me!*"

Know what, though? Such *circumstances* shouldn't make a hill-of-beans difference. What matters most are the personal *choices* that are made — *choices* that still can produce positive *outcomes*.

I made one of my best-ever personal *choices* as a result of what happened on that March afternoon in 1990. It was to *celebrate freedom* and not to *decry injustice*. If life were a car at that point, I ripped out the rearview mirror, focused on the road ahead, and pushed the accelerator to the floor. What was... *isn't!*

At 6:30 the next morning I started my own company, taking control of the *circumstances*. After all, if you're *your own boss*, you can't be fired — unless, of course, you're schizophrenic!

The *outcomes*? This book, for one thing. And for another, the serenity of sunrises with my wife Nancy on the deck of our country home, listening to birds in majestic oak trees, 400 miles from the scene of my former rat-race.

The End or the Beginning?

Some of the happiest people in the world today are people who lost their jobs and made some good *choices* on how to handle the *circumstances*. They chose between roads leading to:

Greater Failure	or	Greater Success
"I was completely devastated and asked the counselor to help me break the news to my spouse. I gave most of my life to that lousy company and this is what I get in return! There's no way I'll *ever* be able to get a job like that or earn anywhere near as much money. My life is ruined! I need a drink!"		"Freedom! Sure I was shocked. Yes, I'm disappointed. But I feel sorry for people who allow their lives to be ruined by job losses! I know my spouse and I can work through this and will come out of it even stronger than before. We will look at every option. We'll do whatever it takes—and *win!*"

It's been said the only difference between the words *bitter* and *better* is "*I*". A subtle difference separates *victim* from *victor*, too. For victims, it's "I-M." Come to think of it, not a whole lot separates *whiner* from *winner*, either.

To add even more good sense to the first three of the 11 words that can make life even better, here are brief quotations from some of my favorite authors:

Choices
The end result of your life here on earth will always be the sum total of the choices you made while you were here.
Shad Helmstetter

Circumstances

Never, ever determine the truth of a situation by looking at the circumstances.

Henry T. Blackaby & Claude V. King

Outcomes
(*Leading back to choices*)

Life is 10 percent what happens to you and 90 percent how you (choose to) react to it.

Charles Swindoll

So there they are — the first three of the 11 words to make life even better. Let's review them:

Life is a series of personal *choices* made under the *circumstances* that surround you, leading to *outcomes* — in keeping with the will of God.

Want, Way, Work

The next three words will help you *make* better *choices* and *produce* better *outcomes*. The three words are easy to remember because they all start with "W".

They pose three extremely important questions:

1. What do you *want* out of life?
2. What's the best *way* to get it?
3. What's the *work* involved and to what extent are you willing to do it and learn how to do it well?

There's an incredible tool you can use to come up with the best answers to these three questions. In fact, the same incredible tool helps you handle your *choices*, *circumstances*, and *outcomes*.

What's the incredible tool? A *computer*!

Let me ask you an important question. Do you carry a computer around with you at all times?

If your answer is "of course not," be careful! I asked you a trick question. I carry a computer around with me at all times and so do you. It's the one tucked between your ears.

That's right, it's your *brain*.

More powerful and more sophisticated than any computer ever designed by humankind, the super-computer God installed in your skull is programmed to analyze *circumstances* and make *choices* including what you *want*, the *way* to get it, and whether or how to do the *work*.

Pre-Programmed for Greatness

I believe every such on-board computer in the world comes pre-programmed by God with what has been described as "seeds of greatness." You and I and everyone have been given the power to control the *input* to our brains, so we also have the power to control the *output* — <u>*choices*</u> that produce <u>outcomes</u>, good or bad; <u>*choices*</u> that can make us winners or losers.

In other words, the brain we're born with includes a phenomenal basic software package that automatically tells us when and how to let people know we're hungry, require a diaper change, need to be held, and the like. Automatic "upgrades" of the software enable us to walk, instinctively avoid certain dangers, etc.

Overriding Our Programs

Parents, teachers, and others try to *override* our programs with input that may be good or bad. At some point, however, we start overriding most everything with our *own* input.

Here's a tongue-in-cheek perspective:

> Children listen just long enough to learn how to talk,
> then give up listening altogether somewhere between
> the age when *you* think they know all the questions and
> the age when *they* think they know all the answers!

For better or worse, then, we become adults with on-board computers programmed to make <u>*choices*</u> based on our <u>*circumstances*</u>, deciding what we <u>*want*</u> out of life, the <u>*way*</u> to get it and whether or how to do the <u>*work*</u>.

As examples of such input and output, here are stories about two people. The first story is sadly symbolic and the second is refreshingly real. Both center on <u>*want*</u>, <u>*way*</u>, <u>*work*</u>.

'Max Fraud'

The first person I'll call "Max Fraud" — a guy who represents many people in the world today.

Max Fraud worked for a large company loading trucks. One day, he dropped a box on his foot.

Since Max had programmed his on-board computer with a software package called "Mega-Loser," Max sued the company for not putting handles on the box he dropped and not reminding him to wear his safety shoes on the day he dropped it.

Max hired a bottom-feeding lawyer who specializes in such matters and, although they couldn't collect the millions of dollars they demanded in the lawsuit, Max *did* get monthly disability payments on the basis that he "no longer could do any work."

To improve his life-style, Max talked his wife into taking a second job. Then he "got on with life," dividing his time between watching trash on television and complaining about the "raw deal" he got when the court didn't award him *millions* for his foot injury.

Max's _want_? Find a _way_ to live without having to _work_.

There are lots of Max Frauds out there, looking for a *free ride* through life. I've met plenty of them, but I've yet to meet *any* of them whose lives are even a fraction as fulfilling as those who _want_ the best life has to offer, find an honorable and effective _way_ to get it, and learn how to *do very well* whatever _work_ it takes to succeed.

Which brings us to the second story.

Bob Wieland

Here is a person who is *real* — not just symbolic — and, in my opinion, is one of the greatest examples of someone whose on-board computer runs a software package called "Mega-Winner."

His name is Bob Wieland and he didn't drop a box on his foot while loading trucks for his employer. No, he stepped on a land mine — a booby-trapped mortar shell, actually — while serving his country in Vietnam.

Both of his legs were literally blown off his body.

Rather than sitting around feeling sorry for himself, Bob decided to get on with a lifelong career goal to become a professional athlete. He made up for the loss of his legs by developing tremendous upper-body strength, working out day after day.

Then he developed a special _want_ — to do something no one else had done. The _way_? Break a world powerlifting record. The _work_ was to develop the mental and physical strength necessary to bench press more and more weight until he broke the record.

Driven by a tenacious will to win and an unflinching faith in God, he worked out month after month until he did it — he broke a world powerlifting record!

Joy Was Short-Lived

But his joy was short-lived. Within moments, he was disqualified, his world record was taken away, and he was banned from powerlifting competition forever.

Why? Because of a rule requiring contestants to *wear shoes*. Bob, of course, *couldn't* wear shoes because he *had no feet*!

What would *you* do if, after months of _work_, you were denied what you _want_ because of a "technicality" in the _way_ to get it? Sink into deep depression? File a lawsuit? Quit?

Or would you do what Bob Wieland did — find another _way_ to get what you _want_ and... get back to _work_?

Bob Wieland became the first person in history to *walk* across America on hands and the stumps of missing legs.

He established a world record that — unlike powerlifting — couldn't be broken in a matter of minutes by someone lifting a few ounces more. Bob Wieland's walk across America set a record likely to go unchallenged forever — three *years*, eight *months*, six *days*.

His <u>want </u>went well beyond doing something unprecedented, too. He used his walk to help raise money to feed the hungry, and to share his unshakable Christian faith with everyone he met.

He went on to write an inspiring book called *One Step at a Time*, to become a great motivational speaker, to become financially independent, and to be an inspiration to millions the world over.

Installing 'Mega-Winner' Software

If you had to put one or the other label on the software *your* on-board computer is running on, which would it be — "Mega-Loser" or "Mega-Winner"? If you're not sure, which *should* you be operating with?

If you're running on "Mega-Winner" software, is it free of "viruses" that might have corrupted all or some of your brain's "operating system"? A "diagnostic" to check your on-board program can be found in the six words you just learned.

You're running on a "Mega-Winner" program free of "viruses" if you can agree completely with these five statements:

1. In keeping with God's will, I am producing positive <u>outcomes</u> in my life by making good personal <u>choices</u> — whatever the <u>circumstances</u> that surround me.

2. I know exactly what I <u>want</u> out of life.

3. I have found — or am actively seeking — a <u>way</u> to get what I <u>want</u> that's *right* in the eyes of God.

4. I accept full responsibility for whatever <u>work</u> is required, not only to *do* it but to do it *well*.

5. I keep the three main inputs to my brain switched to *positive* rather than *negative*.

The 3 Main Inputs

What are the three main inputs?

First, there's what you *read*. Positive input includes Scripture and books that lift the spirit. Negative input includes newspapers, magazines, pulp fiction, etc. that focus on the dark side of life.

Good books are good bread for your head!

Second, there's what you *see and hear*. "Mega-Loser" software automatically turns *on* television and radio for hour after hour of soap operas, talk shows, and all sorts of "news and entertainment" dwelling on perversion, sex, sensationalism, violence, and other trash. "Mega-Winner" software automatically turns *off* the trash, chooses the relatively few *positive* programs that *build* rather than *undermine* the human spirit, and opens a lot of positive books.

Bad television puts a bad stain on your brain!

The third input is the people with whom you associate. Even if you're forced to be around negative people in order to earn a living, you still can keep the input switched to positive by doing everything you can to prevent negative people from influencing you.

And in your personal life, choose to associate with individuals and organizations that lift people up rather than subtly or overtly tear people down.

In my work as a professional speaker, I've yet to find an audience that didn't shout back the correct words to complete the following sentences. You may wish to respond with a pen or pencil:

If you hang around with *losers*, you're likely to become a _____.

If you hang around with *winners*, you're likely to become a _____.

Let's Review the First 6 Words

So now you've learned the first six of the *11 Words for Winning*. Let's review them quickly, starting with the first three:

- *Choices*. Life is a series of personal *choices* made under the
- *Circumstances* surrounding you leading to
- *Outcomes* — in keeping with the will of God.

The second three words pose the three potent questions that will help you make better *choices* and experience better *outcomes*:

- *Want*. What do you *want* out of life?
- *Way*. What's the best *way* to get it?
- *Work*. What's the *work* required and to what extent are you willing to do it and learn how to do it well?

Now let's turn to the last five of the 11 words. They are five *imperatives* that you *must have* if you are to accomplish the *work* that stands between you and what you *want*.

5 Imperatives for Success in Anything

To make these five *imperatives* easy to understand, remember, and apply, I've turned them into the acronym MECCA — an acronym that also is very rich in symbolism.

In its religious context, Mecca is the destination of a journey made by people of faith. As a metaphor, Mecca has come to have a dozen second meanings, including "fulfillment of important life goals," "any place a person longs or desires to be,"and "joy of living."

The five imperatives for success the MECCA acronym represents are *sequential* in that it is necessary to master one before you can get full value out of the one that follows.

Take a hard look at *everything* you want to succeed at — your career, a business of your own, relationships, sports, hobbies, a spiritual walk, or anything else — and apply all five.

M for Motivation.

Without *motivation*, you will get *nowhere*. If you're a highly motivated person, you will work hard to harness the power of the other four imperatives. *Motivation* mobilizes the *will* to succeed!

E for Education.

Education is like the food and water supply for life's journey — nourishment for your brain. If you are motivated you can become educated. *Education* develops the *skill* to succeed!

C for Concentration.

Being motivated to be educated is not enough. You must concentrate *motivation* and *education* on specific pursuits if you are to succeed. *Concentration* joins will and skill to a *way* to succeed!

C for Communication.

All that *motivation*, *education*, and *concentration* are of little value unless you deploy them in the marketplace of ideas and effort. *Communication* puts will, skill, and way into *action*!

A for Achievement.

Motivation, *education*, *concentration*, and *communication*, will bring you the sweet fruits of *achievement* — which also is a powerful motivator. *Achievement* offers self-fulfillment and *success*!

There's much more to it, of course.

It's easy to say "I've got to get motivated." But what does it *take* to be motivated? To be well-educated, etc.?

In Chapter 8, you'll find that each imperative requires five important personal attributes, and that the imperatives and attributes form what I call *The MECCA Matrix*.

You'll have an opportunity to rate yourself on the five imperatives and the personal attributes, and you'll discover hundreds of useful self-improvement ideas along the way.

A Matter of Attitude

Every single one of the imperatives and personal attributes, of course, is a matter of *attitude*. It's "gospel" according to Zig Ziglar and many other great motivators and success gurus that:

Your *attitude* will determine your *altitude*.

No one with a negative attitude can become fully motivated to accomplish positive things. The same is true of becoming well-educated, of concentrating productively on gaining the best life has to offer, of communicating in ways that will build trust and friendships, and in achieving a *life of joy, and success* in its purest form.

11 Words, 3 Factors

In summarizing the *11 Words for Winning*, consider their groupings as important "factors" in getting the most out of life:

• *The Accountability Factor* in which you accept responsibility for the personal *choices* you make, the *circumstances* you face, and the *outcomes* you experience.

• *The Aspirations Factor* in which you *want* the best that life offers, find the best *way* to get it, and do the *work* that's required.

• *The Action Factor* in which you reach your desired destination by applying the five imperatives for success in anything, easily remembered by the MECCA acronym — *motivation*, *education*, *concentration*, *communication*, and *achievement*.

To complete the picture:

• *Accountability*: In keeping with the will of God, your life is a series of personal *choices* made under the *circumstances* that surround you, leading to *outcomes*.

• *Aspirations*: To make good *choices* and achieve good *outcomes*, know exactly what you *want* out of life, find the best *way* to get it, and do the *work* and do it well.

• *Action*: To do the *work* well and be successful, harness the power of *motivation*, *education*, *concentration*, *communication*, and *achievement*.

Chapter 2

The High Cost and History of Bad Choices

- **A Nation's 'Box Score'**
- **8 Decades from Which to Learn**
- **What the 8 Decades Should Have Taught Us**
- **The Age of Accountability**

Question:

If making good <u>choices</u> is the key to producing good <u>outcomes</u> in life, why do so many people make so many *bad <u>choices</u>*?

Perhaps the biggest reason is a decline in the standards of what's bad. How *far* have standards of honor and decency fallen?

- Back in 1939, when Clark Gable used the "D Word" in the movie *Gone With the Wind* ("frankly, my dear, I don't give a d---"), millions *gasped* and many walked out of theaters all across the land. Now, producers seem to believe people won't buy tickets unless they salt their movies with the "F Word" — over and over and over.

- Giving one's word once was considered one's bond. Now lawyers forage for loopholes in even the most ironclad contracts.

- Talking out of turn and chewing gum used to be among the most serious offenses in schools. Now it's murder and hard drugs.

- The key ingredient for success used to be hard <u>work</u>. For many people today, success is getting something for nothing.

What Bad Choices Cost Us

"Inspired" by writing box scores back in my newspaper days, I thought it would be useful to look at what bad personal <u>choices</u> are costing us in annual dollars impact on the economy.

A qualifier: If you don't see some of these <u>choices</u> as bad for you personally (gambling, overeating, smoking, etc.), at least see them as bad for millions of others who *ruin their lives* making them.

A box score of bad <u>choices</u> could be done on every country in the world, but here's one for the United States of America. The best-estimate numbers are so outrageously high that I'm *embarrassed* to put my country's name in the headline. So I'll just call it:

A Nation's Box Score

Bad Personal Choices	Annual Impact on Economy
Alcohol & drug abuse	$ 310,000,000,000
Cheating on taxes	195,000,000,000
Credit card debt	452,000,000,000
Gambling — legal & illegal	550,000,000,000
Health care fraud	100,000,000,000
Overeating & related health problems	100,000,000,000
Sexually transmitted diseases	50,000,000,000
Smoking & other use of tobacco	100,000,000,000
Workplace theft	40,000,000,000
Violent crime	450,000,000,000

That's more than two *trillion* dollars annually of bad personal *choices* — an *enormous* chunk of the world's biggest economy!

How much higher would the total be if we included accidents caused by irresponsible behavior, couples getting easy-out divorces, bankruptcies resulting from someone's greed, pornography, teenage pregnancy, and on and on.

Is There a Positive Side?

"But Tom," you may protest, "what about the *positive* side of those numbers — all the *jobs* that are being created?"

Well, sure. *Millions* of jobs depend on bad personal *choices* — prison guards, casino shills, burglar bar installers, drug counselors, fat-farm operators, and bomb-squad members, to name a few. In fact, if everybody — overnight — stopped making all those bad personal *choices*, we'd have massive unemployment.

But what if, over time, people started making *better choices*? Redirecting much of the two trillion dollars could bring massive tax cuts, boost take-home pay, double teachers' salaries, provide better health care at lower cost, and all sorts of other good things.

That, of course, is but a dream, although there's every opportunity and hope that over the next decade or so, we will come to rediscover better and more responsible ways to live.

Avoid Responsibility: Call It a 'Disease'

How on earth could *anyone* explain away the awesome impact of so many bad personal *choices*? One way especially popular nowadays is simply to declare them *diseases*.

There's a syndrome, phobia, addiction, complex, or "ism" that somehow can be attached to every line item in the Box Score.

Yes, some of the so-called "diseases" may have some basis in fact. Some may even be *real*. But not one of them *completely* excuses personal responsibility — including the bad personal choice of refusing to accept help.

If we are to believe that most any bad personal choice can be excused as a disease, why not cut through the great array of "scientific" labels and apply a *single* label to all of them?

In case no one else came up with it, let me offer "IBD":

Irresponsible Behavior Disorder

Now we can excuse *all* bad <u>choices</u> with a single term!

• Lost the family fortune at the race track? Oh, it's not his fault — he has *Irresponsible Behavior Disorder*.

• Dying of emphysema from smoking cigarettes? Oh, it's not her fault — she has *Irresponsible Behavior Disorder*.

• Shot up a school and blew away some kids and teachers? Oh, it's not their fault — they have *Irresponsible Behavior Disorder*.

• Died of a heart attack 80 pounds overweight from years of pigging out on pizza and ice cream? Oh, it's not her fault — she has *Irresponsible Behavior Disorder*.

• Killed three people in a head-on collision while passing a truck in a no-passing zone? Oh, it's not his fault — he has *Irresponsible Behavior Disorder*.

• Facing bankruptcy from years of buying too much stuff on too many credit cards? Oh, it's not their fault — they have *Irresponsible Behavior Disorder*.

Tune in, for a moment, to someone with a bad case of IBD — in a little monologue I developed a few years back. It's called:

Not *MY* Fault

My boss is always bugging me just because I make a few
    mistakes and show up late for work. *Not MY Fault!*
So all the stress from work is making me smoke and
    drink more and now I don't feel so hot. *Not MY Fault!*
And my spouse doesn't understand me and gets mad
    just because I'm tired and gripe a little. *Not MY Fault!*
So I stopped at a bar after work one night and met this
    great person who *really* understands me. *Not MY Fault!*
And we had a lot of laughs and a few drinks and decided
    to make a night of it. *Not MY Fault!*
And now the only thing *positive* in my life is the result
    of a lab test. *But that's Not MY Fault, either!*

Helping people explain away matters of individual discipline and responsibility as diseases can begin at an early age.

Parents and teachers having trouble getting children to pay attention is nothing new. But in the 1980s and 1990s, there came on the scene a "disease" called Attention Deficit Disorder — A.D.D.

Health-care people in the rest of the world are mostly mystified by a "disease" that seems to strike only *American* children, millions of whom are given regular doses of *prescription drugs* to help them pay attention.

With a new *industry* having grown up around it, dismissing A.D.D. as a cruel hoax is hard to do. But even granting there *is* such a malady, it's clear that far too many children are diagnosed as having it, and far too many drug doses are given to "treat" it.

Paying Attention Takes Work

Having raised two children, Nancy and I are hardly inexperienced with the challenges of getting kids to pay attention. And who knows? Maybe we'd be on the A.D.D. Bandwagon, too:

• If we had delegated much of our children's upbringing to daycare centers and babysitters

• If we had "childproofed" our home, putting valuables out of reach rather than teaching our children from the time they started crawling what was okay to touch and what was a "no-no"

• If we had kept our children quiet as babies and preschoolers by sticking them in front of TV "action cartoons," music videos, and other programs that focus on little, flipping rapidly from one thing to another

• If, when they were old enough to comprehend, we had let our children watch whatever TV programs they wanted to rather than limiting television to a few hours a week of quality programs, most often with one or both parents present

• If we had let them wallow in toys and games strewn all over the house rather than insisting that they focus on a limited number of things — and put them away when they're finished

• If we had let them eat *what* they wanted *when* they wanted rather than make them sit at the table until they had eaten *all* the nutritious (not junk) food put before them

• If we had let them do whatever they wanted to do on school nights rather than setting — and enforcing — *study hours*.

Easy Way Out? At What Cost?

Too often, I believe, stressed-out parents with children who have trouble paying attention will use a readily available A.D.D. diagnosis as an easy way out of what really may be a lack of loving parental discipline.

In the long run, the cost can be dreadfully high and the outcome potentially tragic as children learn early on that the circumstance of having a "disease" can relieve them of responsibility for their own actions — and that being medicated with drugs is an easy answer to problems.

Undermining the Underlying Value

Excusing bad personal *choices* undermines a foundational value on which most other personal values are based:

I will accept full responsibility for my own actions.

We are affected by *decades* in which this foundational value has been undermined *systematically* by government hand-outs, welfare-rights groups, suit-happy trial lawyers, radical educators, and other culprits. And we have only to look at American history to see how values and personal *choices* got to where they are today.

8 Decades from Which to Learn

Let's briefly examine eight decades in which people alive today have shaped their values. Themes and characteristics in each 10-year time block left a *legacy* that still affects us.

Enjoy and learn from this brief venture into "pop history":

The 1920s: A Time to Party & Cast Off Inhibitions

"The Roaring 20s" was the decade following World War I in which we partied, prospered, and experimented with new lifestyles.

There were flappers and bootleggers and "revenooers"; there was Fatty Arbuckle and the Keystone Kops; bathtub gin; the Charleston; gangsters; and vast opportunities to buy stock on the margin.

Legacies and lessons of the 1920s are:

• *Electronic media.* Instant transmission and receipt of information began as millions tuned in to crystal sets and primitive radios.

• *Women's rights.* With the newly won right to vote, women began asserting major influence on the political and economic scenes.

• *Organized crime.* Prohibition shifted demand for alcoholic beverages from legal sources of supply to illegal ones, thus elevating organized crime to the level of big business.

When the 1920s ended, the "party" ended as well.

The 1930s: A Time to Struggle & Help Each Other

A shroud in a single word hangs over the 1930s: Depression.

Unlike today, when families and friendships *disintegrate* over economic problems, relationships in the 1930s usually *got stronger* as people helped each other through hard times.

The darker the days, the bigger the dreams. People focused on positive, uplifting entertainment that, unlike today's bombardment of violence and hedonism, lifted the spirits and underscored personal payback from positive values. Millions got a boost from screen portrayals of glittering wealth, from lilting musical extravaganzas, and from a steady stream of slapstick comedies.

Legacies and lessons of the 1930s are:

• *The welfare state.* For the first time, the federal government played a massive, nationwide role in the economic well-being of individuals. The federal income tax was turned into an instrument of wealth redistribution. Social Security was imposed at a time when few lived long enough to retire. So people came to see it as relief from responsibility to provide for themselves in their "golden years."

• *Large federal debt.* Federal surpluses in the 1920s were making a dent in debt left over from World War I. It was in the 1930s, however, that the federal government set a pattern of deficit spending that ultimately turned the world's largest *creditor* nation into the world's largest *debtor* nation.

While the economy already was recovering by the end of the 1930s, it took what today would be an unthinkable event to bring a return to prosperity: a world war — a *second* world war.

The 1940s: A Time to Unite, Fight, & Revel in Victory

In the 1920s, we learned how to have fun and to be influenced by mass media. In the 1930s, we learned how to make do with little but still have hope — even big dreams. In the 1940s we learned to sacrifice — our lives, if necessary — for a cause clearly and demonstrably greater than ourselves.

Above all, we learned that, with a clear objective, faith in our leaders, and an ironclad national will, we can accomplish *anything.*

Legacies and lessons of the 1940s are:

• *World leadership.* With the devastation of Great Britain and the collapse of the British Empire, America became the most powerful nation on earth, assuming all the obligations and burdens of the role.

• *A world view.* Millions of Americans, accustomed to life within a few miles of where they had been born, experienced other parts of the world and came home with a much different view of life.

• *Industrial power.* We cranked up our old manufacturing facilities, added new ones, and ran them flat out to help our bombed-out allies blast three other industrial powers back into the last century. Then, without modernizing much of our own enormous means of production, we helped allies and ex-enemies alike build modern production facilities that became more efficient than our own.

• *The bomb.* Nuclear weapons greatly raised the stakes in relationships among nations, setting the stage for limited wars with objectives not as clear-cut to us as the crusade against the Axis.

• *The baby boom.* When World War II finally ended and the troops started coming home, we felt *entitled* to the good life. That spawned the greatest legacy of the 1940s: A population explosion called The Baby Boom. Tens of millions of new Americans came into the world in the late '40s. They were born to parents who had experienced *want* in the Great Depression and *pain* in the late great war.

The 1950s: A Time to Fulfill the 'American Dream'

The 1950s represented the last decade in which we clung to "traditional American values." We tried to shed some of those values in the '20s, but the adversities of the '30s and the '40s caused most of us to refocus on strong family units, the work ethic, and faith in God.

Post-war parents showered upon their children all the things they never had. Unknowingly, they placed *time-bombs* under traditional values — time bombs that began exploding when the Baby Boomers started becoming teenagers in the late '50s.

Legacies and lessons of the 1950s are:

• *Television.* It was invented in the 1920s, kept on the shelf in the 1930s because no one could afford it, introduced in the 1940s to wealthy tinkerers who liked to watch test patterns and, in the 1950s, spread like wildfire to nearly every household in America.

• *The automobile.* The 1950s made two-car households the norm, launched the Interstate Highway System, and sounded the death knell for profitable public transit in American cities.

• *Suburban sprawl.* Ex-Seabee construction expert William Levitt carved cloned-home communities out of cornfields. We became commuters, seeking the good life farther and farther from where we worked and shopped. Suburban shopping centers blossomed and urban centers started to decay — a problem that plagues us today.

• *A sense of "gap."* Complacent from being king of the world's mountain, we got a shocking wakeup call named Sputnik in the 1950s. For the first time, we saw a "gap" between ourselves and the Soviet bloc in science, technology and education.

• *The middle class.* Until the 1950s, America's middle class was relatively small. We had an enormous blue-collar and agricultural population and a small percentage of people who were wealthy. In the 1950s, class labels changed from "lower," "middle," and "upper" class to "lower middle," middle," and "upper middle" class.

By 1960, enough over-indulged Baby Boomers ("spoiled brats," some might say) had gotten old enough to cause major migraine headaches for their parents, teachers, police, and draft boards.

The 1960s: A Time to Rebel & Challenge Our Values

It started with the Beatniks in the late 1950s. Unsmiling, often unwashed, and costumed in black, they lamented life, wrote bad poetry, and smoked, sniffed, and injected all sorts of illegal drugs.

Hair was a dominant value of youth in rebellion in the 1950s and 1960s — but unlike the meticulously crafted "duck cuts" of the 50s, the 60s brought on less grease and more dishevelment.

The peace symbol was the dominant rune of the 1960s — on jewelry and jackets, tattooed on various parts of the anatomy, and spray-painted on walls.

But the scariest side of the 1960s was the unprecedented, nationwide call for destruction of American institutions, "justified" by the unpopular Vietnam War and proliferation of nuclear weapons.

Young radicals, urged on by leftist professors and pro-communist agitators, called for the overthrow of the federal government. Fear of anarchy spread as ROTC buildings were set afire and riots and violent demonstrations were organized and sparked by groups whose behaviors were out of synch with their "non-violent" names.

Dr. John A. Howard of the Rockford Institute, putting pen to paper and tongue to cheek, came up with this wonderfully witty yet all-too-true assessment of the 1960s:

Never Mind Over Matter
God is dead! The culture's shot.
The youth, it seems, have gone to pot.
The norms have vanished from the scene.
America will soon be "green."
Hooray for sex! Indulge the ego!
(Just so it's mine, not yours, amigo.)
Whate'er is fun, go have a bunch.
Milt Friedman's wrong, here's your free lunch.
So live it up! Postpone all care!
Your dirty jeans are debonair.
If wisdom is what you would find,
Consult your feelings, not your mind.

Tragically, the 1960s also was the decade of political assassinations. John F. Kennedy, Dr. Martin Luther King Jr., and Robert F. Kennedy fell to assassins' bullets, enshrining heroes greater than their actual accomplishments, and advancing some of their agendas more on waves of emotion than on tides of reason.

Legacies and lessons of the 1960s are:

• *Rebellious youth.* Teenagers who had been showered with much material stuff and sheltered from much discipline, became the first television generation. TV, along with acid-rock music, helped erode what traditionalists called "good order and discipline."

• *The anti-nuclear movement.* Nuclear weapons and peaceful use of the atom became lumped together, costing America its position as world leader in nuclear energy production.

• *Alcohol and drugs.* While booze and "dope" were problems in earlier times, it was during the 1960s that marijuana and hallucinogenic drugs became socially accepted within a large segment of our population. The "drug culture" was firmly established.

• *Degradation of the national will.* America's first "television war" left us torn. We lacked the will not only to win the war, but to maintain our technological and manufacturing edge. Higher-quality foreign-made cars and other goods flooded the U.S. market.

• *The "War on Poverty."* Our costliest "war" in history caused millions to shift responsibility for meeting their needs from themselves and their families to federal, state, and local governments.

• *Progress Toward Racial Equality.* One positive aspect of the 1960s was that nationwide acceptance of racial equality finally began to take root. While some government and private initiatives were ill-conceived, significant progress was made.

Each decade since the 1920s ended with a loosely defined mandate for change. When the 1960s ended, we were anxious to get the Vietnam War behind us and focus on enabling more segments of our population to enjoy the American Dream.

The 1970s: A Time to Anguish & to Change

We began to shift focus from violence to more traditional means of redress, thanks to changes in government but also to the tragedy at Kent State University in Ohio where campus rioting led to the tragic deaths of four students.

While there were many campus demonstrations and protests to follow, the animalistic behavior of Kent State rioters — which included throwing bags of human excrement at National Guard troops — spawned the rudest of awakenings for a generation of self-centered youth in rebellion. The troops opened fire and, across the land, violent temper tantrums en masse virtually ceased.

The 1970s also was the decade in which some of the radicals of the 1960s, who warned their peers never to trust anyone over 30, started — guess what? — *turning 30.*

We hoped that after 1971, when we lowered the voting age from 21 to 18, our youth would turn from protest rallies to polling places. It didn't work out that way. Participation in national elections *grew* in the 40s, 50s and 60s. But with 18-20-year-olds added, the 1970s saw over-all participation *drop* by more than 10 percent.

Legacies and lessons of the 1970s are:

• *Working mothers become the norm.* In the 1940s, women went to work to help win the war. In the 50s and 60s, as living costs and divorce rates rose, many women took jobs to supplement incomes or as heads of households. In the 1970s, a majority of women with children under 18 worked outside the home.

• *Loss of faith in political institutions.* Watergate, the Pentagon Papers, the resignation under fire of first the vice president and then the president, questions about regulatory effectiveness following the Three Mile Island nuclear accident, the Iran hostage crisis, soaring costs of welfare and other entitlement programs, and economic spasms helped us understand that big government can neither solve all our problems nor help us fulfill the American Dream.

• *The end of resource self-sufficiency.* Not since our dependence upon the British for tea in the 1700s had we allowed ourselves to become so dependent on foreign powers for resources as we did for oil.

• *The bitter taste of inflation.* Interest rates soared well into the double digits as the decade ended, with mortgage interest topping 20 percent. We learned painful economic lessons, most notably the need to bring costs of production under control and to become more competitive in the world economy.

The 1970s set the stage for a massive shifting of gears.

The 1980s: A Time to Change Direction

To some, the 1980s was "The Decade of Greed and Excess." To others, it was "The Golden Age of American Capitalism." A single coined-word became the lightning rod of the 1980s: *Reaganomics.*

It's easy to blame Reaganomics for the economic mess of the late 1980s and early 1990s. After all, Ronald Reagan was president and we tend to blame our presidents when bad things happen.

What *was* to blame? I call it "SoFoNo-nomics."

SoFoNo stands for *Something For Nothing* — the dark side of the American Dream. It's belief in the Free Lunch. We *say* we don't believe in the Free Lunch, but our voting habits show otherwise.

To the White House we sent the man who promised *lower taxes*. To Congress we sent those who promised us the *most benefits*.

If nothing else, Reaganomics demonstrated that lower taxes tend to boost economic growth and, as a result, generate more jobs and higher receipts to the federal treasury.

During his successful campaign to be President Reagan's successor in 1988, George Bush described the problem perfectly — but to millions of deaf ears:

Our problem is not that we tax too little but that we spend too much.

Years earlier, Ronald Reagan's fellow movie actor — the profligate swashbucker Errol Flynn — put it less eloquently but in more colorful and personal terms:

My problem is that my net income is exceeded by my gross habits.

In the 1960s, entitlements became a *huge* constant in the federal equation as politicians bought votes by promising womb-to-

tomb benefits — totally opposite President Kennedy's ringing enjoinder to "ask not what your country can do for you — ask what you
can do for your country."

Tax cuts, spending increases, and a mounting national debt
weren't the only objects of economic focus during the 1980s. Many
fingers pointed at massive *greed* in Corporate America.

Chief executives of large American companies entered the
1980s with salaries averaging 25 times those of their lowest-level
workers. By 1989, they were *91 times* that of "Joe Lunchbox."

The 1980s spawned additions to our language as narcissistic
Baby-Boomers wielded corporate power — terms that became syn-
onyms for greed: "greenmail," "golden (or platinum) parachutes,"
"hostile takeovers," "junk bonds," and "leveraged buyouts" (LBOs).

The legacy of the 1980s includes a tipping of the scale from
the potential burdens of government intervention to the potential
bounties of a free-market economy, a big part of that process
involving introduction of a scary concept: *the disposable employee*.

Legacies and lessons of the 1980s had more positives than
negatives, however, among them:

• *Communism collapsed*. As the decade closed, the Soviet
Union collapsed along with most other communist regimes, bringing
the long and burdensome Cold War to an end. Despite its faults, the
U.S. became the No. 1 role model for a greatly expanded free world.

• *The world became safer (at least temporarily)*. As fingers
were taken off nuclear triggers, focus shifted from the dangers of a
nuclear holocaust to the dangers we *bring upon ourselves,* such as
AIDs, illegal drugs, and violent crime.

• *We became more competitive*. On a world scale, the quality of
U.S. goods became the highest since the 1940s. And while painful,
many of the cutbacks, consolidations and restructurings made us all
the stronger to compete in world markets.

• *We became more generous*. The image of greed wasn't the
whole picture in the 1980s. Annual giving to charities by individuals,
corporations and foundations grew 55 percent faster in the 1980s than
in the previous 25 years.

The 1990s: A Slippery Stepping Stone

As we flipped our calendar to the first day of 1990, millions
were seeing dreams fade and, for the first time ever, average
Americans were worse off financially and less educated than their
parents.

Tons of trinkets from the 1980s ended up in a small but
gruesomely symbolic phenomenon of the early 1990s — the "Yuppie
Pawnshop," purveying pre-owned playthings such as Rolex watches,
Gucci apparel, beach buggies, and BMWs.

In 1990, the Gulf War lifted American spirits and provided a payback on the military buildup in the 1980s. The U.S. and its allies *devastated* the world's fourth largest Army in days.

But it didn't take long after Iraqi troops fled Kuwait in panic for Americans to take their eyes off matters of the world and focus them back on matters of their own wallets.

A sign on the wall of Bill Clinton's 1992 campaign headquarters served as a reminder of what the campaign *really* was all about. Forget all that other stuff: *"It's the economy, stupid."*

Once Democrats had control of the White House and *both* houses of Congress, Bill Clinton pushed for a socialization of health-care that would have brought *the biggest transfer of power to the federal government* in this century.

And then? A huge backlash. The 1994 Congressional elections brought the century's *biggest power transfer from majority party to minority party* — Democrats to Republicans. The call was loud and clear: *Less* government, *less* welfare, *more* self-reliance.

The power shift set the stage for fur-flying fights over morality and principle that shaped debates for the rest of the decade.

Legacies and lessons of the 1990s include:

• *Shattered standards of right and wrong.* A scandal-wracked White House. O. J. Simpson's murder trials. Murderers and rapists turned loose. We were left wondering whether right is what you can get away with and wrong is what you can't, based on who you are.

U.S. Military Officer lies about sex: Convicted, loses job.
U.S. Government Doctor lies about sex: Convicted, loses job.
President of the United States lies about sex: Acquitted, keeps job.

• *The end of big government.* The big-government era ended in the 1990s although, like die-hard communists in Russia, many voices continued to cry out for *more* government. Even the dreaded Internal Revenue Service got its teeth kicked in.

• *Demise of the professional politician.* Professionals guided by arrogance built the Titanic, amateurs guided by God built the Ark. In a sense, that describes a big part of the American political scene in the 1990s. Many old-line professional politicians were turned out of office in favor of values-oriented *idea people* who don't want to spend the rest of their lives feeding at the public trough.

• *Generation X.* The 20-somethings who emerged in the 1990s are computer-savvy, self-reliant, and *expect* change. Having grown up with TV remotes as their pacifiers, they focus broadly rather than take things one step at a time. Most believe in *more account-ability* for bad <u>choices</u>. And they're fast taking over leadership roles.

The 1990s just may have shed as much light as heat!

What 8 Decades Should Have Taught Us

Having made a quick review of eight decades of U.S. history that span today's youngest to still-active elderly, there is one question that should nag all of us: "What, if anything, have we *learned*?" What do *you* think, considering:

Decade	*What We Should Have Learned From It*
1920s	Huge problems result when government intervenes too much in human behavior, and not enough through common-sense safeguards on the economy.
1930s	The better road to economic recovery is the road along which people are rewarded for being productive in a robust and innovative private sector, not the road littered with government programs that reward people for not working and punish them for being rich.
1940s	Americans united behind a common cause can do more with less faster than any nation in the world.
1950s	The worst thing we can do to our children is give them the material things we didn't have while denying them what they need most — love, discipline, moral and spiritual values, and the kind of *education* that will help them be productive, self-fulfilled, and successful.
1960s	If we are to have a foreign war, make sure the cause is right and we have the will to win; if we are to have a war on poverty, make sure it's based on people taking responsibility for their own lives rather than becoming wards of the government.
1970s	We can't become all we can be as a nation if we elect to the highest offices in the land people who have strong leadership and weak moral values or strong moral values and weak leadership.
1980s	Governments that suppress people and control production won't last; governments that tax and regulate the least enable people to prosper and be productive.
1990s	With less government to lean on, more freedom to act, and more options available, success depends as never before on being responsible for our personal *choices*.

The Age of Accountability

If nothing else, the 1990s pointed us toward The New Millennium and what I call *The Age of Accountability*.

For *decades*, people who were considered "disadvantaged" were offered a government-subsidized "easy chair." Some welfare families reached *three generations* of non-workers, as politicians, judges, goofy professors, et al, proclaimed that *society* was to blame for irresponsible behavior from glue-sniffing to mass murder.

The 1990s brought the *end* of welfare as it was manifested in the 1960s "War on Poverty." Cries of outrage echoed through the halls of Congress and state legislatures all across America as one welfare program after another was dismantled or radically changed and people were held more accountable for their own lives.

Some welfare bureaucrats were mystified as:

• *Many thousands of people vanished.* When cutoff dates were set and other steps taken to force people to find work, whole segments of the welfare population seemed to disappear. Where did they all go? When the free ride was over, they found *jobs*.

• *Birth rates among welfare women plummeted.* States that put a limit on how many babies the government was willing to pay for saw a substantial drop in birth rates. Men who got welfare women pregnant and came back once a month to get their share of the government checks found themselves cut off, so to speak.

• *Fewer handouts brought more helping hands.* Some money squandered on welfare handouts wisely was redirected to new initiatives that help people stand proudly on their own two feet.

Many other signs of increased accountability appeared in the 1990s, including an often-silly aberration called "political correctness" in which thieves were called "non-traditional shoppers," etc.

And there was an *ambivalent* avalanche of lawsuits. Tobacco companies, for example, were held accountable for lying about the health risks of smoking while people who had *chosen* to smoke (in spite of health-risk evidence dating back to the 1950s) tried to hold tobacco companies accountable for their own bad personal *choices*.

The 1960s were tumultuous, the 2000s will be terrific. I'll characterize the transition this way:

**The 1960s and the
do-whatever-feels-good
Age of Aquarius
has given way to the 2000s
and the do-what's-right
*Age of Accountability.***

Chapter 3

Continuous White Water

- **5 Sets of 'Rapids' to Conquer**
  1. *Intense Competition Everywhere*
  2. *Organizations in Flux or Upheaval*
  3. *Reinvention of Jobs and the Workplace*
  4. *A Nation Awash in Professionals*
  5. *Toxic Environments*
- **It Comes Back to *Choices***

Picture this:

Life is like white-water rafting on a fast-running river, loaded with hazards but offering plenty of opportunities for success and enjoyment before it's over.

White-water rafting is fun, exciting, and reasonably safe. You choose your guide and a river that's mild, wild, or something in between. And even on the wildest rivers, there are some placid spots where you can catch your breath and get set for the rapids ahead.

For many, life today can seem like *continuous white water* — an exhausting continuum of *circumstances* in which people struggle to keep their heads above water. Life becomes one set of rapids after another with little chance to gather strength for things to come.

You're Not Alone

If such an out-of-control scenario describes your life, you're hardly alone. Symptoms abound:

- On average, people spend 80 percent of their waking hours thinking about things related to money.
- The average work week in the U.S. has topped 47 hours — the longest since flat-out industrial production during World War II.
- By the end of their work days, about a third of all employees and business owners say they feel "totally used up."
- The percentage of physical illnesses related to stress has risen to around 85 percent.
- Only 4 percent of *people considered successful* say they are happy in both their personal and their professional lives.

But no matter how tumultuous life seems, it still comes down to *choices*. You can choose to stop paddling like mad, let the raft flip over and, perhaps, drown — and many in life do that.

Or, you can choose to ask your guide (the boss) to yell "eddy out" and head the raft toward calmer waters along the river bank so you can take a break — and many people do that, or at least try.

There are other *choices*, too.

You can find the best time and place to jump out of the raft, swim to shore, get to a place where you can rest up — then choose (a) never to go white-water rafting again, (b) go again but on a river that isn't as rough and/or in a raft that's bigger and more stable, or (c) find a guide who won't make you work as hard. And many make one or more of those *choices*.

Finally, you could choose (d) to *do whatever it takes* to master rafting on even the wildest of rivers, enjoying the thrill of shooting *all* the rapids. Relatively *few* choose to do that.

Whether the "white water" in your life is *continuous* or just occasional, all the twists and turns, rocks and rills, forks and flumes, whirlpools and waterfalls, can be summed up and spelled out in a single word:

C-h-a-n-g-e !

If you are *flat-out excited* about change, you'll *love* life in the 2000s. If you feel *devastated* or continually frustrated by rapid change, you may well *hate* life in the 2000s and look back longingly upon times when things stayed pretty much the same.

The last person to change loses. Period!

5 Sets of Rapids to Conquer

I'll save for the next chapter some important *choices* large numbers of people are making as they seek to handle change in ways that make life more fulfilling.

For now, let's examine five trends — sets of rapids — offering plenty of *continuous white water* for The New Millennium.

1. Intense Competition Everywhere

"Everybody's doing it!"

"Doing what?"

"Doing everything."

"Everything?"

"Well, everybody isn't doing *those* things."

"Why not *those* things?"

"Well, they're so *hard* few people can, or want, to do them."

Competition has become so intense that law-of-the-jungle analogies abound. The gazelle, to cite one such analogy, wakes up in the morning knowing that failure to run faster than the fastest lion will result in being eaten alive. The lion knows that failure to run faster than the slowest gazelle will result in starving to death.

In business, competition continues to get hotter and hotter locally, nationally, and *globally*.

• A company in India wins a contract to process paperwork for a U.S. insurance firm, thanks to communication technology and well-qualified workers willing to do excellent work for less money.

• Growers in Brazil sell oranges in Florida — cheaper.

• Thanks to quality workmanship and competitive prices, there's a waiting list for Harley-Davidson motorcycles — *in Japan*.

• Sugar growers in the U.S. bring in foreign workers. Why? Few Americans are willing to cut cane because the work's *too hard*.

• *Hundreds* often bid on a single request for proposals or to fill a high-level, good-paying job.

Competition for Jobs & People

The strong U.S. economy in the late 1990s brought about a phenomenon not found in much of the rest of the world — simultaneous labor shortages and labor surpluses.

• *Shortage* : Unskilled and semiskilled workers. Wages and benefits rise as employers compete for employees.

• *Surplus*: Middle management people cast out in the restructurings and downsizings of the 1990s, and technicians who didn't keep up with changes in their fields. They must settle for less or stay unemployed.

• *Shortage* : Top-end people in the most sophisticated areas of science and engineering. They're in such short supply that companies seek higher immigration quotas to *import* such talent.

• *Surplus*: College graduates who pursued "soft studies" in "easy" areas such as journalism. If every reporter and editor of every newspaper in America dropped dead tomorrow and journalism students took their places, there would be students left over. And each year, colleges turn out enough broadcast majors to fill every job at every television station in the country.

• *Shortage*: Leaders who lead with inspiration and integrity.

• *Surplus*: Managers who manage by intimidation.

Tough Choices

Long-term success in the global marketplace depends on how you and people everywhere answer some fundamental questions— questions that really pose tough personal *choices*:

• *Are you willing to work harder than your competition?* Americans by the late 1990s were working harder than at any time since 1945. But more and more stressed-out people started "downshifting" their careers so they could spend more time enjoying life.

Who *is* your competition in your quest for success in your

career of business? To what extent are you willing to *do more and do it better* in order to *achieve* more?

> Traffic is always light on the extra mile.

Are you willing to pay the price and go the extra mile?

• *Politically, are you willing to help get rid of government policies and programs that undermine personal and organizational productivity?* Public policy for decades has penalized productive people and rewarded unproductive people.

> In America, we tax work, investment, employment, savings and productivity while we subsidize non-work, consumption and debt. It's time we start to reverse this trend.
>
> Jack Kemp

What people and policies will you vote for in the next election?

• *If you are in business, are you willing to invest in the latest and best technology and methods?* When coupled with hard work and incentives to work harder, the best technology and the best methods will enable you to meet or beat your competition.

But what of the future?

> In the private sector, the biggest obstacle to higher investment is the tax code. The U.S. taxes savings and capital at a higher rate than any other industrial nation, even hitting corporate profits twice — first as company income, second as dividends.
>
> *Wall Street Journal*

What will you invest in? What will you lobby politicians for?

• *Will you invest in* <u>education</u> *— yours and everyone else's?* Unless you will, there's no way you or your country can keep up with rapid change and ever-increasing *global* competition.

> Only 7 percent of U.S. high school graduates are prepared for college-level science courses.
>
> CNN Factoid

Are you willing to become better educated and increase your job skills? What will you advise your children to do? If the school board comes up with a *good* plan to improve the quality of <u>education</u>, will you support it — even if it means paying higher taxes?

2. Organizations in Flux or Upheaval

More than any other single factor, intense competition has brought about the second element of *continuous white water* — organizations of all sorts in a constant flux with some in upheaval.

Back in the "good old days," two surefire rules of thumb were:

(1) the larger the institution, the more stable it is likely to be, and (2) the higher you go in a large organization the more likely it is that you will enjoy great job security.

Both thumbs were smashed in the 1980s. They were *amputated* in the 1990s.

Whole industries have been so shaken by change that onetime bedrocks of security for shareholders and employees alike turned into "silt fines" washed down-river by all that *continuous white water*.

More than two thirds of the 100 largest American industrial companies of the 1950s disappeared from the list by the end of the 1990s. Many of them were broken up, taken over, out of business, or left in the dust by competition.

Secure Industries? No Longer!

There's so much flux and upheaval throughout the once-stable world of large institutions that security-minded employees have few places left to hide. A few examples:

• *Banks & related financial institutions.* To be fired from a bank used to take *effort*. Now all it takes is being in the wrong place at the wrong time.

> Little banks are gobbled up by big banks. Big banks are gobbled up by bigger banks. Little banks are started to provide services that are not provided by big banks. The little banks grow, then are gobbled up.

• *Utilities.* Having spent a big chunk of my career working for large utilities, I can tell you first hand that *they ain't what they used to be*! Telephone giants were broken up in the 1980s. The pieces started acquiring each other in the 1990s. Electric companies, which used to share ideas with each other routinely, now are in dog-eat-dog battles over each others' service territories.

> Long-distance telephone service got so competitive in the 1990s that a practice called "slamming" became commonplace. Customers are switched to another service without their permission. Junk mail, junk e-mail, junk faxes, and irksome phone calls deluge consumers as competition heats up among more and more service providers.

• *Colleges and universities.* Although tenure still protects some professorial sloths, the job-life expectancy of a university president has plunged to an average of less than 3.5 years. Academic excellence and cutting-edge programs abound, but many academicians struggle to keep alive those programs that contribute little to the bottom line.

> "Sorry, professor, but unless you can raise another million dollars and increase your enrollment by at least 100 students, we'll have to close down the Center for Ancient Babylonian Dances."

• *Government.* Getting rid of inept government workers used to be well-nigh impossible. Now whole agencies are eliminated or cut to the bone, often because their work is farmed out to private companies who can do the job better at lower cost.

> Remember Norton? He was the guy on Jackie Gleason's old *Honeymooners* TV series who worked as a "subterranean sanitation engineer." Well, guess what? The city privatized all its sewer maintenance and construction work, and Norton was fired the first time his new employer did an employee productivity audit.

Political appointees always have been vulnerable, of course — especially when caught with hands in the public cookie jar, or when caught belonging to the wrong political party after an election.

Tips for Handling Flux & Upheaval

Here are tips for young people contemplating careers and for older people concerned about what the future will bring:

• *Never count on anything beyond what you are legally owed by your employer.* Vested pensions, funds in a 401K, accrued vacation pay, etc., should be secure. But be wary of even those "entitlements," especially if your employer is in financial trouble or may sell out.

• *Cut expenses and get out of debt.* Do all you can to accumulate enough liquid assets so you and your family could survive for a year or more in the event you suddenly lose your job. Never leave a balance on a credit card and hold other debts to a minimum.

• *Be a reliable, top-producing employee.* Try to be *the last* person your employer would want to cut. But never assume that good performance will protect you.

• *Act as though you plan to stay until retirement.* But update your resume and keep an eye open for situations offering better pay and benefits, working conditions, flexible hours, job security, etc.

• *Consider your job temporary.* Focus on employability, not on survivability. How qualified are you to get a job elsewhere?

• *Diversify your income.* If you and your spouse work for the same firm, decide whether one should find a different employer to keep the axe from falling on *both* of you. Look for *proven* ways to earn income on the side.

3. Reinvention of Jobs and the Workplace

There's much more to organizational flux and upheaval than mergers, takeovers, spinoffs, and cuts in workforces. The nature of organizational design, individual jobs, and the way people relate to each other, continue to go through enormous change as well.

Large or small, private or public, organizations are reinventing the workplace to reduce instability and beat intense competition.

Hierarchical management is being replaced with empowered work teams. Frontline employees are being given more and more accountability for results. Traditional chains of command are being eliminated. Compensation systems are being redesigned, tying rewards to performance rather than to years of service and the cost of living.

And whole categories of jobs are being eliminated through a process summed up by a single word. Coined in 1967 to describe diversion of money into high-yielding direct investments, this little-known word has come to mean much more:

dis·in·ter·me·di·a·tion \ *noun:* the elimination of employees between the customer and the employer's computer.

A classic example of *disintermediation* is the ATM — automated teller machine. Stick your card in the slot, hit some buttons, bypass all the employees, go straight into the bank's computer system and make a transaction. Automated phone systems, direct ordering of products on the Internet and robotic stock-picking machines in distribution centers are all forms of disintermediation.

Will You Be Disintermediated?

A classic bit of whimsy making the rounds during the 1990s was that the factory of the future will be operated by one employee and one dog. The employee's job will be to feed the dog and the dog's job will be to keep the employee from touching the equipment.

But with more jobs available than there are qualified people to fill them— at least in the U.S. — fears that robots would put everybody out of work clearly are unfounded. For one thing, it takes a lot of highly skilled people to make robots and keep them running.

Another unfounded fear, dating to the advent of the assembly line, was that workers would become mindless automatons. Big shortages of "burger-flippers" notwithstanding, the greatest demand now and in the future, it turns out, is for "knowledge workers" — people who can quickly and creatively handle and apply torrents of ever-changing information and ideas.

The illiterate of the future are not those who can't read or write, but those who can't learn, unlearn, and relearn.

Alvin Toffler

Shamrocks & Webs

A 1980s-conceived concept called the "Shamrock Organization" offered an accurate glimpse of how many organizations will get their work done in the 2000s.

Anxious to keep payrolls to a minimum, only about a third of the work is done by full-time employees, according to the Shamrock model. Roughly another third of the work is done by contract specialists on a full or part-time basis. The rest is "outsourced" to vendors, some running cost-effective businesses out of their homes.

Meantime, many organizations seeking to survive have *disemboweled* hierarchical management. Gone, even from some government agencies, are managers to manage the managers managing hard-to-manage managers.

Neatly drawn stacks of lines and boxes showing who reports to whom no longer reflect the way the best organizations operate.

Forget the organization charts! The best of the best now run like organizational webs of working relationships focused on who can do what needs to be done — faster, better, and most *profitably*.

Micro-Careers

Generation X-ers can't imagine why *anyone* would even *want* to spend an entire career working for the same company, let alone working in the same job. Willing to take a hike when they become bored, when things don't go their way, X-ers expect to — and will — make many job changes between graduation and retirement.

> Employment in the future will be characterized by micro-careers. People will find themselves in constantly shifting assignments. We'll work on short-lived projects, with changing sets of coworkers in fluctuating roles that require new competencies.
> Price Pritchett
> *Fast Growth*

For people uprooted from traditional workplaces, career survival will depend on ability and willingness to make personal changes.

As with anything else in life, the people who do the best job of changing with the times and with the organization's needs will succeed. Those with their heads stuck in the past will fail.

Reinvention of jobs and the workplace means:

• *A "traditional education" is less likely to be a good admission ticket.* Deep but narrow specialization was much sought-after when there were lots of jobs demanding specialization. But no longer.

A good *general* education that includes sufficient depth in more than one area of specialization will work best and a blending of *relevant* "hard skills" and *relevant* "soft skills" could be ideal.

• *The ability to get along with people and communicate well will become more important to career success.* Simply mastering technical skills won't be enough. For example, the only way six or so heads can be better than one on an empowered work team is for team members to have good communication skills and work well together.

• *Keeping career and personal life in balance will be tested.* Reinvention of jobs and the workplace will put many a marriage to the test in the 2000s, especially if both partners are immersed in fast-changing work environments.

People in the 2000s will step in and out of fast-paced work arenas in order to enjoy other aspects of their lives. Many will turn down higher-paying and vulnerable management positions so they can have more job security and time with their families.

4. A Nation Awash in Professionals

The special collections room of a big-city's main library holds a telling commentary on the times.

In the Yellow Pages of the city's 1960 telephone directory, there were three pages of attorneys — all listed in discreet lightface type. Ten years later, the lawyers had managed to spill onto a fourth page.

By 1980, the number of pages of legal-eagles had proliferated to 14, thanks in part to the appearance of small display ads.

And now? Well over *100 pages* of attorneys — many more pages than the whole "Automobile" section! Included are full-page ads with blood-red type that seem to cry out:

> Attention all victims, get your due!
> Stop in for a free visit and then let's sue!

The number of lawyers in the U.S. now tops *one million* — far more than advance-degreed scientists and engineers. Most other countries have more top scientists and engineers than lawyers.

During an overseas speaking tour, one of my hosts told me there were only 6,000 lawyers in his whole country. When I asked if he'd like 50,000 or so of ours, he laughed and said: "No thanks!"

The United States is the most litigious nation on earth with well over 20 million lawsuits filed each year, and the implications are far greater than a drag on the economy.

> ...the mere filing of lawsuits has forced industrial plants to shut down, doctors to abandon their practices, playgrounds to close and dads to stop coaching Little League. The defendants decided they simply could not afford to fight all the lawsuits, even though they might well win.
>
> Parade Magazine

It's hard to argue that, like lawyers, the U.S. has too many doctors. Some rural areas have a chronic *shortage* of doctors while, in urban areas, doctors aggressively advertise to drum up patients.

Intense competition among hospitals caused some to close, others to sell to big chains, and almost all to cut staff. "Managed care" programs that control soaring costs sometimes leave patients with lower-quality care and leave doctors, seeing their incomes drop, wondering whether a decade of jumping through costly educational hoops was worth it.

Law and medicine aren't the only professions undergoing great change. Take a look at the accounting profession.

> ...the staid accounting profession has been transformed into a Darwinian jungle. The major accounting firms are reeling from a sharp rise in competition, shrinking audit business in the wake of client mergers, waves of litigation from disgruntled clients, and unprecedented layoffs and partner defections. Accountants are leaving the business in droves. Those who remain are finding that the law of survival of the fittest prevails over generally accepted behavioral principles.
>
> Lee Berton
> *The Wall Street Journal*

What's more, two kinds of reform may *devastate* the U.S. legal and accounting professions in the early 2000s.

• *Tax reform.* Sweeping simplification is virtually assured as more and more people get fed up with a tax system so complicated that 20 accountants can come up with 20 different bottom lines on a single tax return. Clear and simple do-it-yourself tax returns not only will put many accountants out of work, but a legion of tax lawyers as well. Wildlife will join taxpayers in the celebration as fewer forests will have to be cut down to produce all the paperwork.

• *Tort reform.* People outraged by the plethora of lawsuits eventually will break through the phalanx of trial lawyers guarding the legislative halls and force repeal of many "Lawyer Relief Acts" that (1) enable virtually anybody to sue anyone for anything with little or no risk, and (2) make legal procedures and language so complicated that hiring a lawyer becomes a necessity.

Other Professions Changing, Too

Computer-Aided Design and Computer-Aided Manufacturing (CAD-CAM) and other high-tech systems have greatly changed the engineering profession. A single computer now replaces an army of old-fashioned engineers with slide rules.

In the New Millennium, thousands of existing and emerging companies will rise or fall on their engineering and design capabilities. That will assure plenty of high-paying jobs for top-level engineers able to stay on the leading edge, and hard times for a legion of lower-level engineers not able to keep up.

Teaching is the *highest* paid profession in Japan and, except for the ministry, the *lowest* paid profession in the United States.

There is a *huge* need for first-rate teachers. There's also a huge need to pay teachers for *top performance* rather than for longevity and how many times they go back to the world of academia to get their educational tickets punched.

A single outstanding teacher can sow seeds of greatness in even the most culturally and educationally deprived students. The problem is that we have far more poor teachers than truly outstanding teachers, and each day we have to live with the results.

A poor surgeon hurts one person at a time. A poor teacher hurts 30.
Ernest Boyer
People magazine

An Acute Shortage

As much as we need more good teachers, perhaps the most neglected, underpaid, short-handed profession is the one that, in the *continuous white water* of the 2000s, is needed as never before.

We have an acute shortage of *honorable* people to convey the Word of God — deeply caring people who can bring home to individuals buffeted by fast-changing times the *unchanging* message that there really *is* a living, loving God who offers hope and strength to overcome obstacles, no matter how daunting.

Where opportunities in the professions are concerned, none offers so great a challenge than the clergy. For the right person — the sharp and selfless one with a love of God as well as humankind — it can also be the most fulfilling professional calling.

5. Toxic Environments

Demand for cleaner air and cleaner water, worries about global warming, dire outcries over dooming the spotted owl, the bog turtle, the furbish lousewort, etc., all have to do with the *natural* environment — and there's no doubt *that* environment is more toxic than it should be.

But the "toxic environments" I'm talking about have to do with the *human* side of things, from two perspectives — the toxic environment created by the circumstances that surround people and the toxic environment created by the choices they make.

Let's begin by looking at what many people today find as the most toxic aspect of their circumstances:

Crime & Violence

We know crime and violence is a toxic environment when, in spite of thousands of additional police officers, sheriff's deputies, state troopers, and the like; and in spite of locking up a larger percentage of our population than any other nation on earth, crime and violence in America is worse today than it was in the roughest cow towns of the 1870s — even when there was little or no organized law enforcement and virtually every male over 14 carried a gun.

About *five million* Americans are in prison, in detention centers, on probation, or on parole. More than half the states in the union don't even have that many people living within their borders! In fact, there are more than 100 *countries* in the world that don't have that many citizens!

By reading this far, you've found plenty of reasons why crime and violence have become such threats to so many people. But allow me to point once again to the *toxic element* that has become Public Enemy No. 1 to everyone from upscale suburbanites sinking mega-bucks into alarm systems to inner-city single moms hoping to see their kids alive after a day in a violence-wracked school:

T-e-l-e-v-i-s-i-o-n.

In 1939, RCA Chairman David Sarnoff predicted that television, coupled with a universal increase in schooling, could propel the American people to "the highest general cultural level of any people in the world." That forecast ranks right alongside British Prime Minister Neville Chamberlain's pronouncement a year earlier that he and Adolf Hitler had achieved "peace for our time."

Twenty-some years after Sarnoff's rosy prediction, Newton Minow, chairman of the Federal Communications Commission, declared television to be "a vast wasteland."

Study after study has linked television to crime and violence but, unlike all the years it took to show that cigarette smoking caused cancer, little of substance has been done about it — even with a shocking wave of in-school murders.

Thirty years after declaring television a vast wasteland, the former FCC chairman said:

One evening as I watched, with my remote control in hand,
I flipped through the channels and saw a man loading his gun
on one channel, a different man aiming a gun on another channel,
and another man shooting a gun on a third. And if you don't
believe me, try it yourself...In 1961 I worried that my children would
not benefit much from television, but (today) I worry that my
grandchildren actually will be harmed by it.
            Newton Minow in 1991 speech at the
            Gannet Center, Columbia University

And a decade after *that* — in spite of congressional hearings, scathing editorials in the print media, a ratings system of questionable value, and various pledges by broadcasters to clean up their programming, there's *more* violence on American TV than ever!

Television is a drug with a plug.

Many children growing up in front of TV screens consider violence to be some sort of societal norm. They enter their teen years ready to accept the "technical training" that television has to offer —

how to load, aim and fire a gun; where to stick a knife to kill a person, how to loop the wire around someone's neck; and exactly what sorts of delightful screams, blood-splatterings, and painful deaths result from each method.

Study after study shows a direct correlation between television and violence. Remote areas of Canada that were free of television also were virtually free of crime and violence. When television was introduced, crime and violence rose toward levels of violence prevalent in areas where television had worked its wiles for many years.

Television is so effective as a training tool for criminals that there have been thousands of cases from coast to coast in which specific crimes have been traced to specific TV shows.

Excellence Amid Massive Doses of Trash

There's nothing wrong with the *technology* of television. There also are many *excellent* programs mixed in with massive daily doses of trash. The problem is not with the technology, but with a commercial-TV programming process that goes something like this:

Paying for programs requires advertisers. Attracting advertisers and making the most money requires high ratings — and the more people watch a program, the higher its ratings. Luring more viewers means offering violence, sex, and gore in the most sensational ways, for that, unfortunately, is what seems to sell best.

The process can be characterized like this:

Two talk-show hosts are in a ratings battle. They leave no rock unturned to find bizarre, vile, and controversial "guests" who will attract viewer attention. If one talk show features "lesbian hockey players who want to marry their priests," the competition will do whatever it takes to turn up a squad of "transvestite dirt bikers who eat their young."

Even the Children's Shows

The process even extends to children's programming. In the course of a Congressional inquiry into violence on television, the producer of a children's show noted there are two versions of each episode produced — a "violent version" for the U.S. market and a "nonviolent version" for distribution overseas.

Asked why, the producer pointed out that the violent version would be unacceptable to stations in foreign markets but was necessary in order for the show to attract viewers in the U.S.

If we agree television programming is a major cause of unprecedented crime and violence, and if we also agree outright censorship is not realistic in a "free country," how do we solve the problem?

Parents assuming full responsibility for the viewing habits of their children and setting a good example by reading more and watching only programs that reflect positive values would help reduce America's inexcusable crime rate to return to pre-TV levels.

The odds of *that* happening are even less than of returning to censorship laws. There are too many dysfunctional families, "latchkey kids" on their own, and parents whose priorities are elsewhere.

What *can* be done?

• *Apply public pressure.* Find a way to persuade legislators, network executives, and others to limit crime, sex and violence in programming — especially explicit material that glamorizes violence.

• *Go after the sponsors.* Boycott or at least publicly chastise businesses that *pay* for programs devoted to crime, violence, foul language, and illicit sex. Recognize companies that sponsor good programs and help them promote viewership.

• *Isolate toxic programming.* If violent and sexually explicit programming can't be banned altogether, at least make it an optional extra rather than standard fare. With most people saying they don't approve of violent and sexually explicit programming, why not make those who want it pay extra to get it rather than making those who don't want it pay extra for keeping it out of their homes?

• *Encourage viewership of quality programs.* Work through parent-teacher groups and school boards to encourage viewership of programs that contribute to education. Support efforts to bring more educational channels and educational programming into the home.

The 'Criminal Injustice' System

There's much more to fighting crime and violence than cleaning up television programming.

The criminal justice system in America — the one that "provides justice for criminals and injustice for their victims" — also is in need of reform if we are to clean up our toxic environments.

Maximum sentencing laws, aimed at slowing the revolving door through which convicted criminals too quickly end up back on the streets, have contributed to prisons jammed to capacity. When prisons become overcrowded, other laws kick in that result in inmates — some of them violent — being turned loose.

On average, four *years* was added to the sentences of nonviolent offenders, often resulting in nonviolent criminals spending more time behind bars than violent criminals.

The odds of a "white-collar criminal" mending his or her ways after a short sentence is greater than someone convicted of a violent crime — especially if prison is perceived by the white-collar criminal as something awful and by the violent criminal as little more than a refresher course in criminal behavior in a setting that "ain't as bad as the neighborhood I come from."

What sort of deterrent is a prison sentence when 70 to 80 percent of convicts end up back in prison within two years of parole?

One question hotly debated is whether prisons are too hard or too soft. To anyone who has lived comfortably with no intention of ever committing a crime, even the "nicest" of prisons would seem too hard. But to one who has grown up in the worst of conditions and has been hardened by violence and deprivation, prison life may not seem all that bad. Such a person may view crime as a "no lose" situation:

> If I get away with it, I get to live better. If I don't get away with it,
> I *still* get to live better — and have lots of time with guys who will
> help me figure out how to get away with it the next time.

Our society's concept of "cruel and unusual punishment" contributes mightily not only to crime, but to the billions of dollars it is costing us each year to run our ever-expanding prison system.

Is requiring able-bodied men to convert large rocks into small stones the old-fashioned way cruel and unusual punishment? Is imprisonment without TV, air conditioning and wall-to-wall carpet cruel and unusual punishment?

Should prisoners be given law libraries and unlimited time to cook up frivolous lawsuits — such as the inmate who sued because he wanted crunchy rather than creamy peanut butter?

Other Toxic Environments

I've focused on the toxic environments of crime and violence, television, and flaws in the criminal justice system, but there are other toxic environments to deal with as well.

• *The home.* If you're a parent, what sort of environment do you create for your children? What sorts of TV programs, magazines, books, and other material do you allow in your home? How do you treat your spouse? Your parents? Other family members?

• *The workplace.* Water coolers, among other places, often become "character assassination zones" where employees gather to condemn, complain, or criticize. Do you contribute toward a toxic environment at work? Do you stay above it all? Try to stop it?

• *The social arena.* Are you a gossip-monger? Do you try to make yourself look and feel better by putting other people down?

Clean up your toxic environments! I challenge you to do this:

> From the time you get out of bed tomorrow morning until you go to
> sleep tomorrow night, do not criticize, condemn, or complain — not
> once, and not about anyone, anything, or any situation. Instead, use
> every opportunity to smile, edify everyone, and avoid all the toxic
> people and situations you can.

If you couldn't manage to get through a day without criticizing, condemning, or complaining, keep trying until you've done it, then keep doing it. You'll find your environment a lot less toxic!

It Comes Back to *Choices*

Where the five *continuous white water* challenges are concerned, what *choices* will you make? To what extent do these challenges represent threats? How about opportunities?

No matter what *circumstances* you face, *outcomes* of success and happiness depend almost solely upon the personal *choices* you make, including what you choose to do and whom you choose to be.

Your Checklist

Activity: Circle a number on the scale of 5 to 1 to rate the effects of each *continuous white water* challenge on you. (5 means very much, 1 means not at all, and 4, 3, or 2 are somewhere in between. For each challenge, write one or two *choices* you will make to overcome it or keep it from affecting you.

Challenge	Effect on You
1. Intense Competition Everywhere	5 4 3 2 1

I choose to: _____

_____

2. Organizations in Flux or Upheaval	5 4 3 2 1

I choose to: _____

_____

3. Reinvention of Jobs & the Workplace	5 4 3 2 1

I choose to: _____

_____

4. Awash in Professionals	5 4 3 2 1

I choose to: _____

_____

5. Toxic Environments	5 4 3 2 1

I choose to: _____

_____

> **People are always blaming their circumstances for what they are. I don't believe in circumstances. The people who get on in this world are the people who get up and look for the circumstances they want, and, if they can't find them, make them.**
> **George Bernard Shaw**

Chapter 4

An Ongoing Search for Stability

- **5 Places People Search for Stability**
    1. *In Down-sized Dreams & Lowered Expectations*
    2. *In an Avalanche of Entrepreneurship*
    3. *In Bunkers, Barriers and Backrests*
    4. *In a Quest for Better Solutions*
    5. *In a Return to Many Traditional Values*
- **A Perspective on Change**

Forget it!

There's no such thing as a completely stable life, even though many people spend much of life searching for one. Will a day come when you are *completely stable*? Absolutely! It's the day you die and rigor mortis sets in.

Some people go through life *excited* about change and would be *bored stiff* — a kind of living rigor mortis — if life were *too* stable. They quickly find ways to shake things up. Sadly, though, *most* people seek a "comfortable rut" in which to *just get by* in life. A rut, you may already know, is "a grave with the ends knocked out."

> Most people die at age 25 but their bodies don't catch up until they are 65 and can be buried together.
>
> Benjamin Franklin

Healthy Havens of Stability

Remember from the last chapter the differences between white-water rafting and the *continuous white water* many people are caught up in these days? One *big* difference is that, on a rafting trip, there are stretches of placid water — *stable* areas— in which to become rejuvenated and prepared for more rapids to come.

Life is like that.

• If you're struggling with *continuous white water* at work, a stable, loving family to come home to can help you go back to work and dig your paddle deeper into the fast-running currents.

• If you're going through the *continuous white water* of adolescence with a torrent of temptations from your peers, having the stability of a loving mom and dad to confide in can make a huge difference in which way you steer your "raft of life."

• If your marriage is headed for the rocks, the stability of a good counselor can help you get past the rocks to calmer waters.

• If any or even *all* aspects of life have you careening toward a deadly water fall, you always can turn to the greatest source of strength and stability in the universe — a living, loving God.

Seeking Stability in the Wrong Ways

Many believe they can bring stability into their lives by:

• *Controlling others*. By exerting enough *power* over people, they reason, life will be better — more stable — because they will be in control. At worst, such people are workplace tyrants, child and spouse abusers, and even murderers. At best, they are well-mannered manipulators and charming con artists.

> The only person you *really* can control is yourself. When you take control of yourself and become a better you, people notice and it's amazing how often they are inspired to do likewise. Situations and relationships can turn from stressful to stable.

• *Not caring or pretending not to care*. "If I care or people *think* I care, I might get hurt," goes the rationale, "so I'll be indifferent to most everything and everyone."

The 1990s were even *labeled* by some as "The Decade of Indifference," with many finding it *cool* not to care.

Millions sat glued to TVs one Thursday night in 1998 to find out how the comedy sitcom *Seinfeld* would end after nine incredibly popular years on the air. The last-ever episode of the "show about nothing" was a funny but all-too-true commentary on life today.

Jerry, George, Kramer, and Elaine — the show's four main characters — stood on the sidewalk of a small New England town indifferently videotaping an armed robbery across the street.

Arrested for doing *nothing* to help the hapless robbery victim, they ended up in a "show trial" aimed at upholding the new Good Samaritan Law they had violated. Called as witnesses against them were people the four had treated badly or with indifference during dozens of episodes over the years.

The series aptly ended with the main characters going to

prison for what many millions of people everywhere could be tried and convicted of quite easily:

This court finds you, the defendants, guilty of *Criminal Indifference.*

5 Places People Search for Stability

Controlling yourself more than others, and caring about others more than yourself, are two of the *surest* ways you or anyone can create havens of stability in times of *continuous white water*. More about *those* ways later on.

But let's look at five other ways people — rightly or wrongly — pursue their *Ongoing Search for Stability.*

1. Down-sized Dreams & Lowered Expectations

Barry Joye is an ex-$6-an-hour house painter I know who became a millionaire before he was 30. A *master* at helping people expand their dreams and expectations, he came up with an incredibly clear analogy to explain how people down-size their dreams and settle for less than what life has to offer.

"Every one of us is born with two 'wheels' in our heads — a *dream wheel* and a *settle-for* wheel," Barry Joye explains.

When children are young, he continues, their dream wheels spin like mad. They think they can *have* anything, *do* anything, and, when they grow up, *be* anything they want.

At an early age, however, their settle-for wheels are set in motion and their dream wheels slow down. They start learning they *can't* have, do, or be anything they want.

Many things cause dream wheels to slow or stop. Maybe it's a parent afraid a child will be hurt by trying to achieve too much. Maybe it's a teacher who proclaims: "you will never amount to anything!" Maybe it's TV programs showing life at its worst.

Surveys of inner-city neighborhoods show a *majority* of teenagers expect to die by gunfire before age 21. So it's easy to understand why they stop dreaming of success and happiness, and settle for drugs and other ways to kill the pain of having a life with no future.

There comes a time in the lives of *all-too-many* people when the once-spinning dream wheel gets rusted out and turns hardly at all, but the settle-for wheel grinds on and on. This used to happen later in life; but now, unfortunately, it happens much earlier.

Rather than want and expect more out of life, they reason, it's easier and less painful to simply want and expect less.

Settle for Less, Just Get By

Put in terms of <u>want</u>, <u>way</u>, <u>work</u>, many people *by their mid-20s* have figured out that it's easier to give up on what they <u>want</u> —

their dreams — and settle for whatever *way* is readily available and whatever minimum amount of *work* is required to get by.

The best many of them can do is give that rusty old dream wheel a creaky turn or two by "treating themselves" to things the settle-for wheel won't let them afford. Maybe that's why more than 20 percent of the average American household's disposable income goes to pay for ever-greater amounts of credit-card debt.

Great nations and happy families are built on great dreams by great dreamers — people with vision, confidence, faith, and a *passion* for *achievement*. These are people who believe:

> Dreams *do* come true, and my dreams *will* come true!

Sadly, though, we're living in times when far too many people have rewritten that classic call to action:

> Well, there's no way I'll ever be able to *do* it,
> so why should I bother to *dream* it?

When your dream wheel is spinning, it means you're alive with hope for a better tomorrow. You're *excited* about life, and stand out in a crowd of *"sheeple"* — to use the comparison to sheep — whose collective settle-for wheels emit a depressingly dull drone.

Downsized Dreams Are Unnecessary!

No matter how indifferent they seem toward life and the world around them, Generation X'ers — people in their 20s and 30s — are a bit more willing to spin their dream wheels than their forebearers.

They're saving more money for retirement than their parents because they don't believe Social Security and other entitlements will even *exist* by the time they want to retire. "Sophisticated survivalists" who adapt quickly to change, they're also more likely than their parents to take risks and seize opportunities.

They lend credence to what I believe to be true:

> It is not necessary for people to downsize their dreams and lower their expectations if they are willing to open their minds to new ideas and subject themselves to healthy doses of self-discipline. Virtually *anyone* can become a millionaire if, for a long time, he or she will trade *instant* gratification for *delayed* gratification and work both hard and smart. Some of the richest people in America, and in many other countries, were penniless immigrants willing to work, save money, and invest wisely — and many never went to college.

Studies of millionaires in America show that relatively *few* got their money through inheritances or hitting lotto jackpots. Most of them — including many immigrants who started with nothing —

became rich by *living below their means* and having a strong <u>work</u> ethic. Over *years* of consistent, persistent effort, they never rewarded themselves with too much too soon, and just kept plugging.

They became millionaires largely by living frugally. Many *always buy used cars*, letting *someone else* take a new car's big first-year loss of value. Many buy their clothes at discount stores. You'd never guess many are wealthy — and they *prefer* it that way.

In a nutshell, they put *savings* ahead of *status*.

Two other traits stand out. They learned to handle change and *most* of them started their own businesses.

> A fast-changing society poses major dangers for people who have difficulty adjusting to new situations, but it is a wonderland for entrepreneurs — those imaginative and energetic self-starters who can recognize emerging needs and create ways to fill them.
> Edwin Cornish
> World Future Society

Which leads me to introduce the second of the five ways many people pursue *An Ongoing Search for Stability*:

2. An Avalanche of Entrepreneurship

Being in business for yourself long has been the dream of people the world over.

Business ownership fits an almost inbred need for independence. It also underscores the great truth that working for yourself to fulfill *your* dreams is much more likely to bring success and happiness than working for others so they can fulfill *their* dreams.

One reason this may well be the *best* time to start a business is the tremendous and growing need for personalized services.

The more that big organizations eliminate the personal touch in their dealings with people, the greater becomes the market for putting some *humanity* back into relationships — between businesses and their customers, top management and disgruntled employees, etc.

In the last chapter, I gave you what may have been a word totally new to you — *disintermediation*, in the sense of getting rid of employees between the customer and the employer's computer.

Well, I've coined the following word to underscore money-making opportunities from the often-unwise practice of replacing human beings with machines. With tongue-in-cheek, here it is:

> an·ti·dis·in·ter·me·di·a·tion·ism \ *noun:* rebellion by customers fed up with automated systems devoid of contact with human beings.

Opportunities to offer a human touch go well beyond people

being sick and tired of jumping through voice-mail hoops when calling businesses — or even social-service help lines.

> Welcome to the fully automated suicide hotline. Listen carefully to the following 27 options: Press 1 if you are planning to use a gun, Press 2 if you have a fast-acting poison, or 3 if you have a poison that will take two or more hours to kill you. Press 4 if you plan to jump from a building 20 or more stories high, and 5 if you....

Anyhow, let's get back to the *Avalanche of Entrepreneurship*.

As great as the opportunities to start your own business may seem to be, there are harsh realities to contend with:

• If you're like most people, you'll choose a business that, at least for the first year or several, involves trading more of your time for fewer bottom-line dollars than would be the case if you had kept working for someone else.

> First you trade your time for *no* dollars to get started and drum up business. Then you trade your time for *some* dollars on the business you drummed up. Then you try to collect payment on services rendered, all the while trading more time for no dollars to drum up more business.
> Consultant after one year in business

• Overall, the odds of succeeding in a new business are against you. Some 80 percent of small businesses fail in the first 18 months, and a *much higher* percentage are history within the first five years.

> Is the American Dream owning your own small business? I did that. Made a million dollars. And it cost me $1.2 million to do it!
> Burke Hedges
> *Who Stole the American Dream?*

What is the underlying reason so many small businesses fold so quickly? It's simply that, in pursuing the age-old wisdom that "you have to spend money to make money," the *spending* part quickly overwhelms the *making* part.

If you're planning a traditional business, the start-up and general operating costs can be awesome — rent or mortgage, electricity, municipal fees and permits, advertising, liability insurance, security systems, furnishings, equipment — and a biggie: *employees*.

Officeless Offices, Storeless Stores

Technology and tax laws make at-home businesses very attractive, indeed — the "officeless office" when services are involved, and the "storeless store" when products are involved.

Not only does a business at home avoid the considerable

expense of setting up shop elsewhere, but tax laws allow deductions for properly allocated residential space that's used exclusively for business. This avoids business expense while saving on household and transportation expenses.

Rapid advances in technology, along with declining costs of acquiring it, have helped create a burgeoning cottage industry. Even large corporations are recognizing the advantage of letting employees work part of the time (or even all of the time) out of their homes.

Well over 40 *million* Americans work full or part-time out of their homes. Some are on payrolls but *most* run home-based businesses, either as their primary sources of income or as supplements to their incomes.

Fulfilling Dreams Through Entrepreneurship

If you have big dreams and want to fulfill them through entrepreneurship, you have a limited number of realistic options.

I've grouped these options under five key questions. Each question has a logical series of *choices* that may or may not be right for you.

1. *What is the best way to make plenty of money?*

> Win millions playing Lotto, break the bank in a casino, hit the big one at the track, etc.

> Except for a few genius-level professionals who end up being banned from casinos, gambling is a heavy tax self-imposed upon people who don't understand mathematics. Your odds of hitting a big lottery jackpot, for example, are less than being hit by lightning.

> Play the markets: stocks, bonds, commodities, and such.

> To become rich on investments requires having enough money to invest in the first place and not many people do. With interest rates on "safe" investments pretty low, and throwing darts at stock listings often yielding better results than some of the country's best investment gurus often get, how productive would it be to bet on speculative investments — even if you had the money?

> Sue somebody.

> Lots of people are doing it nowadays, but it usually requires you to suffer and not everyone is up to it. The more you suffer, the more you might win in a lawsuit. Of course, your lawyer is going to walk away with a big chunk of the money without having to suffer nearly as much as you will. And if your suffering isn't genuine, you may get a chance to trade lots of time for a few dollars making license plates.

> *Work* for it.

> Aha! This option *always* has been the most obvious and most likely avenue to wealth, despite all the monumental efforts to avoid it.

2. *If you agree that working for it is the best choice, then you are faced with two more* <u>choices</u>*:*

> <u>*Work*</u> for someone else.
>> We've already hammered on this one but, for the record, it can lead to financial freedom. Just be *exceptionally* good at what you do, be prepared to change jobs many times to get to the top, and put a big hunk of your earnings into a good investment strategy to cushion against downsizing, a takeover, periods of unemployment, etc.

> <u>*Work*</u> for yourself.
>> In spite of the high failure rates of new businesses, the odds of becoming very wealthy — a goal actually achieved by fewer than 2 percent of the population — are higher working for yourself than for someone else. And if you can start your business *part-time* while still having the security of a paycheck, not only are your *odds* improved, but your *risks* are reduced as well.

3. *If you choose to* <u>*work*</u> *for yourself, then you must choose from among several economic sectors. Which one is the most likely to yield success?*

> Agriculture.
>> Forget it. Millions have gotten *out* of farming and many of those who are left would *love* to sell you their farms — cheap.

> Manufacturing & Inventing.
>> Although there are people who have started in their garages and gone on to run mighty factories, the odds of becoming wealthy by that route are pretty slim. What bank in its right mind would bankroll a manufacturing plant for someone who hasn't already demonstrated success as a manufacturer? And if you're clever enough to invent something that can become a marketplace hit, the odds are you won't also be clever enough to manufacture and market it. Best bet: invent something and get *someone else* to make and sell it.

> Real Estate & Construction.
>> Lots and lots of money has been made in real estate and construction when things are booming, and lots and lots of money has been lost when the real estate and construction markets have gone bust. And competition can be brutal, especially when business is bad.

> Services.
>> Like other countries, American history is a succession of economic eras — from agriculture in the 1700s and 1800s, to manufacturing in the 1800s and 1900s, and on to the "service economy" of the late 1900s. More fortunes were created in the 1980s by finding better services to provide and better ways to provide them than in any other sector. From easy-access computer networks to overnight

package delivery to 24-hour banking to horoscopes via 900 numbers, there is good money to be made in services. But competition is fierce. Spend lots of time and money coming up with a new service, and the fickle consumer may or may not respond. If the new service is a success, people and organizations with more resources than you have will be there in a heartbeat to compete with you.

> Distribution.

Once upon a time, 85 percent of the cost of a product was in making it and 15 percent of the cost was in distributing it. Manufacturing has become so efficient it's now the other way around with 85 percent in distribution. That creates an enormous opportunity for people who can find better ways to bring products and services to consumers. More fortunes were made in distribution over the last couple of decades than in any other economic sector and that will continue.

3. *If, up to now, you decided the best way to make plenty of money would involve working for yourself in the distribution sector, which of the following choices would work best for you?*

> Become a wholesaler.

Yeah, sure — just when everybody and his uncle is "bypassing the middleman" to cut costs and become more competitive. Sam Walton became a *gojillionaire* getting rid of almost *everyone* between the manufacturers and his Wal-mart stores.

> Open a traditional retail outlet.

Decide on a line of merchandise that is likely to sell, then find a good location that isn't awash in competition. Rent a store front, buy inventory, do some advertising, hire a clerk or two. The odds of this one leading to financial success are a little better than starting a family farm. There are more than 4,000 abandoned shopping malls in America, and retail stores are closing in droves.

> Buy someone else's traditional retail outlet.

Watch it! If you're buying someone else's *successful* retail outlet you may pay top dollar for walls on which the seller sees the handwriting but you don't. Think of how many popular restaurants have changed hands, then went out of business. Some of the most successful retail entrepreneurs make big money by knowing when to get out as well as when to get in. And if you buy someone else's *unsuccessful* retail outlet, make sure your turnaround strategy makes *more* sense than the fire-sale price you're thinking about paying.

> Buy a Franchise.

It may come as a surprise, but more than 25 percent of all U.S. businesses are franchises. That means *someone else* owns the name, cooked up the formula for success and, hopefully, provides top-notch training and support as part of the package. The odds of success are vastly greater with a first-rate franchise than with trying to do your own thing. But franchises cost money and, like working for someone else, involve trading lots of your time for dollars.

> ## Start your Own Franchise.

Many fortunes have been made by people clever enough to do this well. But the combination of skills needed to create a new business and turn it into a successful franchising operation are rarely found in the same body. Remember that Ray Kroc was *not* the founder of McDonalds. He bought the business from two guys who knew how to make hamburgers, then turned it into the most successful franchise on the planet.

> ## Go Into Network Marketing.

This may be the best choice for people short on marketing skills or who are unwilling or unable to take large financial risks. The sad fact, though, is that most people who get into network marketing do *not* make money. They may get into a network with low potential for success. Or they get into a high-potential network, then don't treat it like a serious business. But for people who *do* find a good network, *do* treat it like a serious business, and *do* make the commitment of time and energy, the odds of making a lot of money are very good.

4. *If you've decided to <u>work</u> for yourself in the distribution sector of the economy with network marketing as the vehicle, you must make one of four more <u>choices</u> that will greatly affect your prospects for success:*

> ## Start your own network.

There's no doubt this option could produce a huge financial return. But like starting your own franchising business, it will take a lot more up-front money, a combination of product and networking expertise, and a considerable risk. Hundreds try it every year, and the failure rate is very high. And trying to improve the odds by venturing into the "illegal pyramid" area is a great way to spend time behind bars.

> ## Get in on someone else's new network.

Careful! Start-up networks often make get-rich-quick promises based on "getting in on the ground floor." Check the company and its sales and marketing plan very carefully. Will it be one of many to disappear (with your money) in a year or so? Remember: "If it *sounds* too good to be true, it probably is."

> ## Join an established network with goods and services in demand.

There are successful networks that have helped many thousands of people earn good extra income working out of their homes. What they all have in common are top-quality products and services for which there is great demand and a bonus program that rewards distributors well. Your odds for success are least in a network with a few products that must be sold literally "door to door." Your odds may be best in a network that offers high-demand products and services— so good money can be made by simply teaching people a better means of buying what they're already buying regularly.

Advantages & Words of Caution

There are people who can make money on every one of the business options laid out on the preceding pages because they have the right combination of time, money, experience, ingenuity, and ambition. But I believe network marketing offers the *best* money-making opportunity for:

(1) People who *don't* have the time, money, experience, ingenuity, and ambition to make a traditional business work well, or

(2) People who *have* those attributes but want to spend less time *making* money and more time *enjoying* it.

And now for some words of *caution*. Before getting into a network marketing business, make sure it:

• Is backed by a financially sound company with a good track record and reputation.

• Has a sales and marketing plan that either has formal government regulatory approval or meets the approval criteria.

• Doesn't make you carry a large inventory of products and will allow you to return marketable products for a full refund.

• Offers products and/or services that are in great demand, not just specialty items for which the market is very limited.

• Rewards you well for your own success as well as for helping people you sponsor succeed in their businesses.

• Has income based on the flow of products and services, not on recruiting new distributors (a practice that's usually illegal).

• Provides a large national or international marketplace in which you can build your business.

Be Realistic

Many people go into network marketing looking for big bucks in a matter of weeks. Like any business, network marketing tends to be "front-end loaded." You have to put time and money into the front end if you are going to see the rewards down the road.

If someone promises you big bucks at the front end, run for cover. "Get-rich-quick" schemes may enrich some of the folks doing the luring, but almost *never* work for the people lured into them.

And never let yourself be *pressured* into a network marketing program — or any other kind of "business opportunity," no matter *how* good a deal it seems to be.

In examining the questions and the *choices* associated with the avalanche of entrepreneurship, you may think by now that network marketing is the key to success for everyone. It isn't.

There are *many* avenues to financial freedom through entrepreneurship. At a time of rapid change and much uncertainty, what would give you the *best* opportunity to become financially free?

Only *you* can answer that question.

3. Bunkers, Barriers, & Backrests

When psychologist Abraham Maslow developed his "Hierarchy of Needs," he placed on the bottom tiers of his pyramid survival needs such as food and water, and needs related to safety and security.

Until those foundational needs are met, Maslow claimed, people won't do much to meet higher human needs such as love and, ultimately, self-actualization or transcendency (being all you can be).

In the 1980s, many people focused on a higher-level tier of Maslow's hierarchy called "Ego Needs." Status and conspicuous consumption reigned supreme.

With economic ups and downs, rising crime and violence, insecurity in the workplace, and other forms of *continuous white water*, however, many turned their attentions toward *survival* needs and away from *status* needs.

'Life in the Bunker'

A search for stability often results in *fortified environments* wherein people can feel relatively safe from the world around them. "Life in the bunker" is nothing new. People in big-city apartments started adding extra locks and deadbolts many years ago. But rising levels of fear bring more and more effort to create "secure areas" in which to feel secure — even comfortable.

> On average, people 70 and under in the U.S. lose more years of their lives to violence than to heart disease. In the workplace, deaths from homicides now exceed deaths from machinery accidents.

Sales of guns still set records in some areas. The lock-and-burglar-bar business continues to boom. Alarm systems are becoming household necessities with demand for greater and greater sophistication. Martial arts classes are more popular than ever, and women are carrying Mace and learning how to kick attackers where it hurts.

People spend more *time* in their bunkers, "entertaining" themselves with television, which continually reinforces — guess what? — the need to stay in the bunker and add more layers of fortification!

Running Out of Places to Hide

The people of America and many other countries where violence is prevalent are running out of places to hide.

For those who move to some far-off paradise or another, it's only a matter of time before that area, too, is plagued with the very problems that caused people to flock there in the first place.

> In 1940, an American college professor was so fearful of all the violence and insecurity in the world that he sold everything and moved his whole family to a remote, faraway island. It was a quiet, peaceful little island in the Pacific Ocean — an island called *Guadalcanal.*

We build communal bunkers, too. Upscale families seek shelter in condominiums with well-trained security staffs. Real estate agents specializing in condominium sales recognize security as an alluring feature, especially when dealing with prospects who have gone through a home invasion or other forms of neighborhood crime.

The number of "gated" communities continues to rise. A fortified bunker inside a fenced community with a single guarded gate has great sales appeal, especially when there's a first-rate police force patrolling the surrounding area.

A couple of decades after coining the word, futurist Faith Popcorn provided an update on "cocooning" — an update that still holds true:

> We are going into emotional as well as physical withdrawal. Our answering machines were screening *all* our calls. If anything, the early 90s have brought us into a time of heavy-duty *Burrowing,* digging in deeper, building ourselves a bunker — *Cocooning* for our lives.

> Faith Popcorn
> *The Popcorn Report*

Is bunkerization, cocooning or burrowing the way to meet your safety and security needs? Will sitting with a shotgun across your lap behind triple-locked doors in a "home" with an alarm system that dials the police department make you *that* much more secure?

Of course not! Why? For the same reason the French failed to protect themselves from the Germans at the start of World War II by hiding behind their tremendously well-fortified Maginot Line. The Germans simply went *around* the fortifications and attacked from the rear.

And that's what happens in millions of households everywhere. While focusing on perimeter alarms and burglar bars, crime and violence pours into the house electronically — through hour after hour of violent television programming and stereo systems blasting "gangsta rap" and the like.

In other words, we bar the enemy at the door and welcome the enemy through "The Tube."

Even settings that should bring families and friends to-gether in much joy and happiness can turn sour:

> Police Say Groom Shoots Bride
> During Wedding-Day Food Fight
> Newspaper headline

I'm constantly amazed at how so many people are *mystified* by all the crime and violence in society, and how they can point so many fingers at everyone and everything but the boob tube and their own family viewing habits.

> The best predictor of violent behavior at age 19 is what kind of television programs were preferred at age 8.

Barriers That 'Balkanize'

A companion to living in bunkers is building barriers to people who, for one reason or another, are *different*. It's a sad fact of human behavior that when people feel deprived or threatened, or see themselves as victims, they tend to seek acceptance, security and status by joining a group that espouses anything that would seem to provide protection and feelings of greater self-worth.

Under such <u>circumstances</u>, people are drawn to cults, gangs, and other groups that help them feel superior. Whether it's members of an ethnic group banding together to the exclusion of other kinds of people, or members of a hate group who think they can find a better life by ridding the world of one or more ethnic groups, the effect is to build barriers, to cast blame and, ultimately, to generate grief.

From the beginning of civilization, people have tried to feel better about themselves by denigrating those who are "different." The result can be anything from the tragedy of a holocaust to the silliness of social snobbery.

> Columnist Russell Baker once described a vacation island in Maine on which a distinct pecking order allowed owners to feel superior to renters, seasonal renters to feel superior to monthly renters, etc. At the bottom were the "dreadful" people who came over on the ferry to visit (and spend their money) for only part of a day.

Street gangs long have provided early-life experiences in barrier-building. Raised largely by themselves in neighborhoods where many see life as cheap, young people seek safety and acceptance within the "security" of a gang. They're willing to trade freedom and relative safety for a sense of belonging and a chance to feel superior.

The problems of "Barriers that Balkanize" are worldwide, not limited to the United States. While the U.S. has more than its share of strife with a government that's relatively stable, many other countries have more than their share of strife under governments that are highly *unstable* — and that's nothing new.

Could violence and divisiveness in the U.S. ever reach the point where the world's longest-running democracy falls apart? Probably not. But within our cities, there are a few similarities to my fictional version of a world-news story that has become all-too-familiar:

> For many years, a powerful national government prevented upheaval among what used to be a hodge-podge of small independent states. Within months of the government's fall, ancient rivalries were renewed by power-hungry people, to the dismay of those who had learned to live well together, even to intermarry.
>
> The worst conflict, a bloody civil war, broke out between Tumultia in the north and Bashnos-Mobrulvia in the south. Thousands died in the fighting until, with U.N. intervention, the land was partitioned into small states that were like ethnic enclaves.
>
> With the Tumultians held at bay by U.N. forces, the Bashnoses and the Mobrulvians began arguing over who had the greater right to govern. Warlords cut off food supplies. People starved. But thanks to secret arms deals and intense ethnic pride, the Mobrulvians slaughtered the Bashnoses.
>
> Two days after the victory celebration, the Mobbites got into an argument with the Rulvians over what to call the main street in the capital. Fighting broke out again. Total defeat of the Mobbites brought much exhilaration among the Rulvians, for surely peace *finally* had come to the land. But when the Rulas tribe took control of the central water supply, the Vian clan armed itself and launched a bloody attack, wiping out the entire Rulas army.
>
> Recent news dispatches from what's left of the country report that an attempt to design a new flag resulted in an outbreak of violence between the Vi's and the An's. Now out of ammunition, the two factions are holed up in their respective caves. Every night they send out raiding parties to beat each other with clubs.

Obviously, building bunkers and barriers that balkzanize ultimately makes matters worse in our *ongoing search for stability*. So why do so many people keep digging more bunkers and building more barriers?

Mostly because of:

Behavioral Backrests

Keeping others *out* of our lives is easier than bringing them *in*. In other words, it's easier to *board up* than to *reach out*.

And so, once having built our bunkers and barriers, we develop "behavioral backrests" against which to lean, comfortably disconnected from the world around us. Some examples:

• *The Backrest of Fear*. It's easier to live in fear than develop the strong and abiding faith it takes to *overcome* fear. Take precautions? Absolutely. Let fear control your life? *Never!* Begin by understanding that most fear turns out to be unfounded.

> FEAR is an acronym. It stands for False Evidence Appearing Real. The antidote for fear is *faith*. Fear lives in the mind. So does faith.

• *The Backrest of Non-Involvement*. It's easier to hide from bad things happening around us than to become involved. Support crime watch programs. Support opportunities for young people to find positive alternatives to crime and violence. Get to know the police who patrol your area. Let them know you *appreciate* their efforts to keep the neighborhood safe.

> You can increase your safety a little by working with a screwdriver to change your locks. You can increase your safety a lot by working with other people to change your neighborhood.

• *The Backrest of Isolation*. It's easier to avoid enemies than it is to make friends. Work on relationships. If that's a problem, it can be overcome by seeking and accepting help.

> A person who makes many friends rarely has enemies.

• *The Backrest of Intolerance*. It's easier to stick with our "own kind" than to befriend people who are different. Reach out to people of different ethnic, socioeconomic, and religious backgrounds. Promote multiculturalism.

> If any one word characterizes American Society, it is *diversity*. The American experiment is, in a fundamental sense, a test of whether a common political culture can succeed based on the principle that freedom, justice and equality are the inherent rights of all human beings. In spite of enormous strides, we find ourselves struggling daily with this test.
> The National Conference

4. A Quest for Better Solutions

In terms of "supply and demand," there always has been an abundant supply of problems that create strong demands for solutions. As you may have concluded from reading Chapter 2, *The High Cost & History of Bad Choices*, "solutions" too often do little more than produce new problems. To wit:

Problem	Solution	New Problem
Too much drunkenness.	Prohibition of alcohol.	Organized crime.
Ominous threat of war.	Appease the enemy.	A more-costly war.
Low pay, benefits, etc.	Unions, demands, strikes.	Layoffs, job exports.
People living in poverty.	Big welfare programs.	Indolence, crime.
Children *want* more.	Give them all they *want* .	Spoiled children.

There are countless other examples, but I offer those five simply to illustrate this point:

It's easy to find solutions to problems if you
ignore the problems created by the solutions.

There's a greater-than-ever demand for new and *better* solutions to problems because so many solutions once accepted as "conventional wisdom" simply don't work.

In my view, truly *better* solutions to major problems must include three principles:

1. Less government involvement
2. More personal responsibility
3. People caring for each other

Let's examine these one by one:

Less Government Involvement

Every time a government agency or political body steps in to solve a problem best left to individuals or private-sector organizations, it's a safe bet that as much or more focus will be on the opportunity to expand government as to solve the problem.

As some great wit observed a decade or so ago:

If rats were the problem and government were called upon to hire a rat catcher, in no time at all the rat catcher would become a "rodent control officer" and would have no intention of killing rats, because they had become his constituency.

With due respect to the many dedicated public servants, there is little or no motive for a government body to form a lean, gung-ho team of people that acts quickly and efficiently, then disbands itself as soon as its mission is fulfilled.

Politicians approach problem-solving as new opportunities to garner votes, and that can bring solutions that may be good or bad. But let professional bureaucrats get into the act, and the problem-solving effort too often goes from bad to worse.

Private companies operate on a profit motive, and while that *also* can pose problems, a company operating within a system of free enterprise has far more incentive to deliver the best for the least than a government agency with little or no competition.

More Personal Responsibility

For centuries now, arguments have raged over where to draw the line between the rights and responsibilities of people as individuals and the rights and responsibilities of people as a group.

Over the years, much responsibility for personal well-being and success has been shifted from individuals to government programs, employers, and even "society" as a whole.

U.S. Social Security, for example, never was intended as a substitute for personal savings, but helps undermine individual responsibility to provide for old age. "Oh, I don't need to worry because Social Security will take care of me," says the 50-something while making minimum payments on seven or eight credit cards.

Employer-provided health benefits, along with government and private health insurance systems, help undermine personal responsibility for one's own good health. "Oh, I don't have to worry about my health that much because the company (etc.) covers all that," says the overweight couch potato slurping another beer.

"Passing the buck" of individual responsibility extends to many other areas, too. I'll side with the teachers on this one:

> Surveys show most parents believe responsibility for teaching values should rest mainly with their children's teachers. An even bigger majority of teachers, on the other hand, believe the responsibility for teaching values lies squarely with the parents.

Burglars sue victims for injuries from anti-burglar devices. Students get falling-down drunk, then sue colleges and universities for their injuries from falling down. Well-off individuals and companies with little or no responsibility for accidents are forced to pay millions in damages because they have the "deepest pockets."

"Society" is blamed for the behavior of criminals — in other words, anyone can be relieved of responsibility for bad personal *choices* as long as their *circumstances* are bad enough.

> When everyone is responsible for everything,
> no one is responsible for anything.

A few suggestions for *The Age of Accountability*:

• *Take charge of your behavior.* Accept full responsibility for the personal *choices* you make and never use bad *circumstances* as excuses for doing what is wrong.

• *Take charge of your health.* Understand that any promise of unlimited "free" health care is an empty promise. If you smoke, quit. If you're a fast driver, slow down. If you're overweight, get trim. If you're a sofa slug, start a sensible exercise program. Have regular checkups. If you need treatment, don't delay.

• *Take charge of your destiny*. The only person on this earth who can make you a success is *you* — not your boss, not your business clientele, not your relatives, friends, or advisors. Not even *God* is likely to *hand you* success. God provides food for the birds, but He doesn't make daily free deliveries to their nests.

• *Take charge of your legacy*. If you're a parent, *be responsible* for your children, for they're your immortality. Set a good example. Ban forever the hypocrisy of "don't do as I do, do as I say." Spend plenty of quality time with them. Teach them positive values at every opportunity. *Never* cover up for them when they do wrong, for you rob them of valuable lessons in personal responsibility.

Care for One Another

For the first 157 years of U.S. history, there were *no* massive government welfare systems and entitlement programs. Support was four layers deep *without* government aid.

First, we took care of ourselves. To the extent that we couldn't take care of ourselves, our families pitched in. To the extent our families couldn't take care of our problems, our churches helped out. When even the churches couldn't get the job done, we developed the world's largest and best system of charitable organizations.

The search for solutions to our problems will reach the happiest ending when the only role left to government will be to fill those needs we truly *can't* meet ourselves — *not* the unending passel of needs we've been *unwilling* to meet ourselves.

It comes down to rebuilding a strong sense of community.

We have to start thinking of America as a family. We have to stop screeching at each other, stop hurting each other, and instead start caring for, sacrificing for, and sharing with each other. We have to stop constantly criticizing, which is the way of the malcontent, and instead get back to the can-do attitude that made America.

Gen. Colin Powell
My American Journey

How can you become more a part of the solutions and less a part of the problems? Some suggestions:

• *Support the political process*. Keep up with the issues. Focus on the big-picture and long-term good, rather than narrow self-interests and short-term "fixes." Get to know candidates. Support the ones with common sense and integrity. Run for office. Vote!

• *Support education*. Do what it takes to assure a quality *education* for *all* children. Join a PTA and be active. Run for the school board, or get behind a good person who will. Demand an end to unruly behavior and permissiveness in schools. Fight for the right to have good *choices* on where and how children receive their educations.

• *Support free enterprise.* The engine that pulls the economic train is free enterprise. Government adds heavy cars that slow the engine down. Help correct what's wrong with business, championing high standards of integrity, a strong social consciousness, and fair treatment of employees. Then focus on what's *right* about free enterprise, and the boundless opportunities it provides.

• *Support charitable organizations.* Fewer tax-supported government solutions to problems brings a greater need for privately supported non-profit organizations that offer *practical* solutions to problems. A strong, well-managed system of non-profit organizations provides higher levels of social services at lower overall costs than government at any level.

Less government involvement! More personal responsibility! People caring for one another! And that points to the fifth and final component of *An Ongoing Search for Stability*:

5. A Return to Many Traditional Values

For generations, tens of millions of American children took to heart the childhood example of George Washington for whom punishment was preferable to telling a lie. The great majority of Americans grew up with an innate sense of honesty — the belief, strongly practiced, that it is wrong to lie, cheat, or steal.

Simple, basic honesty was a time-honored, traditional American value. Yes, our past is checkered by the corruption of those whose greed overshadowed this simple virtue. But for *most* people during the nation's first 200 years, honesty *clearly* was the best policy.

To be a good American was to be a good citizen. Good citizens were scrupulously law-abiding and honest. But today?

> We are a nation of lawbreakers. We exaggerate tax-deductible expenses, lie to customs officials, bet on card games and sports events, disregard jury notices, drive while intoxicated — and hire illegal child-care workers...
>
> Stephen J. Adler & Wade Lambert
> *Wall Street Journal*

The antithesis of traditional American integrity, it seems, is "situational ethics." We break the law or violate the rules when we believe the *situation* justifies it.

We believe it's all right to cheat on taxes because the taxes are too high. And yet, if *no one* had cheated on federal taxes over the past 40 years or so, the additional tax revenues would have been enough to have *avoided the entire national debt* and taxes would be much lower.

We believe it's all right to exceed the speed limit because we're in a hurry — or the speed limit isn't high enough for the road we're traveling or the car we're driving. And yet, we're quick to complain when someone drives too fast through our neighborhoods or our own teen-agers push the family car past the legal limit.

We believe it's all right to help ourselves to the supply cabinet at work or to some of our employer's property, yet we complain bitterly when our salaries are cut or our jobs are lost because excessive costs have more than wiped out the company's profits.

Lying, Cheating, Stealing

Studies abound and statistics vary widely, but it appears that the average American lies at least once a day.

Where cheating is concerned, children do it in school routinely — and, what's worse, many of them believe that cheating isn't wrong so long as they don't get caught.

Is it *wrong* to steal? Yes, most people say. But many *don't consider it stealing* when they pad expense accounts, remove a few bucks from the wallet of a family member, take paper and pens from the supply cabinet at work for their child's school project, etc.

Whether it's lying, cheating, or stealing, dishonesty compounds itself and becomes a habit.

> I took it because I needed it.
> I took it because I wanted it and couldn't afford it.
> I took it because even though I *could* afford it, I wanted
> to use my money for something *else* I wanted.
> I took it because everybody else is taking stuff.

Do most people still see honesty as the best policy?

Yes and no, according to conflicting survey results. Yes, in the sense that honesty should be *everyone else's* best policy. No, when faced *personally* with bad <u>circumstances</u> or good opportunities in which a little lying, cheating, or stealing would result in a gain.

So honesty has come to depend on the <u>circumstances</u> and, in an age of loopholes in the law, convictions overturned for lack of a comma in a transcript, plea-bargaining, and the like, what's *legally* right often triumphs over what's *morally* right.

> When the legally right and the morally right are aligned, it's mere coincidence.
>
> Veteran attorney on why
> he stopped practicing law

Hard-Working? God-Fearing?

Much wealth and national success over the past two centuries has been attributed to the so-called "Protestant Work Ethic," a term which is quite *politically incorrect* in an age when lazy people are called "the motivationally dispossessed."

The term also is a major misnomer in that hard-working (and lazy) people always have been abundant in *all* religions. If nothing else, though, the term points to a union among honesty, industriousness, and *all* religious conviction.

The traditional value known as "the work ethic" is alive and well in America and elsewhere no matter how many sleeping street people you have to step over on the way to work in the morning.

The problem with <u>work</u> in America is not in *whether* to do it, it's in *how* and in *why* — too often morally shortcutting one's way to success, or shortchanging loved ones by working for the wrong reasons.

Whole books have been written that decry the demise of traditional values, and so many ain't-it-awful stories appear that it's easy to believe we're all in the proverbial handbasket making a rapid descent to a particularly hot place.

Reasons for Optimism

I believe there's plenty of reason for optimism, though.

Just as the people of England overcame a long period of moral decay in the 19th Century and returned to traditional values, I *really believe* the people of America and other countries rife with moral decadence also will return to many traditional values.

Here are a few predictions with some clear indicators:

• *Better Parenting.* The first generation of Americans to grow up without the full-time attention of at least one parent has many in its ranks who would *love* to make it the *last* such generation.

— Books, courses, support groups, and the like on how to be a better parent are becoming more and more popular.

— Surveys show an increasing number of working women would rather be full-time moms, and working men and women are willing to make sacrifices to spend more time with their kids.

— Public opinion and, sometimes, even the courts favor holding parents more responsible for the actions of their children.

Childhood should be an apprenticeship, not a joy ride.

• *Better Schools.* I believe we are turning the corner toward doing a much better job of educating our children. Schools are getting better, often by returning to some "old-fashioned" concepts:

— Boys and girls are put in separate classes, grades go up and behavior improves.

— Uniforms are required, violence usually drops.

— Children are made to sit up straight and made to stand when called on by teachers, respect for authority increases.

— Phonics is brought back, language skills rise to levels not seen since the advent of "new English."

— Older children help teach younger children, learning improves and a new sense of personal responsibility is gained.

— Ex-gang members become national calculus champions.
— Schools once written off as hopeless "war zones" become outstanding places of learning and achievement.

Every child in America has the right to expect three things from our educational system: a safe learning environment, a school that teaches basic skills, and instruction that reinforces rather than undermines traditional values.

Contract With the American Family
Christian Coalition

• *Better Work Life*. Job security in exchange for employee loyalty was a traditional value that died back in the 1980s. In its place came low morale and unprecedented worker mistrust. So many employers, faced with a shortage of talented and *loyal* people, are trying to win back the trust and confidence of employees.
— Flex-time, job-sharing, on-site day-care centers, and other programs help accommodate employee needs for more family time.
— Companies that once *fired* people for sleeping on the job now encourage naps, which reduce stress and increase productivity.
— Telecommuting and helping employees become independent outsourcing contractors instead of wage slaves is becoming a bigger and better win-win for employees and employers alike.
— Companies are redoubling efforts to involve employees in decision-making and to improve internal communication.

Every employer's creed should include these principles: (1) Treat people right, (2) Heed their opinions, (3) Keep them informed.

• *Celebration of Honest Acts*. As always, news organizations will continue to focus on what is *wrong*. But, hopefully, they will continue to offer more and more stories exemplifying what is *right* in their communities, featuring such things as:
— Schools honoring students for acts of integrity.
— Courses on ethics and civility being established.
— People of integrity being recognized at ceremonies organized by the increasing number of *centers for ethics*.
— Employers rewarding people for exemplifying positive organizational and community values.

When a homeless family in California found a wallet containing credit cards, a thick wad of $100 bills and a $1,500 plane ticket, they returned it to the owner simply because it was the right thing to do — and became instant national heroes. Job offers poured in from employers wanting to put someone that honest on their payrolls, and the family was deluged with gifts, including free housing.

• *Better Role Models*. America is starved for heroes, and so is much of the rest of the world — people of integrity who can serve as role models.

— Increasingly, our biggest heroes will be the *overcomers*. They are people who have beaten all the odds and succeeded anyway. Ever cheering for the underdogs, we will edify even more the people who succeed in spite of incredible handicaps.

— Decreasingly, our heroes will be the sports figures who rake in millions of dollars a year and live shameful personal lives.

— A forgiving people, we also will count among our heroes people who have made major mistakes in their lives, admitted them, asked for forgiveness, *made amends*, and then dedicated themselves to helping others avoid the same mistakes.

— The White House once again will be a place of honor, not just a place of scandal, as voters demand much more of elected officials than slick-lipped promises and silver-tongued excuses.

> Example is the school of mankind and they will learn at no other.
> Edmund Burke

• *Victories Over Crime*. Crime rates go up and down, but I believe there will be many more victories over crime as the problem is attacked on two main fronts: in the homes and on the streets.

— In the homes, parents will take more responsibility for the behavior of their children, if for no other reason than being held more accountable for their children's behavior.

— TV will be reigned in. V-chips and other limits will be placed on what children watch. Sponsors of programs that undermine basic values will be boycotted. Networks, producers, and sponsors will be sued more often when destructive behavior can be linked directly to their programs.

— On the streets, police agencies will keep getting the upper hand on criminals. "Relentless pursuit" is becoming the order of the day with high-tech computer systems and incredible sleuthing by police labs taking many more criminals off the streets.

> For years sociologists and politicians have told us that police cannot have much effect on crime because crime is a product of economic and social forces beyond their control. New York has proved otherwise. If police can slash crime in the nation's largest and most complex city, they can do it anywhere.
> Reader's Digest

A Return to Strong Spiritual Values

Perhaps the biggest part of a return to traditional values is a return to strong *spiritual* values.

The values set forth in the religions of Jews, Christians, Muslims, and others underlie all other major values. If the teachings of the great religions were universally practiced, there would be no crime, no use of drugs, no widespread destruction of family units, no government welfare programs, no wars, etc.

Religion is coming back in a big way. Increasingly, people can't cope effectively with life devoid of a spiritual base. They're looking upward as well as inward for relief.

While two-thirds of the Baby-Boom generation left the religions of their upbringing, most Baby-Boomers continued to believe in God. Such people became known as "believers but not belongers."

But now, more and more people not only are drawn toward believing but belonging as well — especially to religious bodies offering stricter, more traditional interpretations of God's Word.

The "graying of America" is contributing to the resurgence of religion. But people of all ages are finding religion to be a powerful buffer to modern-day tribulations, and a way to find greater meaning and fulfillment in life.

Pray More, Live Longer

A strong religious faith can reduce pressures of daily living to the extent that physical well-being actually is improved. For example, insurance statistics show that people who attend services regularly live more than five years longer than those who don't.

Other items of interest:

• Of 44,000 inmates in a state prison system, only 14 came from traditional Jewish families — families with a strong father figure, constant affirmations of their children's future success, and feelings of shame if the family is dishonored.

• More and more business and self-improvement books embrace religious themes and espouse traditional religious principles.

• An increasing number of employers are bringing prayer into the conduct of business, and are providing time and facilities for employees to attend to daily devotionals.

• Bible study programs abound and new ones are being started almost everywhere.

• Religious revival meetings are setting attendance records all around the world.

• Newer programs such as Promise Keepers and Youth Alive are filling stadiums and making a powerful difference in the lives of their targeted audiences.

• Growing in number rapidly, Muslims soon will outnumber their Jewish cousins in America. Strict adherence to the traditional values of Koranic scripture leaves no room for drugs, crime, and a host of other sins, and a strong Muslim presence in inner-city neighborhoods often results in a reduction in crime of all sorts.

• Christian denominations able to connect the Gospels to handling the stress of contemporary living enjoy soaring membership. Meantime, some denominations that have not made that connection continue a long and steady decline.

• More children are being moved from public schools to private schools run by Jewish, Christian, and Muslim organizations — schools where religious values can be taught openly.

• Prayer, meantime, finally is re-entering public schools.

Movement back to religious faith is indisputable. There are, though, many modern adaptations, ranging from interactive Bible studies on CD Rom, to web sites covering virtually all religions, to Muslims being called to daily prayers by alarms on their computers.

The bottom line is a spiritual uplift that transcends the ages and people of every race, national origin, age group, etc.

Four words made it through the "God is dead" movement of the 1950s and 60s.

The four words also endured long and bitter separation-of-church-and-state battles — and the screwball idea that prayer and the expression of religious values should be banned from public schools, courthouses, and the like because the U.S. Constitution won't let government set up and run its own church.

Through it all, the four words have been repeated *billions* of times as coin and currency continues to flow from U.S. mints. The four words say as much about the future as they do about the past:

In God We Trust

Questions for The New Millennium

Here are three questions for the 2000s:

1. How big a renaissance of traditional values will there be? Will there be a rebirth of *The American Spirit*?

> We believe it's time to reclaim America. To take a stand for what's right. To re-establish the fundamental principles upon which this nation is founded; principles such as faith, family, free enterprise, freedom and future. When it's all said and done, it's the Resurrection of the American Spirit.
>
> Dean Sikes
> The Spirit of America Foundation

2. What kind of people will we elect to lead us? How much will we care whether our future presidents had numerous sexual escapades, whether they lied to cover them up, whether they were involved in illegal deals to be elected, etc.? Will we elect more convicted felons to positions of trust? Will we demand *better* of our leaders — or, if not, will we simply get the leaders we deserve?

It is not genius or acuteness of intellect that are so important, rather it is the simple virtues of character: honesty, courage, and common sense. In a democracy like ours, we cannot expect the stream to rise higher than its source. If the average man or the average woman are not of the right type, your public (servants) will not be of the right type."

President Theodore Roosevelt

3. Will a moral resurgence fuel greater prosperity? Will there be prosperity with ample opportunities for everyone, or will there be pandemonium with ample opportunities for corruption?

America is great because America is good. If America ceases to be good, America will cease to be great.

Alexis deTocqueville

A Perspective on Change

It's been said that "change is the only certainty in life."

When an eastern monarch asked for the wisdom of the world to be summed up in a sentence, his advisors came up with six words:

And this, too, shall pass away.

Let me offer 10 precepts which attempt to put the matter of stability into context. The precepts set the stage for Part 2 of this book, in which you'll be offered a *process* that will help you make the most out of life in turbulent, fast-changing times.

10 Precepts for Achieving Greater Stability

Stability for most people is preferable to continual *change*

Change will continue to accelerate, producing ever greater *impact*

Increasing impact will diminish conventional avenues to *self-fulfillment*

Self-Fulfillment will come more to those willing to make good *choices* in life

A choice in life increasingly important is developing an *effective personal plan*

An effective plan is written, tracked, updated and worthy of *support by others*

Support by others depends on the quality and strength of *relationships*

Relationships are strengthened best by developing *enduring values*

Enduring values increase the ability to handle continual *change*

Change well-handled produces a sense of greater *stability.*

Your Checklist

Activity: Circle a number on the scale of 5 to 1 to rate how much you are engaged personally in each of the *ongoing search for stability* trends, offered here as positive statements. (5 means very much, 1 means not at all, and 4, 3, or 2 are somewhere in between). For each trend, write one or two *choices* that will help you make the most out of your life.

<u>Trend</u>   <u>Your Involvement</u>

1. I have big dreams and high expectations   5 4 3 2 1

    Choices: _____

_____

2. I am in an entrepreneurial pursuit   5 4 3 2 1

    Choices: _____

_____

3. I avoid bunkers, barriers, & backrests   5 4 3 2 1

    Choices: _____

_____

4. I support good solutions to public problems   5 4 3 2 1

    Choices: _____

_____

5. I promote & exemplify traditional values   5 4 3 2 1

    Choices: _____

_____

The last person to change for the better loses — period.

Part 2

The Process

- The 3 Aspirations Words
- A Simple Way to Plan Well
- The 5 Action Words

Aspirations get you nowhere without planning and action. After all, a dream without workable goals attached to it is only a fantasy.

In Part 2, you will put your aspirations in the perspective of the three most powerful words to launch *any* sort of planning process.

Then, you will discover a simple, step-by-step life planning process that challenges you to find your own best answers to five crucial questions.

Finally, you will learn to apply the five action words — your *imperatives* for success in anything.

11 Words for Winning

Chapter 5

Start With the Right Questions

- **3 Questions for the Preparation**
- **5 Questions for the Journey**

Quick review:

In Part 1, you considered *The Accountability Factor*. It was summed up as the first three of the *11 Words for Winning*: "Life is a series of personal *choices*, made under the *circumstances* that surround you, leading to *outcomes* — in keeping with the will of God."

That, in my view, is a context for *anyone's* journey through life, and you and I and everyone become fully accountable when we accept the fact that the *outcomes* have far more to do with personal *choices* than with personal *circumstances*.

Everything you do in life, you do *in a context*. It is *context* that influences each decision you make, right or wrong. It is *context* that surrounds every experience, good or bad. It is *context* that sheds the light of meaning on every outcome of every decision and experience.

You may find it hard to maintain *any* sort of strong and positive context for life. The world is more complex and offers more options, producing *circumstances* vastly different than in the past.

Would You Trade Contexts?

Maybe you'd *never* trade contexts with your parents, grandparents, or ancestors. Or, maybe you're among those who really believe they *would* find a more stable and more positive context for life's journey somewhere in the past.

Life is as good as you choose to *make it* today and tomorrow, not as good as it *would have been* if only you lived in times gone by.

Enjoy pleasant memories, but *never* take your eyes totally off the present and the future. Remember the headline as you began reading this book? "*What Was Isn't, What Is Won't Be.*"

When Nancy and I lived in Florida, we were among so many *elderly* folks that we began wondering whether "The Sunshine State" really *is* "God's Waiting Room." But while we found many in the *widespread ranks of the wrinkled* living in the past, we saw others getting the most out of the present and looking to the future.

As I write this, the media is reporting the delightful story of a bubbly great-grandmother who, cheered on by her family and many friends, celebrated her 82nd birthday by making her first-ever parachute jump. When it was over, she told reporters it was a lot of fun — and she plans her *next* jump for her *92nd* birthday!

> We are living in an age of scientific, technological, and sociological miracles that give us more and greater opportunities to live longer and better than at any time in history!

So much for the context. Now let's plunge into Part 2 and a powerful *process* in which you and anyone can find *Certain Success in an Uncertain World*. It's a process that starts with what I believe to be the right questions for life's journey. But first, there are:

3 Questions for the Preparation

Remember *The Aspirations Factor*? It consists of the second three of the *11 Words for Winning* — the "W" words that pose the preparation questions:

- What do you *want* out of life?
- What's the best *way* to get it?
- What's the *work* involved and to what extent are you willing to do it and learn how to do it well?

Underlying each "W" word and preparatory question are vital elements I call *The ABC's of Want, Way, Work*. The ABCs are:

Attitude. Your attitude as you approach each of the three "W" questions is the mindset through which you can accomplish major goals and make your dreams come true.

> A successful person is not someone with a good set
> of *circumstances* but someone with a good *attitude*.

The more *positive* your attitude, the more you can build...

Belief. To be successful, you must *believe* in yourself and *believe* in what you're doing. As many wise people will tell you:

> If you believe you *can*, you're right.
> If you believe you *can't*, you're also right.

Armed with a positive mental attitude and powerful *belief*, you're ready to make a strong...

Commitment. The bigger the dreams and goals, the more *commitment* is required. With *total* commitment you are almost certain to achieve anything that's achievable. With *less than* total commitment, you'll quit when the going gets tough.

> A commitment really isn't a *lasting* commitment unless you continually *re*-commit to the commitment!

Here's how the ABCs relate to the three "W" words:

THE ABCS OF WANT·WAY·WORK

WANT	WAY	WORK
ATTITUDE Big dreams & goals *can* be fulfilled & I am worthy of earning all that they offer!	**ATTITUDE** The best *way* to get what I *want* exists! With an open mind & persistence, I'll find it!	**ATTITUDE** The *work* not only is worth doing & doing well, but will give me great fulfillment!
BELIEF I have the *potential* to achieve all of my dreams & goals!	**BELIEF** The *way* I found is the *best* & I have what it takes to make it work for me!	**BELIEF** I am capable of doing this *work* & overcoming every obstacle in my path!
COMMITMENT I *will* achieve my dreams & goals starting with finding the best *way*!	**COMMITMENT** This is the vehicle to get what I *want* & I will do whatever *work* is involved!	**COMMITMENT** Believing in the *way*, I will do the *work* & do it well, driven by what I *want*!

Take a Closer Look

Now let's revisit the three preparation questions, taking a closer look at them and giving you an opportunity to rate yourself.

1. What do you *want* out of life? How could you possibly *succeed* in life if you have no inkling of what you *want* out of life?

> Going through life without knowing what you *want* is like going to sea without knowing where you're headed.

Winners in life have big *dreams*. Losers, at best, have big *fantasies*. What's the difference?

A big fantasy envisions attaining what you *want* without focusing on the *way* and the *work* involved in getting it.

> Some day my ship will come in. It will be filled with much treasure and I'll be set for life!

A big dream envisions not only what you *want* in life, but also the *way* to accomplish it and the *work* that's required.

Ships pass by here all the time, some filled with treasure. I'm going to find out which ship holds the treasure and stop sitting around waiting for it to come in. I'll get in the water and *swim out to it!*

Dream *big*, like the most successful people do. Answer the first question thoroughly. Then apply the ABCs to the fullest.

Rate Yourself
(Circle 5 for absolutely yes, 1 for absolutely no, or 4, 3, 2 for in between)

- I know what I *want* out of life   5 4 3 2 1
- I have the strongest, most positive
  Attitude toward getting what I *want*   5 4 3 2 1

  Belief in my potential for getting it   5 4 3 2 1

  Commitment to setting big dreams & goals   5 4 3 2 1

2. What is the best *way* to get what you *want*?
Having pinned down what you *want,* what is the best *way* to get it? What *way* are you pursuing now? If you're not getting what you *want,* is it because you haven't found the best *way* — the right *vehicle?*

You're about to start a 100-mile road race through the mountains. Your only opponent is a three-time European grand prix auto-racing champion. This is the first time you've ever been in an auto race. You slide behind the wheel of a brand new, turbocharged, factory-tuned sports coupe. Your opponent gets into a 1953 Divco milk truck with a cracked cylinder head and two flat tires. Who is going to win?

Like the milk truck, you may be in a vehicle that won't get you what you *want* no matter how good you are or how hard you *work*. Or, like the turbocharged sports coupe, you might have found a vehicle that may help you overcome even some major shortcomings, such as a lack of racing experience.

But there's still *work* involved, and you must be willing to do it and do it well, no matter how good your *way* may be.

Rate Yourself
(Circle 5 for absolutely yes, 1 for absolutely no, or 4, 3, 2 for in between)

- I have or am seeking the best *way*
  to get what I *want*   5 4 3 2 1
- I have the strongest, most positive
  Attitude toward the *way* I found or seek   5 4 3 2 1

  Belief that the *way* will get me what I *want*   5 4 3 2 1

  Commitment to the *way* & the *work* required   5 4 3 2 1

3. Are you willing to do the _work_ and do it well? If you know what you _want_ and have found the best _way_ to get it, to what extent are you willing to do the _work_ and learn how to do it well? Do you tend to abandon a _way_ — or what you _want_ — when the _work_ seems too hard? If you're looking for a business opportunity, are you chasing after one get-rich-quick deal after another trying to find a _way_ to get what you _want_ without having to do the _work?_

> The only chance to start at the top is to dig a hole.
> Og Mandino

Unless you expect to inherit a fortune, the _way_ to get what you _want_ is certain to involve _work_. And the more you _want,_ the more _work_ is likely to be involved.

If you found the right _way_ to get what you _want,_ are you _really_ willing to do the _work_ that's required — to do whatever it takes? If you're in a vehicle that won't get you what you _want_ no matter how hard you _work,_ are you willing to do _whatever it takes_ to find a new vehicle with a _work_ plan that's right for you?

Rate Yourself
(Circle 5 for absolutely yes, 1 for absolutely no, or 4, 3, 2 for in between)

- I am doing the _work_ to get what I _want_
  and I am doing it _well_   5   4   3   2   1
- I have the strongest and most positive
  Attitude toward the _work_ I do   5   4   3   2   1

Belief in my ability to do the _work_   5   4   3   2   1

Commitment to keep on doing the _work_   5   4   3   2   1

5 Questions for the Journey
The three "W" questions were an important part, but the bigger and even _more_ important part of your _internal_ context for life's journey are five _crucial_ questions which only you can answer.

These five questions are so important that I've devoted an entire chapter to each of them. I also devoted more than five years to figuring out the process through which you can come up with your own best answers.

No matter how rough things are, no matter how serious your problems may seem to be, no matter how far you may have slipped into despair or how close you already are to true happiness, finding the _best_ answers to these five questions can bring you _total_ success:

1. Where are you now & where do you want to be?
This is the classic planning question, whether for life's journey or for

developing a good business strategy. It is the question that must be answered first if the other four questions are to have full value and meaning.

A good answer to this question is essential for identifying the *overall* context for your life as it is now and a new context for life as you *want* it to be in the future.

> If you don't know where you are, and
> don't know where you're going, it makes
> no difference what road you're on.

But if you know exactly where you are and where you want to be, the road you take will depend upon your answer to the second question:

2. Whom do you choose to be for the journey? This is the *toughest* of the five questions. Sadly, many people go through life *never* coming up with a good answer.

They often take a wrong road through life, stumbling along, often reversing course, never quite sure *who* they are, what they *want* out of life, and what is most and least important.

You have the power to *define yourself* in a way that will make attainable the destination you identified in your answer to the first question. You have the power to change the way you think...to be a victor or victim in life...to choose how far you want to go in anything you pursue.

> It is not enough to understand what we ought to be, unless we
> know what we are; and we do not understand what we are,
> unless we know what we ought to be.
> T.S. Eliot

But no matter *whom* you choose to be for life's journey, achieving self-fulfillment and *certain* success will depend upon your answer to the third question:

3. What will it take to reach your destination? Simply identifying a good destination for life's journey isn't enough. Neither is a good self-definition.

The answer to the third question gives you *The Action Factor* — the last six of the *11 Words for Winning*. They are the five *imperatives* for success, easily remembered by the MECCA acronym.

These five imperatives offer you the *personal power* to get most anything you *want* out of life. But if you're like most people, you will have to strengthen some important personal attributes if you are to harness the power of the five imperatives.

Motivation is the prerequisite to *education*. No one can be educated unless they first are motivated. *Concentration* enables you to focus the power of *motivation* and the substance of *education* on a single task or a life's work. But all is for naught without *communication*, for life is a journey that cannot be made successfully alone. The reward for commitment to the imperatives is *achievement*, which is among the mightiest of motivators to achieve even more.

What it will take to reach your destination also requires a "road map," which means coming up with your own best answer to the fourth question:

4. How should you chart your course? The people most successful in life are those who *plan* well. A good answer to this question results in an effective personal plan.

Having answered the first three questions, you're now ready to get specific on such important aspects of planning as your Personal Mission in life, your specific Vision for the Future and your Key Objectives which, when achieved, will result in getting whatever it is that you *want* by finding the best *way* and, step-by-step, getting the *work* done well.

In an army, it's said the best way to get lost is the combination of an eager second lieutenant and a map. In life, the best way to get lost is being an eager person *without* a map.

Success is confirmed, underscored, assessed, and reinforced by the fifth question:

5. When will you know you've arrived? Many think they've "arrived" when they attain an important position at work, build a business to a certain level, move into a fancy house, etc.

Arrival as confirmed by the fifth question means you've reached the attitudinal "location" identified in the first question. That location is not an *end* to your journey through life, but the best place in which to *continue* it.

Making sure you've arrived in the location you set out to reach avoids the problem of the nuclear submarine captain who announced to his anxious crew that, after being submerged for six months, they were surfacing at last — and soon would see the skyline of either New York or Rio de Janiero.

When you've answered the fifth crucial question well, you've positioned yourself for *ongoing success* and self-fulfillment.

Process Is Hard, Lack of It Harder

No matter how symmetrical and easy to understand, this or any other career and life-planning process is *hard*. In the long run, though, living life *without* such a process can be a whole lot *harder.*

That means you've come to a *fork* in the road.

One route leaves the book at this point and offers the seemingly easier alternative of "winging it" through life. The other route starts in the next chapter with a process that, if followed, will give you greater control of your life and a firmer fix on where you're going.

The process also will enable you to take your place among the *less than one percent* of the adult population that has developed a well-conceived, *written* career and personal plan.

> When you come to a fork in the road, take one.
> Casey Stengel

Do you know people who "have it all together?" They're the ones who know where they're going and who focus on getting there. They're successful in their jobs, professions or businesses; and *still* have a good family life with time left to enjoy recreation, hobbies and other such pursuits. They exude self-confidence.

On the other hand, do you know people who lead lives of utter *chaos*? They're the ones who either fail at one thing after another or always seem to be hanging on by a thread. They go from job to job, marriage to marriage, friendship to friendship, constantly complaining about never having time to enjoy *anything* in life. They always seem frazzled and out of breath.

> When this latest crisis is over, I'm going to have a nervous breakdown.
> I earned it, I deserve it and *nobody* is going to keep me from having it!
> Popular sign for the wall

What's the difference? Why is it that some people seem to be in total control of the <u>circumstances</u> in their lives and others allow the <u>circumstances</u> of their lives to be in total control of them?

Quite simply, it's that the people who seem to be in control have developed better answers to the questions raised in this chapter than people who are *not* in control.

You don't want a million answers as much as you want a few *forever* questions. The questions are diamonds you hold in the light. Study a lifetime and you will see different colors from the same jewel.
Richard Bach
Running From Safety

Chapter 6

The First Question:
Where Are You Now and Where Do You Want to Be?

- **5 Cities and States from Which to Choose**
- **A Road Map for the Present and Future**

Question One:

It's that eons-old question to kick-start *any* planning process, whether for a huge multinational corporation or for you personally. It simply identifies conditions now and conditions as they will be, given successful accomplishment of whatever steps are required to go from where you are now to where you want to be.

"Where are you now and where do you want to be?"

Gosh, that's a *simple* question, isn't it? I wish it were!

Organizations step back, look *objectively* at the big picture, pick the best forms of measurement, and ask themselves that question all the time. The fact is, though, very few *individuals* are willing or able to do likewise.

"Where am I now and where do I want to be? Well, uh..."

Totally Clueless?

To use some Generation X vernacular, when it comes to answering such a profound question, most people are *"acluistic"*. That means *totally clueless.*

Oh, sure, they'll pick out some *slice* of life. Maybe they'll say they're living in a bad part of town now and want to live in a good part of town — someday; or, that they're working as a wick-twister now and want to own a lantern factory — someday.

Maybe *you* see the question that way, as *I* once did. It's much easier, after all, to address the first question in the context of whichever slice of life has your attention at the moment.

The context for each slice may be positive or negative, depending on your perspective — and that, of course, takes us back to the first three words and the kinds of _choices_ you make, how you view your _circumstances_, and what sort of _outcomes_ you expect.

Where Are You Now?	_Where Do You Want to Be?_
Single and lonely	Married and happy
Living in an apartment	Living in a beach house
Trainee welder	Journeyman welder
Business student	CEO of a corporation
A nobody	Leader of a gang
Hopeless duffer	Scratch golfer
English-speaking	Multi-lingual
In prison	Free — to get even
In prison	Free — to make a new life
Stuck in traffic	Commuting by helicopter
Seamstress	Fashion designer
Flat broke	Multimillionaire
Cancer victim	Cured, pursuing a full life

Those are only _slices_ of life — goals, perhaps, viewed as keys to success and happiness. They may be worthy or unworthy, realistic or unrealistic.

Step back, for a moment, and reflect on a _broader_ context for your own life. What do you _want_ out of life: Happiness? Contentment? Joy of living? These suggest intangible states of being.

Or, do you identify what you _want_ out of life in more _tangible_ terms: Wealth? A bigger house or a better neighborhood in which to live? Titles? Status?

So there are two parts to the first of the five questions for your journey through life. You may find the first part fairly easy.

• _Where are you now...?_

Your answer may be a matter of deciding how _off_ you are — anything from "I'm very well _off,_ thank you," to "I'm very badly _off._"

"Well-_off_" seems like an oxymoron. If you're _well,_ how can _off_ put you in a positive state? "Well _off_ the main highway," for example, could put you in the middle of a swamp. Or how about this: "I'm well-_off_ in life but today is one of my _off_ days."

If you are doing really, really, really well, especially in a material sense, should you be regarded as well-_on?_

You also may look at the first part of the question in terms of your general state of mind — anything from being extremely happy to being totally miserable. Or, perhaps you could frame it in institutional terms, such as "in college" or "in mid-career."

Or how about psychological terms, such as "mid-life crisis"?

It's possible, of course, to be floundering so much in life that your "Where are you now?" answer may be like many people's today: "I have no clue." Sadly, a lot of people simply are *lost* in life. Not only have they no idea of where they are going, they have no idea of where they are *now*.

Like everything, the "where are you now?" part of the question is a matter of perspective — of *context*.

> Many miles off course, a balloonist descends to within shouting distance of a farmer working in a field somewhere in Vermont. The balloonist leans out of the basket and shouts: "Where am I?" The farmer looks up, thinks for a moment, and yells back: "Yer in a balloon, ya darn fool!"

What of the *second* part of the question? It may be harder:

• *Where do you want to be?*

You may see your direction in life as a *continuation* of your "state of *off*." You might say, "I'm well-*off* now and will continue to be" or "I'm not well-*off* now, but I'm going to be well-*off* in the future" or "I'm badly-*off* now and see myself as being worse-*off* in years to come."

While having some sort of grasp on where they are now, many people today haven't a clue as to where they want to be.

They may have vivid dreams of fame and fortune or obscure notions of future happiness. They may be caught up in pure fantasies, envisioning themselves as mega-winners in lottery games, or having their every need met by a Prince Charming or a rich widow.

They may believe that "the Lord will provide," interpreting that to mean they simply can sit back and wait for it all to be handed to them.

How about you? How do *you* answer this two-part question? Do you agree that coming up with the best possible answer is an important first step in becoming happier and more successful in life?

Identifying a destination in answer to this question is vital.

> If a man does not know what harbor he is
> headed for, no wind is the right wind.
> Seneca, 4 BC

5 Cities & 5 States from Which to Choose

I think you'll find the question *easier* to answer if you think of it in the form of a road map connecting five "cities."

I call the uppermost city on the road map the *City of Joy*. Lots of people are happy, at least some of the time, but relatively few live lives of pure joy all or most of the time.

City of Joy is the place most people are likely to *want* to be. It is the culmination of positive life experiences. It is consummate joy of living. It is being all you can be. And, it connotes a *spiritual direction* for your life, whatever your religious beliefs may be.

At the bottom of the road map, at the other end of life's spectrum, is a city I call *Hades Gulch*. It represents ongoing misery with little or no hope. Another name for it would be "Pure Hell."

3 Other 'Cities'

Moving up the map from Hades Gulch toward *City of Joy* are three other places to describe life overall:

Purgatoria, a place of unhappiness and upheaval that at least offers *hope* for something better; *Malaisia,* a kind of "rut" where people *get by* in life but don't *get far*; and *Fat City,* which can be a "gold-plated rut" with plenty of ego satisfaction, lots of material goodies but, quite possibly, a feeling that something's missing.

If you are living in or near the *City of Joy*, a major problem in one part of your life shouldn't send you careening all the way down the road to Hades Gulch; unless, of course, there is very little to your life *other than* the part in which you are having a big problem.

There are, to be sure, those who seem to have *everything* go wrong in *all* aspects of their lives — all at once. Without the positive attitudes to deal with such *continuous white water*, people in that situation join the millions who, tragically, have taken up residency down at the bottom of the map in that place I call *Hades Gulch*.

Here is an overview of the five cities and their characteristics:

City of Joy
Self-actualization
Spiritual fulfillment
Attitude of gratitude

Fat City
Material comfort or success
Ego satisfaction / Status
"Conventional" happiness

Malaisia
Moving in circles, going nowhere
Endurable pain
Complain, then watch TV

Purgatoria
Ongoing change / Upheaval
Hope / Striving for something better
Pain and/or unhappiness "for now"

Hades Gulch
Misery
Little or no hope
The ultimate rut

Before taking a closer look, let's put in perspective the concept of the five cities and the road that connects them.

Life is a *journey* and finding joy and happiness in life has more to do with the journey than with reaching a particular destination. So in viewing the five cities, it's important to understand that "taking up residency" in no way inhibits your journey through life.

Your journey *continues* no matter what city you're living in. When you move from one city to another, you change residences but your travel continues.

Put another way, the cities represent *attitudes* or states of mind. A *City of Joy* resident, for example, lives a life of self-ful-fillment that comes with being in a very positive attitudinal state.

So in a broader "geographical" context, consider each of the five *cities* as the capital of an attitudinal *state*. From the bottom of the map to the top, the lineup looks like this:

The city of	*Is the capital of*
Hades Gulch	**The State of Despair**
Purgatoria	**The State of Anxiety**
Malasia	**The State of Mediocrity**
Fat City	**The State of Affluence**
City of Joy	**The State of Grace**

Now I invite you on a tour of the five cities and attitudinal states, seeing what life is like in those places and letting you hear from some of the people who live there.

Let's start with:

Hades Gulch (The State of Despair)

The worst part of living in Hades Gulch is that you have little or no hope. The best part? There is none.

Sadly, many millions of people live most or parts of their lives in Hades Gulch. If you're one of them, you probably see your life today summed up perfectly by a popular bumper sticker:

Life Is Tough, Then You Die

Most days are bad at best, awful at worst. Nothing seems to go right at work (if you have a job), at home (if you have one), or any-where else. The future is bleak. When something *does* go right, it only underscores all the *other* things that are wrong.

Where jobs are concerned, Hades Gulch includes the chroni-cally unemployed whose despair dispels interest in finding a job.

But you'll also find among Hades Gulchians the chronically *over*-employed. These are people who work days, nights, and weekends just to pay bills or keep up appearances. They have been doing this and getting nowhere for so long that life has become one, long, miserable *drag*.

Hades Gulch is the *ultimate rut*. It's the rut that is hardest to climb out of because the people who live there, seeing little or no hope, have scant reason even to *try* moving on.

Being around citizens of Hades Gulch can make it harder to reside in any of the cities higher on the road map. Denizens of Hades Gulch drag other people down.

> Misery loves company. I'm miserable, so pull up a chair.

They replicate the classic observation of crab-fishing: "Catch one crab and put it in your basket and it will climb out. Put a second crab in the basket and neither crab will climb out, for they constantly pull each other down."

Adapting to the environment in Hades Gulch is a form of masochism. Citizens there can develop a *taste* for suffering, perhaps a certain perverse pleasure in day-to-day pain. Often, they allow plenty of time to reinforce their misery.

> The secret of being miserable is to have the leisure to bother about whether you are happy or not.
> George Bernard Shaw

The primary avocation in Hades Gulch is a game called *Ain't It Awful*. Even positives can be negatives through awfulizing:

> After all I've done for that rotten company, they give me a lousy
> 3 percent raise. Oh sure, I didn't get the axe like half the others
> in the department, but now they want me to do some more work.
> I told my boss it wasn't fair, and she had the gall to tell me I have
> a bad attitude!

Dual-income Hades Gulch spouses come home after their bad days (that's just about *every* day) and play a variation on a theme of *Can You Top This?*

> You think *you* had a bad day! Well, *my* day was so terrible that I have
> a splitting headache that starts here and goes all the way around to...

People living in Hades Gulch commit most of the domestic violence and *all* of the suicides. There is a great deal of mental illness among the residents. *But*:

Just because you're not violent, suicidal or mentally ill doesn't mean you haven't taken up residency in Hades Gulch. The city also abounds with people who simply have very negative outlooks on life.

And many people living higher on the map suddenly land in Hades Gulch following a major shock or setback. It could be the sudden end of a relationship, or the loss of a job, or getting the worst-possible news after a physical exam.

Some such people move back up the map on their own. Some are helped back by loving residents of other cities or professional counselors. Some move quickly, others take months or years.

What's Most Tragic

What's most tragic about Hades Gulch is when life *ends* there.

Some people, however — no matter how much *ruin* they've brought to their own lives and to the lives of others — reach the end believing they were totally blameless for all the tragic <u>outcomes</u>; that, somehow, it was *other* people, or the world itself, that was to blame.

> ...my trust has been misused by many people. Disloyalty and betrayal have undermined resistance throughout the war. It was therefore not granted to me to lead the people to victory.
> Adolf Hitler
> April 1945

Is there anything more tragic than nearing the end of life bitterly blaming others for life's miseries?

Yes! It's nearing the end realizing that the tragedy is, indeed, *of your own making* — that you put *yourself* in Hades Gulch and it's too late to do much about it...that you've frittered life away...that you didn't become all you could be because you *didn't try hard enough*.

> A man once successful in business lost it all by making some bad decisions and having what he regarded as a lot of "bad luck." He lost his fortune, then he turned to alcohol and lost everything else — his family, his home, and his self-respect. He lived on the street, begging money to buy cheap wine. Quite ill, he lay in the gutter clutching one final bottle of muscatel. A Rolls-Royce stopped in traffic a few feet from where he lay. A chauffeur was at the wheel and, in the back seat, were a well-dressed couple in happy conversation, apparently heading for the theater. The derelict reflected back on his life and on the gutter in which he lay. Turning his eyes toward the man in the Rolls-Royce, he muttered the six saddest words of all: *"There but for me go I."*

What will be the closing thoughts of *your* life if you are living it in Hades Gulch? What will *you* look back upon with regret? What words will *you* use to coomplete the one sentence — or string of sentences — that begins with the words *"If only I had...?"*

Denial is one of two common characteristics in Hades Gulch.

There's nothing wrong with *me*. It's the *world* that's sick. Okay, so I don't walk around with a phoney-baloney smile telling everyone how great things are. The fact is, things *aren't* great and there's no use trying to pretend that they are!

The other common characteristic is a need for help. Fortunately, some recognize that need and go after it, or accept one of the helping hands so often extended by people who care.

There are many good avenues of treatment available and many excellent professionals who can give a big boost to a better place on the road map. The most powerful help can come from above through prayer, facilitated by caring people who already have found great strength in the spiritual dimension of life.

No one should consign one's self — or be consigned by others — to life in Hades Gulch, no matter *what* the *circumstances*!

Where are you now? If you agree that, overall, your life is one of misery and little or no hope, then you are living in Hades Gulch, smack in the middle of the State of Despair. That's the bad news.

The good news is that you can step back and take a hard, fresh, honest look at your life and decide that while Hades Gulch is where you are now, it's neither where you want to be nor where you will be.

If you don't want to stay in Hades Gulch, where *do* you want to be? Onward and upward — *all the way to the top?*

Was this all life would ever mean to me — working at a job I despised, living with cockroaches, eating vile food — and with no hope for the future?

Dale Carnegie
Recalling the start of his career

What an *improvement* it would be, just to move up — for now, at least — to the next city and state on the map:

Purgatoria (The State of Anxiety)

Welcome to Purgatoria. Like Hades Gulch, you may find much "pain and suffering" here. But there are five major differences :

1. If you live in Purgatoria, you *have hope* for something better. If you live in Hades Gulch, you have little or no hope.

2. In Purgatoria, you are *moved to action* and are strengthened by hope. You are willing to *work* toward making life better. In Hades Gulch, whatever hope there may be depends on external *circumstances* such as winning a huge lottery jackpot. *Not* winning, week after week, reinforces the misery of living in Hades Gulch.

3. Having a good measure of hope, you regard your residency

in Purgatoria as temporary. In Hades Gulch, having little or no hope, you probably feel resigned to live there permanently.

    4.   Residency in Purgatoria may have resulted from a conscious decision you've made to pursue a particularly arduous, or even painful, course of action in order to bring about something better in life. If you're living in Hades Gulch, it's *not* because you've made a conscious decision to live there. You may even live there a long time without realizing it.

    5. If you are suddenly faced with tragedy — loss of a loved one, a crippling accident, sudden termination of a job or the like — you may land in Hades Gulch. But you'll move up the road to Purgatoria the moment you decide to *overcome* your loss and get moving with whatever actions are necessary to recover, no matter how painful.

    The temporary nature of Purgatoria is underscored by the doctrine of the Roman Catholic Church. Purgatory, the doctrine holds, is a place where, having received the grace of God upon death, a sinner undergoes punishment and atonement in preparation for Heaven.

A Temporary State

    In a secular sense, Purgatory has come to mean a *temporary* state of misery or suffering. Put another way, Purgatory — or the City of Purgatoria, in this case — may be a place of darkness but, like a short tunnel, it clearly has a light at the end.

    Purgatorian: "I'm finally seeing light at the end of the tunnel!"
    Hades Gulchian: "Yeah, but I bet it's the headlight of a locomotive."

    If you're like me, you've spent *some* parts of your life in Purgatoria and the State of Anxiety, and maybe that's where you are now.

    You may even have moved to Purgatoria *voluntarily,* perhaps by immersing yourself totally in the pursuit of a goal that you have accepted weeks or months of pain in exchange for significant gain.

    Many an Olympic Gold Medal winner spent a *long, long time* in Purgatoria's gyms and practice fields, enduring every hardship just for the *prospect* of winning the gold. The sunlight at the end of the tunnel shines very brightly, indeed!

    If you've served in the military, you may have spent some number of weeks in a notorious neighborhood of Purgatoria called Boot Camp. Or you may have volunteered to live for awhile in an even *tougher* neighborhood so you could earn greater responsibility and the privilege of becoming a leader.

    Purgatoria, however, should not turn into a lifelong struggle. In every relentless pursuit of something better, there should come a time when the quest itself will produce a strong sense of self-fulfillment — even exhilaration. In other words, one person's *Purgatoria* can become another person's *City of Joy.*

You haven't lived until you've lived *some* parts of your life in Purgatoria. It's not healthy, though, to live large amounts of your life there.

Whatever Purgatoria's hardships are for you, they should result in *outcomes* that enable you to pack your emotional bags and move to a better place on the road map.

If, like an Olympic athlete, your voluntary residency in Purgatoria could go on for years, the constant striving and continuous improvement should bring the kind of refreshing excitement and joy that puts you at or near the top of the map.

'Runner's High'

Marathon runners know this phenomenon as "runner's high." There's pain in all-out running, but there comes a point when a certain kind of euphoria sets in — an exhilaration from the run itself.

Being in Purgatoria voluntarily is the consummate expression of *no pain, no gain*. If your quest for self-improvement is limited to only those things that are easy or convenient, you haven't decided to take up temporary residence in Purgatoria.

Having the will to endure the pain of Purgatoria *voluntarily* in order to achieve something better requires not only being able to see sunlight at the end of the tunnel, but learning to break goals down into manageable pieces, mastering the art of living one day at a time and making the best of it.

> While serving as chaplain at the U.S. Naval Academy, I remember a young man who came to my office wanting to resign. It was "Plebe Summer" and he had been there about two weeks. "I can't take 300 days of this," he said. I asked him whether he could stand it until tomorrow. He said he could and I told him to come back to see me. The next day I asked him if he could stand it for one *more* day, explaining to him that he doesn't have to handle all 300 days at once, only one day at a time. He got the point and got through it — all 300 days of it — one day at a time!
>
> The Rev. Chuck Greenwood
> Captain (Chaplain), U.S. Navy-Retired

Being in Purgatoria voluntarily is one thing. *Involuntarily* landing there is quite another.

Losing a loved one through a long, terminal illness can make anyone face the depths of despair. Those who *never* recover from the anguish have consigned themselves to Hades Gulch. Those who do, spend some time in Purgatoria, then move on.

Perhaps the worst tenures in Purgatoria were endured by prisoners of war in Vietnam — men held captive under conditions so horrible that it's hard to imagine so many survived the ordeal and were able to get on with their lives after they were freed.

First-rate military training played a major part in the ability of so many POWs to stand up under physical and mental torture lasting eight years and even longer.

Some lapsed into the hopelessness of Hades Gulch, for there were suicides, breakdowns, and some long-term mental disorders. The remarkable resiliency of so many others, however, has been attributed to *more* than just "good training."

> Each man's values, from his own private sources, provided the strength enabling him to maintain his senses of purpose and dedication. Our values systems had in common the fact that they were based on rules, that they placed unity above self and that they precluded self-indulgence.
>
> Vice Admiral James B. Stockdale
> *A Vietnam Experience*

Navy Captain Robert Mitchell, a flight surgeon, conducted a long-term study of the men who spent years as prisoners in Vietnam. He examined many of the men shortly after their release and matched them with men of similar age, experience and physical characteristics who had *not* been held prisoner.

Fifteen years later, Capt. Mitchell and his colleagues were startled to learn that the ex-POWs were in generally *better health* than those who had *not* undergone the ordeal of captivity!

Heart Attacks Down, IQ Scores Up

There were fewer heart attacks, attributed to being without red meat for a long period, and the increase in IQ scores was higher among the ex-POWs, probably due to mental exercises and creative activities that helped them endure captivity.

The ex-POWs also tended to have no long-term psychiatric problems and were found to handle stress better than those who hadn't suffered at the hands of the North Vietnamese.

This suggests that, given the right training, values systems, personal courage, and deep and abiding faith, even in so terrible a place as a North Vietnamese prison camp a person can become stronger and more able to overcome life's challenges.

Hades Gulch is a rut — the deepest rut of all. Purgatoria should *not* be a rut; rather, it should produce the kind of self-renewal and strength that enables you to *move straight through* the next city on the road map. It's a *huge rut* in which reside many, many millions of people. It's called:

Malaisia (The State of Mediocrity)

Malaisia can be a *trap* for people experiencing the joy of breaking out of Purgatoria.

One day, the months or years of struggle and hard work pay off.

Graduation at last!... Finally! The Gold Medal you've worked so hard to achieve!... *Yes*! You've starved yourself and suffered for three months to get your weight down to this level and *you did it*! Years of putting up with *stuff* and *finally* you got the job you've always wanted!

You made it! A grand and glorious leap from weeks or months or years in Purgatoria, all the way to this exhilarating *moment* in the City of Joy or a romp through the gold-plated avenues of Fat City.

But *now* what? For most people, when the celebrating stops and the joy of <u>achievement</u> wears off, it's a descent right back down to the City of Malaisia, capital of the State of Mediocrity.

The streets of Malaisia go around in seemingly endless circles and the signs that mark them are long-faded.

President Jimmy Carter inspired the name for this city when he warned in a 1979 speech that America's two greatest problems were energy and malaise.

By energy, he was referring to fuel supplies; but, just as well, he could have meant energy fueled by ambition and self-discipline.

By malaise, he was referring to a weakening of the American spirit and a kind of vague sense of ill-being that accompanies lack of action, moral decay, and societal decline.

Malaisia, like Hades Gulch and Fat City, is a rut. It's simply a more *comfortable* rut than Hades Gulch, although it lacks Fat City's big bucks, expensive toys, and gilded lifestyles.

An Endurable Pain

There's some pain in Malaisia. It's not the deep and enduring pain found in Hades Gulch, nor is it the intense and temporary pain experienced in Purgatoria.

It's an *endurable* pain and it quickly becomes an *acceptable* pain. The stores in Malaisia sell a lot of sofas, hammocks, recliners, big-screen TV sets, aspirin and other painkilling home remedies — all to enhance the endurability of the dull pain associated with "just getting by" in life.

> An old dog lay on the front porch of a house, woefully letting out a low yowl now and then. A visitor inquired of its owner why the dog was lying there yowling. "He's lying on a nail," the owner explained. "Why doesn't he move to a more comfortable spot?" the visitor queried. "Well," answered the dog's master, "he probably figures it hurts more to move than it does to just lay on the nail and yowl."

Residency in Malaisia represents the "settle-for" style of living. Part of the endurable pain associated with living there is that, deep down, Malaisians *know* they can achieve more in their lives, but it's easier just to settle for what life hands them. After all, a mediocre life is *very acceptable* in Malaisia — among so many mediocre people.

While there's a high rate of employment, there's also a huge amount of *under*-employment and untapped potential in Malaisia.

People go back and forth from home to job, oblivious to opportunity and impervious to invitations to make more of themselves.

Life is much the same throughout Malaisia, except that the ruts in the higher-income areas of town are more comfortable than the ruts in the lower-income areas.

Avoiding the Need to Think

Television is the main source of entertainment in Malaisia and the more mindless the programming the better. After all, what could be more fitting after a day of less-than-maximum effort than to spend an evening on a sofa avoiding the need to think?

This doesn't mean everyone in Malaisia is lazy. Like some folks in Hades Gulch, there are people who hold down two or three jobs trying to keep up with the bills or with "the Joneses." But there is little likelihood of becoming successful at any single pursuit, because Malaisians tend to lack focus.

The deepest belief among Malaisians is in the Free Lunch. The city, and the State of Mediocrity surrounding it, is a thriving market for every kind of get-rich-quick scheme and offer of something for nothing.

Unlike the people who live in Hades Gulch, there is a fair degree of hope among the residents of Malaisia. But the source of that hope lies more in *something coming along* rather than in *making something happen.*

> *Calvin*: "I don't want to pay any dues in life. I want to be a one-in-a-million overnight success! I want the world handed to me on a silver platter!"
> *Hobbes*, rolling his eyes: "Good luck."
> *Calvin*, angrily: "Surely you concede I *deserve* it!"
> Bill Watterson, cartoonist
> *Calvin and Hobbes*

When stopping to ask directions, most Malaisians ask for the Path of Least Resistance. Sometimes, residents will work very hard at finding the *easy* way around a problem — exerting, in the process, more energy than would have been required if the problem were attacked head-on in the first place.

Procrastination reigns supreme in Malaisia.

> *Visitor* : "Your roof's leaking. Why don't you fix it?
> *Host* : "It's raining."
> *Visitor* : "Why don't you fix it when it's *not* raining?"
> *Host* : "Well, then it's not leaking."

Relationships among Malaisians are more superficial than deep and genuine. Often, they center on routines — bowling every Friday night with the same people, the bingo hall two or three nights a week with the same crowd, going to religious services every week to sleep through spiritual messages and *appear* to be believers.

Many people spend most of their lives living in Malaisia and the State of Mediocrity, hoping someone will give them a free ride up the road to a better place.

Average? Yes and No

From a geographical perspective, the city's location — in the middle of the road map — suggests that it's *average*. But from a psychological perspective, there's no challenge to Malaisia's claim as capital of the State of Mediocrity.

> Mediocrity is a region bounded on the north by compromise, on the south by indecision, on the east by past thinking, and on the west by a lack of vision.
>
> John L. Mason
> *An Enemy Called Average*

By today's standards, living in Malaisia and the surrounding State of Mediocrity too easily is regarded as *normal*. It's normal to spend evenings glued to the boob tube. It's *normal* to stay home on most election days. It's *normal* to take the path of least resistance in careers, in <u>education</u>, in relationships, in the practice of religion, and in other aspects of life.

You are living somewhere in the State of Mediocrity if you are minimally to reasonably comfortable and would rather complain about life's shortfalls than go out and *do* something about them.

Do residents of Malaisia aspire for a better life? Of course! But it's a matter of having better luck, or of some long-lost uncle leaving a wad in his will, or of hitting the big jackpot Saturday night, or of being given a big raise or promotion at work based on length of service rather than outstanding performance.

And if one of those "strategies" ever *did* pan out in a big way, it could mean a free ride all the way up the road to:

Fat City (The State of Affluence)

Those who live in Malaisia and eventually choose to find a better place, as well as those who take the expressway from Purgatoria and go straight through town without stopping, find a fork in the road just beyond Malaisia.

One road leads to City of Joy and the other goes to Fat City. To be undecided on which road to take is to stay in the City of Malaisia.

Most often, travelers on the roadway made their decisions on which city to head for *long* before reaching the fork in the road. The decision may have come on a sofa in Malaisia while fantasizing about life as it *should be*. Or it may have been the very focal point of tremendous effort and sacrifice back in Purgatoria.

Those motivated by fame and fortune and status probably never noticed the City of Joy sign as they left Malaisia and headed for Fat City. Their destination never was in question.

Occasionally, City of Joy is the *vision* but, suddenly immersed in fame and fortune, there's a sudden swerve to the glamor of Fat City.

The sign at the edge of town is fully gilded: "Welcome to Fat City, Capital of the State of Affluence."

Life in the Fast Lane

People who live "in the fast lane" invariably are on the road to Fat City. Once there, they find a full range of material comforts and ego-massagers befitting "Lifestyles of the Rich and Famous."

Main Street is loaded with BMWs, Jags, Corvettes and other cars reflecting "arrival." There are more exclusive clubs in Fat City than any other place.

Wine consumed in Hades Gulch may be from a brown paper bag. In Purgatoria, it may not be consumed at all, especially by those undergoing rigorous training. In Malaisia, the wine often is the best that money can buy on a coupon at the discount store. And Fat City? It's the most impressive label available, preferably served where there is both a red wine steward *and* a white wine steward.

People who brag about being "self-made" live in Fat City.

The problem with self-made people is that they worship their creators.

There are a lot of titles in Fat City and great sensitivity to how they are used. Residents usually don't wait for someone to bestow the titles in conversation, but rather are quick to bestow the titles upon themselves.

Cocktail parties in Fat City offer abundant opportunities to engage in first-person-singular communication. Listening is simply waiting for the right moment to resume talking, or tuning out of conversation long enough to concoct another barrage of impressive patter:

I really am glad to meet you because as I was telling your charming spouse just a moment ago, I enjoy getting to know people who share my opinions on economic matters, especially since I became president of the Society for the Advancement of Arbitrage and had the opportunity to conduct a briefing at the White House for which I received a presidential citation that resulted in my picture being on the front-cover of *Debt Today* magazine...and by the way, what did you say your name was?

In and of itself, *wealth* is not the problem in Fat City. There are wealthy people in the City of Joy as well, along with many people who are simply rich in spirit. The difference is that a certain *level* of wealth is a requirement to take up residency in Fat City.

There are two roads out of Fat City.

One leads back down the roadway. If the departure from Fat City is due to a sudden loss of the material things on which residency depended, it may be a fast plunge all the way down the road into Hades Gulch.

The other road goes on to the City of Joy. This road is open to those who, without having to lose it all, come to believe there's much more to life than the conventional happiness and material success that Fat City has to offer.

There also are people lost in the fog somewhere between Fat City and the City of Joy. These are the people who are not sure *where* they are from one day to the next.

> Within my earthly temple there's a crowd.
> There's one of us that's humble; one that's proud.
> There's one that's brokenhearted for his sins,
> And one who, unrepentant, sits and grins.
> There's one who loves his neighbor as himself,
> And one who cares for naught but fame and pelf.
> From much corroding care would I be free
> If once I could determine which is *me*.
> Edward Sandford Martin

Fat City is a rut. Although gold-plated, the rut can be even deeper than Hades Gulch.

The biggest principle of life that's lost on people living in Fat City is that happiness can't be bought. If you're living in Fat City, that hasn't *fully* occurred to you. And why should it, so long as there are the resources to enjoy a never-ending supply of *things*?

Conventional Happiness

Life can be happy in Fat City, at least in a "conventional" way. But carried to its extremes, life there can be especially tragic.

From the movies comes a compelling illustration. It was the extraordinary film by Orson Welles of the poverty-to-power climb of a newspaperman who, in a material way, really *did* end up having "everything."

> "For what shall it profit a man if he shall gain the whole world and lose his soul." See Citizen Kane for details.
> *New York Times* film review, May 2, 1941,
> citing *The New Testament*

Don't be misled by the extreme cases, though. The fictional Mr. Kane and real-life role models notwithstanding, many Fat Citians *do* find life there pretty good — even *very* good, and even for long periods.

Those inwardly driven in a quest for *more,* however, often are unable to find much *self-fulfillment* in Fat City.

For the people who live there, happiness is far more related to *satisfaction* than deep and spiritual self-fulfillment. Perhaps that's because too much wealth came too soon, or that the focus on the material aspects of life has been so strong for so long that a kind of boredom sets in. The pursuit of happiness may require more and more novel, or even *bizarre,* experiences.

Relationships Change Often

Relationships are likely to change more often in Fat City than in other cities on the road map.

> There's a ritzy neighborhood in California where 5 out of 4 marriages end in divorce. How can *that* be? So many people get divorced 2, 3 or 4 times that the average lifelong commitment never took place!

Although there's a relatively high divorce rate, Fat Citians pride themselves in being quite civilized about such matters. Pre-nuptial agreements, out-of-court settlements, joint custody and boarding schools for the kids are not unusual.

Lawyers do quite well in Fat City. Most of them, in fact, also *live* there.

Economic downturns are especially hard on Fat Citians, forcing many back down the road to Purgatoria or even all the way down to Hades Gulch.

Rarely are refugees from Fat City content to set up housekeeping in Malaisia, however. More likely than accepting a *settle-for* life in the State of Mediocrity, they choose Purgatoria for another run at fame and fortune. If it works, they're back in Fat City. If it doesn't, the new destination may be Hades Gulch in the State of Despair or yet another "go" at Purgatoria.

'Will Consult for Food'

When times are bad, you might even find an ex-Fat Citian in a pin-striped suit on a street corner holding a briefcase in one hand and, in the other, a sign reading: "Will Consult for Food."

The lower road out of Fat City can be pretty crowded when there's a big economic downturn. High rollers with a lot of debt usually pass through bankruptcy court on the way down the road.

The upper road out of Fat City is the road to the City of Joy and represents a totally different direction in more ways than one.

Choosing *that* road abandons the notion that money is the root of all happiness.

It begs the difference between rich in pocket and rich in spirit. It leads toward a whole new perspective, rooted in the realization that even people *totally lacking* in material wealth can find a joy of living that's true and enduring.

> Some have too much, yet still do crave;
> I little have, and seek no more;
> They are but poor, though much they have,
> And I am rich with little store:
> They poor, I rich; they beg, I give;
> They lack, I have; they pine, I live.
> Edward Dyer

Traffic conditions on either road leading to the City of Joy are described in the title of an extraordinary book:

> *The Road Less Traveled: A New Psychology of Love, Traditional Values and Spiritual Growth*
> M. Scott Peck, MD

In this context, you'll find the roads less traveled lead to:

City of Joy (The State of Grace)

If you think Fat City is where the *truly* powerful and successful people live, think again. The trappings of success and power may be everywhere in Fat City, but much is missing.

Getting some Fat Citians to acknowledge something missing may not be easy. With lots of material stuff, what *could* be missing?

What's most-often missing in Fat City (besides humility) is *enough*. There is an endless quest for more. Sometimes, though, when the quest for more doesn't bring a hoped-for level of happiness, a Fat Citian may discover what so many in the State of Affluence find hard to pinpoint: That the "missing something" is an understanding of where power comes from and how it should be used and appreciated.

> Invariably, when asked the source of their knowledge and power, the truly powerful will reply: "It's not my power. What little power I have is but a minute expression of a far greater power. I am merely a conduit." I have said that this humility is joyful. That is because...the truly powerful experience a diminution in their sense of self.
> M. Scott Peck, MD
> *The Road Less Traveled*

The City of Joy is a place of *spiritual* fulfillment, with "spiritual" covering a wide range of meanings far beyond the confines of a single religion or brand of philosophy.

City of Joy is not a "gated community" like Fat City, for people who live there may see *no* gates or, if they do, see them as beyond-life and, perhaps, pearly.

Like the other cities on the roadway, the City of Joy also is a capital. Hades Gulch is the capital of the State of Despair, Purgatoria is the capital of the State of Anxiety, Malaisia is the capital of the State of Mediocrity and Fat City is the capital of the State of Affluence.

City of Joy is the capital of the *State of Grace*.

Living Beyond Yourself

To be in the State of Grace is to be in a state of joyful living, and to be in a state of joyful living is to be in a state of living beyond yourself. Citizenship in the City of Joy cannot be bought, nor can it be earned. *Anyone* can live there, for citizenship is a gift *offered* to everyone but *accepted* by few.

Wherever you are now, you are there because you have granted yourself permission to be there. If you are in a place of unhappiness, it is by your own <u>choices</u>. No one — and no <u>circumstances</u> can make you unhappy without your permission.

Grace is a gift offered to the undeserving. It cannot be earned, only accepted. It is no more an entitlement than is happiness.

The gift of grace granting City of Joy citizenship is a divine gift. If the God of your understanding is a loving God, the divine gift of grace is *unearned* and *unmerited*. It is a gift offered equally to anyone willing to accept it and live in it.

Some seek to accept this gift in part. Few accept it in its entirety, for it requires a selfless spirit and unravels the web of conventional wisdom.

New Heights of Intolerance

Take excellence, for instance. The frenzy for excellence, spawned by a deluge of excellence books and other forms of unending exhortations, has created new heights of intolerance and fear throughout much of Corporate America.

There's no margin of error among the most avid disciples of excellence, and many a career has been ruined over interpretations of what constitutes excellence and what level of deviations should be professionally fatal. The same is true of excessive lust for winning.

Americans love a winner and will not *tolerate* a loser!
General George S. Patton Jr.

Excellence and winning are essential qualities in successful people. What distinguishes the Fat Citian from a resident of the City of Joy? Intolerance and an unforgiving spirit.

Intolerant and unforgiving people cannot live in the State of

Grace, for they lack not only the ability to extend gifts of grace to others, but they lack the ability to forgive themselves for their own shortcomings. Thus, they deny themselves the ability to accept a divine *gift* of grace.

> The many uses of the word in English convince me that *grace* is indeed *amazing* — truly our last best word... The world thirsts for grace in ways it does not even recognize; little wonder the hymn "Amazing Grace" edged its way onto the Top Ten charts 200 years after its composition. For a society that seems adrift, without moorings, I know of no better place to drop an anchor of faith.
> Philip Yancey
> *What's So Amazing About Grace?*

Does this mean the people in the City of Joy are weak and unsuccessful? Not at all! Unlike the whiners often found in other places, City of Joy citizens are able to deal with problems — their own and those of others — without having to "leave town."

> Actually, I'm grateful for all my problems. As each of them was overcome, I became stronger and more able to meet those yet to come. I grew on my difficulties.
> J.C. Penney at age 95

An occasional stressful situation to one side, people who live under *continual* stress are not — and cannot be — residents of the City of Joy. Tragically, more than half of all Americans suffer from hypertension by the time they reach their 50s.

> Never let life become an ongoing emergency!

If you live in the City of Joy, you do not live a stressful life. You have a deep and abiding faith that helps you overcome the fears that *cause* stress. Your faith enables you to accept life's lack of guarantees and overcome life's problems with a spirit that's both good *and* strong.

In the City of Joy, you are happy to live in a single neighborhood that extends beyond the city limits and embraces the entire State of Grace. There are no wealthy sections of town, nor any tracks where you may live on "the other side."

Rich in Spirit

Your neighbors are *all* rich — in spirit and, perhaps, in material blessings as well; and, living where "status" is of no importance, you accept people for themselves rather than for what they represent.

Fat City *can be* a city of *happiness,* but the City of Joy lives up to its name. What's the difference between joy and happiness? Don't those two words really mean the same thing?

Happiness is a state of good fortune and contentment most-often stimulated by favorable *circumstances* or by other people. Some people are happier than others because they have created for themselves a greater *capacity* for happiness and because favorable *circumstances* bring out in them a greater sense of well-being.

Joy is a different matter, for it depends much less on *other* people and on *circumstances*. Joy wells up *within* people who radiate a zest for living and harbor a compulsion to share their joy with others, *no matter what.*

Joyful people are unsinkable!

People living in the State of Grace are joyful people. Their happiness is inward, deeply rooted and *contagious.* Look around you. Do you *know* such people? If so, get closer to them. If not, seek them out. "Catch" some of their contagious joy!

In Fat City, there are people who are, at various times, happy, contented and satisfied. But unlike the City of Joy, Fat Citians depend mainly on *external* factors, putting fulfillment at risk if the stimuli disappear. And they may become bored if the stimuli *don't* disappear.

Here are a few ways to distinguish between people living in Fat City and in the City of Joy:

In Fat City, people mostly...	In the City of Joy, people mostly...
Focus on themselves	Focus on others
Show pride in their success	Are humble about success
Love things, use people	Love people, use things
Lead with authority	Lead by example
Give to get recognition	Give for the sheer joy of it
Are conscious of status	Are statured in conscience
Put trust in facts	Put trust in faith
Seek good connections	Seek good relationships
Have high self-image	Have high self-esteem
Take time out to relax	Take time out to live
See death after life	See life after death

City of Joy as a destination is not a final resting place but is the ultimate base camp from which to pursue a joyful, enriching and totally fulfilling continuation of life's journey, richly blessed with a sense of ongoing renewal— whatever the *circumstances*.

We cannot dream of a Utopia in which all arrangements are ideal and everyone is flawless. That is a dream of death. Life is tumultuous — an endless losing and regaining of balance, a continuous struggle, never an assured victory.

John W. Gardner

A Road Map for the Present and Future

Now it's time to *answer* the first question. Answer it in the context of *life overall,* not just a part of life that may be the burden or blessing of the moment. Consider *all aspects* of your life.

Activity: Draw a large dot in one of the cities, or along a road between cities, to describe "where you are now" *in life overall.* Then draw a star in the place that identifies "where you want to be."

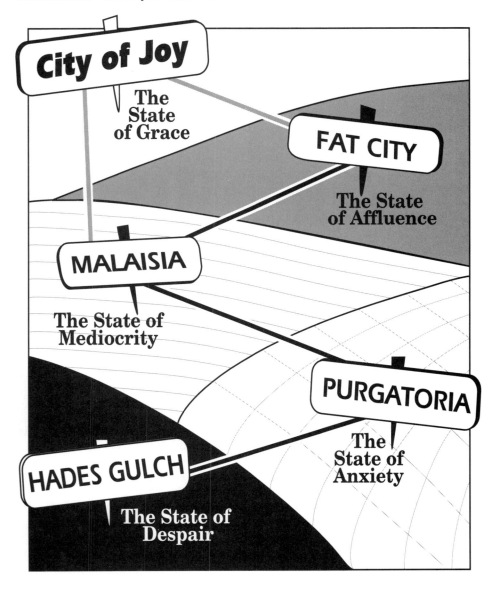

Where Have You 'Lived' During Your Lifetime?

Activity: Now look back on your life, identifying the cities in which you have "lived." This will help you get to where you want to be, especially if there's a wide gap between your dot and your star. Put a check mark in one of the three spaces next to each of the five cities.

I've Lived In:	*Much of the Time*	*Some of the Time*	*None of the Time*
City of Joy	____	____	____
Fat City	____	____	____
Malaisia	____	____	____
Purgatoria	____	____	____
Hades Gulch	____	____	____

Why Did You Place the Dot Where You Did?

Activity: List at least three good reasons why you placed your dot where you did.

1. _____

2. _____

3. _____

4. _____

5. _____

What Would It Take to Reach Your Star?

Activity: List in order of importance at least three changes in your life that would be necessary in order for you to reach your "destination."

1. _____

2. _____

3. _____

4. _____

5. _____

In workshops related to this book, feedback from participants consistently shows a gap — often a *wide* gap — between where people are now and where they want to be.

A session for senior-level managers attending a conference in Washington, D.C., for example, showed *nearly 20 percent* of the participants to be in Hades Gulch and *none* in the City of Joy.

As to where they *wanted* to be, all but one in that session put their stars squarely in the City of Joy. The exception was a committed Fat Citian who would "have it all" if given some winning lottery numbers in advance.

In the workshops overall, a little over a third of the participants providing feedback reported citizenship in Malaisia or some nearby spot in the State of Mediocrity. About 12 percent declared Fat City to be "home," another 10 percent reported they are in Hades Gulch and, but for a fraction of 1 percent in or near the City of Joy, the rest said they are in Purgatoria

98% Want the Best Life Has to Offer

As to where people said they *want* to be, *no one* said they preferred Malaisia or points lower on the map. Preference for the City of Joy was overwhelming, with *98 percent* saying that's where they want to be. Only two percent said, in effect, "just give me plenty of money (Fat City) and life will be great."

So now *you* have answered the first and *easiest* of the five questions for making a successful journey through life: "Where are you now and where do you want to be?"

Get ready to tackle what, for most people, is the *hardest* question of all — the second question: Whom do I choose to be for the journey?

The greatest discovery of my generation is that a human being can alter his life by altering his attitude.
William James

Chapter 7

The Second Question:
Whom Do You Choose to Be for the Journey?

- **Programming, Habits, Priorities**
- **Who You Have Been Up to Now**
- **5 Personal *Choices* for Whom You Will Be**
    1. *To Be a Victim or a Victor*
    2. *How to Think*
    3. *What to Aspire To, Expect, and Feel Entitled To*
    4. *How Far to Go*
    5. *How to Define Yourself from Now On*

Question Two:

Just who *are* you, anyway?

I'm not asking you to give the sort of superficial answer most people give: "butcher," "baker," "candlestick maker..." It's so easy, when asked a question like that, to blurt out your occupation — or, in military terms, to offer no more than "name, rank, and serial number."

And, no, I'm not trying to send you off on one of those deeply ethereal contemplate-your-navel exercises, either.

I tried navel contemplation once, back when various gurus were saying it was an important thing to do. To my surprise, though, I actually discovered something and learned something from the effort. What I discovered was a hunk of navel lint. What I learned was that I needed a shower!

Okay, so much for silliness from the 1960s.

A Valid Question

The second question is a *valid* question when asked in the right context and when framed in an effective way.

The right context, in my view, is its important position between the first question and the third question.

You just answered the first question — *Where are you now and where do you want to be?* Using the road map of five cities and

111

five states, you marked the map to show where you are now and you drew a star to reach for a place you want to be in the future.

Oh, how tempting it is to skip over the second question and dig right into the third — saying, in effect: "Okay, I know where I want to be, so tell me quickly how to get there."

You'll never get full value out of your answer to the third question until you've thoroughly answered the second — whom do you *choose* to be for this journey called life.

> The secret of getting from where you are now to where you want to be is in figuring out who you are now and who you want to become.

Skipping Question 2 would be like declaring your life's work to be finding a cure for cancer without first defining yourself as a medical researcher. Without such self-definition, how could you get the most power from Question 3's five words for winning: *motivation*, *education*, *concentration*, *communication*, and *achievement*?

Programming, Habits, Priorities

You are who you are *programmed* to be.

That may sound robotic, but it's true. As described in the first chapter, the "on-board computer" called your *brain* runs on "programs" that are like computer software packages, ranging all the way from *Mega-Winner* down to *Mega-Loser*.

Some of your programming is influenced by genetic factors. For example, you were born with certain physical features. The owner of the first nose pressed against the maternity ward window starts an endless debate over which relative you *really* look like.

Speaking of noses, if you're blessed with a particularly big one, your on-board computer — through the nature of its programming — considers your nose and related *circumstances* and makes personal *choices* which guide your behavior, habits, and priorities.

Both the legendary swordsman Cyrano de Bergerac and the old-time comic Jimmy Durante declared their humongous proboscises to be symbols of greatness. Make fun of Cyrano's, however, and he'd *kill* you. Make fun of Jimmy's and he'd join in the laugh, saying: "Hey, *'The Nose' knows*!"

> Your programming is the sum of the familial, social, cultural, and physical conditions in which you have made your journey through life from infancy up to this moment. By age 10, most of your *basic* values are programmed, including an underlying work ethic (or lack thereof), concepts of right and wrong, and a sense of order (or disorder).

If you grew up in a positive household surrounded by positive people and avoid harmful influence of negative peers, your initial programming most likely will be positive. If your upbringing was in a negative environment, it most likely will be negative.

If you are the child of successful, *positive* people who helped program you to be successful, your odds for success are greater than if you grew around *negative,* naysaying losers.

The worst of behavior, as well as the best, often can be attributed to childhood programming. Most spouse abusers, for example, grew up in households where there was spouse abuse.

> It has often been reported that when abused children grow up, they become troubled adults, likely to pass the suffering on to their own children. This is another of America's secrets, perhaps our saddest.
> James Patterson & Peter Kim
> *The Day America Told the Truth*

Over the years, your programming undergoes much buffeting and changing, however. Significant emotional events can cause you to change your programming — sometimes *totally*.

For example, if you grew up scoffing at danger, constantly taking risks and throwing caution to the winds, the sudden death of a close friend in a car crash could change your programming from reckless to cautious overnight.

Many a soldier with lifelong programming as an atheist or agnostic has emerged from combat as a believer in God. And, for better or worse, many a child of affluence has undergone substantial programming changes with the loss of the family fortune.

Your programming has everything to do with where you are now and where you want to be, and whom you choose to be for life's journey. Your programming also will determine whether and how you reach your destination.

The *bad* news is that success on the journey may be no greater than the quality of your programming. The *good* news is that you can *change* your programming and *choose* to be whomever you want to be.

> Your past cannot be changed, but you can change tomorrow by your actions today.
> David McNally
> *Even Eagles Need a Push*

Your Habits Reflect Your Programming

What are your habits? What behaviors have become so ingrained that you act with little or no thought to doing otherwise? Which are good habits and which are bad habits?

Smoking is a habit. So is exercising and eating healthy food. Watching mindless trash on TV is a habit. So is nourishing your brain with tapes and books on how to live a happier, more fulfilling life.

Are you habitually late or habitually punctual? Do you habitually toss papers on piles, then spend hours trying to find them; or, do you habitually file papers so you can retrieve them immediately?

Consider the things you did yesterday without thinking. Were you on your feet at the first sound of the alarm, or did you groan through three or four gropes for the snooze button?

If you're married, did you share a *genuine* hugs-and-kisses affirmation of love before leaving for work, or did you simply bound out the door, late as usual, expressing nothing?

Your work habits will determine your degree of success at your job or in running your own business.

Do you habitually finish projects on time or are you always having to explain why they're late? Do you habitually compliment or criticize the people with whom you work — or do you habitually say nothing?

Winning is a habit and so is losing. Winners habitually hone their programming in positive, goal-oriented ways. Losers habitually reinforce their negative programming.

Bad habits *resist* change for the better. Good habits *seek* change for the better.

> ...Many people settle for — and actually practice — their limitations. They practice them so constantly and for so long a time that the limitations become habits.
>
> Norman Vincent Peale
> *How to Handle Tough Times*

Your programming influences the nature and the tenure of your habits. Your habits point toward a third element, the one that helps you answer the second question:

You Are Your Priorities

Your programming drives your habits and, together, your programming and your habits drive your priorities — what you consider most important in life.

So... what in life *is* most important to you right now? What sits on top of all that programming and habitual behavior?

If, in answering the first question, you found a gap between where you are now and where you want to be, what priorities, habits, and programming will you have to change?

You may have one pursuit in life that is so important that little else matters. Or you may have one or more relationships that you seek to balance with a particular pursuit. Or, like many people, you may have a dozen or more things constantly fighting for attention, with "most important" changing from day to day.

If you were to make a list of all the things that are important in your life as of now, you'd find that every item on your list would fit mostly or entirely into one of three categories:

Material Wealth: Money, houses, cars, jewelry, investments, and other tangible possessions. Call this *Having*.

Work and Other Activities: Careers, jobs, hobbies, avocations, and all the things that consume time in the pursuit of income or self-satisfaction. Call this *Doing*.

Relationships: Love, rapport, positive or negative interaction, and all manner of communication with other people, with God, and even with *yourself*. This is the essence of *Being*.

Your list probably will have more than one item in each category. And you are almost certain to have one category that is dominant. Not only will one become dominant because of the *number* of items listed, but because of the extent to which the items represent important *needs* in your life.

This process of *self-definition* is at the center of your answer to the second question: Whom do you choose to be for the journey?

Perhaps the way you define yourself as of *where you are now* in life is exactly right for getting to *where you want to be*.

More likely, though, getting to where you want to be will require changes in how you define yourself. Without making these changes, you will either be unable to reach your destination or your journey will be needlessly hard.

> It is not enough to understand what we ought to be, unless we know what we are; and we do not understand what we are, unless we know what we ought to be.
>
> T.S. Eliot

Question 2's process of self-definition invites you to take a hard look at how you define yourself now and how you *will* define yourself in the future, given a commitment to reaching the destination you identified in Question 1.

Taking inventory of what's been *most important* up to now may not be easy. Like most people, you may not have thought much about it — unless some important aspect of your life is threatened. Even then, the focus most likely would be on *what is threatened* rather than on the full menu of what you consider important and how you define yourself.

The first step in discovering how you define yourself as of now is to make a list of what is most important to you in each of the three categories. Consider whether items should be listed separately or should be combined. For example, if you're a great lover of sports, you could list golf, tennis, softball, scuba diving, and rock climbing separately, or could lump them into an item called "outdoor sports."

The second step is to distinguish between items that are *needs* in your life and items that are *wants*.

Figuring out what is a need and what is a want may not be easy. Your programming largely will be responsible for how you perceive needs and wants, but your perceptions should fall somewhere between necessities for physical survival and how a comedian defines a "need" in this classic laugh-line:

A need is any luxury your neighbor has that you don't have.

Here are definitions that should help you distinguish between needs and wants:

Need: Something of importance in your life that, if suddenly lost, would result in a major reduction in your overall happiness and sense of well-being.

Want: Something of importance in your life that, if suddenly lost, would be disappointing but would *not* result in a reduction in your overall happiness or sense of well-being.

And, don't get ahead of the process! Don't declare a need to be a want because — now that you think about it — it really *should* have been a want all along. If you've *treated* it as a need, it's a need.

The third step in determining how you define yourself now is to decide whether each item on your list is secure or is at risk.

You brought nothing into the world and you will take nothing out. In that sense, *nothing* is secure. And, like everyone, you have no guarantee that your life is totally secure from one day to the next.

So here are two more definitions to help you understand what I mean by the two terms:

Secure: Something that you are not concerned about losing because there are no significant threats to it.

At Risk: Something that may be lost as the result of significant threats you have identified.

While few jobs — at least *real good* ones — are very secure nowadays, consider yours secure if you *see* no significant threats to it. If your home is on the list, consider it at risk if you are having trouble making payments, if it sits in the path of a future highway, etc.

Who You Have Been Up to Now

So now it's time to take a thorough inventory of what, up to this moment, has been most important in your life.

Activity: On separate sheets of paper, list what is of greatest importance in your life as of now. Assign each item to one of the categories. Decide which are needs and which are wants. Write them below in priority order by category, being sure to list needs ahead of wants. Circle the **N** to identify needs and the **W** to identify wants. Circle **S** if the item is secure and **R** if it is at risk.

Needs vs. Wants			Secure vs. at Risk	

Material Wealth (Having)

N	W	1. _____	S	R
N	W	2. _____	S	R
N	W	3. _____	S	R
N	W	4. _____	S	R
N	W	5. _____	S	R

Work / Activities (Doing)

N	W	1. _____	S	R
N	W	2. _____	S	R
N	W	3. _____	S	R
N	W	4. _____	S	R
N	W	5. _____	S	R

Relationships (Being)

N	W	1. _____	S	R
N	W	2. _____	S	R
N	W	3. _____	S	R
N	W	4. _____	S	R
N	W	5. _____	S	R

Picture Yourself as a Pie!

Now that you've made prioritized lists of what's been most important in your life up to now, get ready to *illustrate* the categories of greatest importance by creating a three-slice pie chart based upon your lists.

Figure a percentage of importance for each slice, making sure the three numbers add up to 100 percent. Then draw the three slices according to the percentages and label them *Having* (material wealth), *Doing* (work and other activities), and *Being* (relationships).

But before doing your own pie, "practice" on a few others.

Activity: On notepaper, draw four circles. Then do pie charts on:

• Ebeneezer Scrooge (*before* that life-changing Christmas Eve). As a greedy old miser, how big would his *Having* slice be? He spent all his time working to accumulate wealth but took more pleasure in *Having*, so how big a slice would you assign to *Doing*? Is there *any* slice of *Being*?

• Albert Einstein. His life was in *Doing* his work, his relationships were mostly with other scholars, and he cared little about *Having* material wealth.

• Mother Teresa. Her relationships with the dying in Calcutta, with God, and with her many supporters were as legendary as the work she did.

• 1960s Hippies. *Doing* work was the last thing most of those "flower-child" *Beings* wanted. They decried *Having* much beyond beat-up VW buses.

Activity: Now do your own pie chart bewlow, writing in the percentages and then labeling your three slices as *Having*, *Doing*, and *Being*:

THIS PIE IS "I" *NOW*

MATERIAL WEALTH
———————— %

WORK / ACTIVITIES
———————— %

RELATIONSHIPS
———————— %

Take some time to reflect upon your pie chart. Is the relative importance you have placed on *Having*, *Doing*, and *Being* consistent with reaching (or remaining in) the place *where you want to be* on the road map you marked in answering the first question?

If your pie chart consists of an enormous slice of *Having* with lesser slices of *Doing* and *Being*, how successful will you be in moving from where you are now to where you want to be, especially in light of the 10 trends identified in chapters 3 and 4?

Or how about if you are in the rut called Malaisia, if you want to move up to the City of Joy, and if your pie chart is one big slice of *Being*? Will you *ever* reach your destination without increasing your slices of *Doing* and *Having* — at least a little?

If, in answering the first question, you are not *already* where you want to be, the pie chart you've drawn probably needs to be changed. In other words, you will have to *redefine* yourself — at least to *some* extent — if you are to reach your destination.

Late in life, even Ebenezer Scrooge redefined himself in a huge way after the ghosts of Christmas created the sort of significant emotional events that enable people to *transform* themselves.

> He became a good friend, as good a master and as good a man as the good old city knew, or any other good old city, town, or borough, in the good old world.
>
> Charles Dickens
> *A Christmas Carol*

Scrooge lived most of his life as a Human-*Having* in Hades Gulch, trying to work his way to Fat City but was destined never to get there, because (1) there never could be enough money in his counting house, and (2) he never figured out how to *enjoy* his wealth.

Scrooge's pie chart changed drastically on Christmas morning. The consummate Human-*Having* became a joyful Human-*Being*. And when the pie chart changed, so did the destination for his journey through life. He found the previously undreamed of City of Joy.

5 Personal <u>*Choices*</u> for Whom You Will Be

Having determined who you have been up to now by listing what has been most important and illustrating it with a pie chart, it's time to make five <u>*choices*</u> — the last of which is whom you *will be* from now on.

Before starting that process, though, consider these points:

- A single dominant slice that all but squeezes out the other two will not enable you to reach either the City of Joy or Fat City.

Too much of anything is not good for you.

A person whose self-definition is 98 percent *Having* lacks the sort of emphasis on *Being* and *Doing* that will make living in Fat City out of the question. Fat Citians need to be *Doing* things to attain their conventional happiness. They also need *relationships,* as superficial as they may be, to satisfy their egos.

• Trying to balance the three slices equally won't get you there, either — unless your destination is Malaisia. To balance the slices equally is to live a life of mediocrity.

If you do everything equally, you will do nothing well.

• There's no way to live in the City of Joy without a big enough slice of *Being* to enable joy of living. How many truly *joyful* people do you know who lack strong, abiding, loving relationships? Probably none. And as I can tell you from personal experience:

True joy is being married to your best friend.

Here are five sets of *choices* to help you develop your best answer to Question 2 — whom do you choose to be for the journey?

1. Do You Choose to Be a Victor or a Victim?

I alluded to "victimhood" in earlier chapters. America, for one, has become a *nation* of victims with people often blaming others or their *circumstances* for their own shortcomings and lack of success.

If you're like most people, you probably at least have *felt* like a victim at one time or another. And, like most, you no doubt have pointed a finger at other people when your own efforts fell short.

Point a finger at someone else and three other fingers point back at you.

People who regard themselves as victims are more likely to live in Malaisia or Hades Gulch than in Fat City or the City of Joy. Victims also are more likely to focus on *Having* rather than *Doing* or *Being*. In fact, I believe *broke* people usually are much more money-oriented than rich people — and, in that sense, more materialistic.

Money is a terrible master but an excellent servant.
P.T. Barnum

Whom have you chosen to *be* up to now? A victor or a victim?

Activity: On the next page are five pairs of statements, each with a row of numbers in between. Read each pair carefully, then circle a number. If the statement above the numbers fits you *completely,* circle the "5" or if it comes pretty close circle the "4." If the statement below fits *completely,* circle the "1" or if it comes pretty close circle the "2." Circle the "3" if both statements apply equally.

I have the power to shape my life and I take full responsibility for my personal *choices* and where I am in life today.

5   **4**   **3**   **2**   **1**

I'm at the mercy of forces beyond my control and feel powerless to change the *circumstances* of my life.

I readily accept responsibility when I am wrong and work hard at learning from my mistakes.

5   **4**   **3**   **2**   **1**

I'd rather avoid responsibility for mistakes; I'm good at coming up with ways to show they weren't mistakes at all.

I find joy in the success of those around me, even those who may not have my capabilities or work as hard as I do.

5   **4**   **3**   **2**   **1**

Others succeed by luck or "pull"; I resent people getting ahead of me, especially when they lack my qualifications.

No matter how bad things get, I know I have the power to endure and, eventually, to produce positive *outcomes* in my life.

5   **4**   **3**   **2**   **1**

There's no use in beating my head against the wall; quite often, it's better just to give in and settle for what I've got.

My success is mainly the result of help I have received from God and/or other people.

5   **4**   **3**   **2**   **1**

I get things done in spite of other people or a higher power; when I succeed, I deserve full credit for my success.

Add up the numbers you circled. If the total is:
- 22 to 25, you're programmed as a Victor — congratulations!
- 18-21, you're *mostly* programmed as a Victor but should work on the areas you scored "4" or less.
- 13-17, you're too much of a Victim and have a lot of work to do. Pursue self-help books, tapes or programs and consider professional counseling.
- 12 or below, you are programmed as a Victim and need more help than you can get from books, tapes, and seminars. Seek professional counseling!

Even when they use their victimhood to gain victories, victims ultimately fail. Their negative thinking undermines even the greatest of victories.

If you expect to fail and you succeed, you've failed again!

Examples abound of down-and-out people wrapped in their own victimhoods who've won huge gambling jackpots. It didn't take long for many of them to squander the money and return to what, for them, is normal — victimhood.

In America, many victims of the system are actually volunteers who are cooperating in their own failure.
Dr. Denis Waitley
Seeds of Greatness

Examples also abound on the other side of the equation. There are countless people who, even in the *worst of circumstances*, refused to consider themselves as victims. They were determined to be victors and, backing belief with hard *work*, went on to achieve great things.

Victors are overcomers. A study of 300 world class leaders showed *75 percent* had a physical disability, were abused as children, or grew up in poverty!

Consider Abraham Lincoln. *He failed at everything,* from school to storekeeper to his first four runs at political office — but then went on to become America's greatest and most-beloved president.

If you have a streak of victimhood or are a *total* victim, you can still *choose* to be a victor. But that choice will depend upon how you handle the *second* set of *choices*:

2. How Do You Choose to Think?

You *are* what you have chosen to *think* up to now and you *will be* what you choose to *think* in the future. To change your *life* for the better, change for the better the way you *think*.

Thinking will determine your success or failure, underscored by a simple-yet-profound observation that people who succeed almost always *think* they'll succeed, and those who don't succeed almost always *don't think* they'll succeed.

How you think and what you think determine your level of happiness as well. If your destination for life's journey is Fat City, it is your thinking that will activate the conventional happiness that goes with the territory. And if your destination is the City of Joy, your thinking will determine whether you can turn conventional happiness into *sheer joy.*

To be joyful, you first must be happy, recalling that joy is innate — within you and self-generating — and happiness is circumstantial, often depending on what other people do with you or for you.

Your mind is the processor of perceptions — the thinking machine — that places you on the road map in or near Hades Gulch, Purgatoria, Malaisia, Fat City, or the City of Joy.

> The mind is in its own place and in itself can make a heaven of hell or a hell of heaven.
>
> John Milton
> *Paradise Lost*

If you aren't already convinced that *Choosing How to Think* is the key to reaching your destination for life's journey, consider three blockbuster quotations from three very diverse sources. When considered together, these quotations make it obvious that you *can* choose how to think and the <u>choices</u> you make are directly related to where you are on the road map.

The first quotation is from Joseph V. Bailey, president of the Minneapolis Institute of Mental Health. Bailey and his staff train substance-abuse counselors. In his book *The Serenity Principle,* Bailey lays the foundation:

1. **Thought creates our psychological experience and thinking is a voluntary function.**

You can choose to think or not to think. For better or worse, you can plunge deep into thought. At the other extreme, you also can choose to "vedge out" or, in the latest vernacular, "collapse in front of the boob tube and just *rot.*"

As I've underscored earlier, television is the primary tool with which people *avoid* the need to think. There are other tools as well, such as Rap and various forms of "music" usually played at an ear-numbing volume that makes thinking, let alone meaningful conversation, impossible.

So if you *volunteer* to think, you're ready to consider the second of the three blockbuster quotes. It drives home the potential <u>outcomes</u> from *what* you think and *how* you think.

The point has been made in the teachings of many religions and philosophies, but this version — from Buddhist scripture — says it succinctly and well:

**2.   We become what we think... Suffering follows
an evil thought.**

By engaging in that voluntary function called thinking, you have determined who you are and, by continuing to *volunteer,* you are determining who you will become. If your thinking is evil or — in the modern context — "negative," you bring upon yourself suffering, be it a little or a whole lot.

People are negative because, in volunteering to think, they choose to think negative thoughts. Negative thinking brings unhappiness and denies the glories of joyful living.

Cynical commentators in the news media excepted, negative thinkers rarely succeed in their career pursuits any more than they succeed in finding joy of living. You'll find negative thinkers stuck in the rut of Malaisia, struggling with little result in Purgatoria, and sunk in the mental mire of Hades Gulch.

News flash: The world is a mess! Stayed tuned for details.

Positive people are the ones who *will* find happiness and even joy in life because, when they volunteer to think, they find ways to think positive thoughts. If they're living in Purgatoria, struggling to better themselves, it won't be for long. And when they do move higher on the road map, they are unlikely to get bogged down in the mediocrity of Malaisia.

If you *still* haven't fully grasped the importance of continually *volunteering* to think positive thoughts, the third of these blockbuster quotes should bring a blinding flash of discovery.

It was a revelation that launched a movement called "Psychology of Mind" — an approach to improving the human condition that is favored by a growing number of psychologists. It was a statement that, shared by a friend, changed the life of Sydney Banks, a Canadian welder with no background in psychology, who founded the movement more than two decades ago:

3.   You're *not* unhappy. You just *think* you are.

Wow! It's so obvious and so true — and so many people are so totally *oblivious* to it!

Unhappiness is unnecessary. It results from negative or "evil" thoughts that you voluntarily choose to let enter your mind. There is no reason on earth why you should *ever* be unhappy.

Like everyone else, you will have moments or even prolonged periods of sadness in your life, such as the loss of a loved one. But *unhappiness?* Why?

Unhappiness is strictly the result of your own thinking — *stinking* thinking, to be sure. You *become* what you think, and what you think dictates your attitude and your actions. To be unaware of *that* simple truth is to be on an emotional treadmill.

> When we are unaware that our thoughts create reality, we become victims of our belief system and can only respond through our habits. This is a concept of sincere delusion.
> Joseph V. Bailey
> *The Serenity Principle*

Plus, your attitude and actions can have a big impact on what *other* people think and *their* attitudes and actions toward you — just as you allow the attitudes and actions of other people to influence how and what you think. It's a cycle that, too often, is needlessly vicious.

If you think you're unhappy *because* of your marriage, you can choose to be happy *in spite of* your marriage. Your new-found happiness may even have a positive impact on your marriage partner and — who knows? — could even remove the conditions that you blamed for your unhappiness.

After all, the *only* person you can control is yourself.

The same can be true of your job or even of a life-threatening illness, as shown by "terminally ill" people who literally *laughed* their way back to health.

> A merry heart doeth good like a medicine.
> Solomon
> *Proverbs 17:22*

Happy people tend to be incurable optimists. Unhappy people have chosen the pathway of pessimism — or, even worse, the narrow corridor of cynicism.

You *choose* to think or not to think. You *choose* how to think and what to think. You *become* what you think. If you're unhappy, it's because *you've chosen* to *think* you're unhappy.

The most famous adjective associated with "thinking" is the word "positive." In his landmark book, *The Power of Positive Thinking,* Dr. Norman Vincent Peale offered techniques that, if accepted, would elevate even the most negative of thinkers from victim to victor.

These techniques include ways to believe in yourself, develop peace of mind, create your own happiness, generate an inflow of new thoughts, and harness the power of prayer. To choose *positive* thinking is to choose what Dr. Peale called "a victorious life."

Another adjective associated with *thinking* is the word *effective*. Dr. Gerald Kushel, president of the Institute for Effective Thinking, offers three elements of what he calls *Uncommon Success*.

> "Uncommon Success" means simultaneous success in three significant dimensions: (1) Successful performance on the job, (2) High level of personal satisfaction at work, (3) Success in personal and family life.
>
> Dr. Gerald Kushel
> *Effective Thinking for Uncommon Success*

Dr. Kushel says it's not unusual to find people who are successful in one or even two of the dimensions, but it is *rare* to find people who are successful in all three.

In his research of 1,200 people regarded as successful in what they do, only *four percent* said they also were *happy* in what they do *and* are happy in their personal lives. That's only *48 of the 1,200*!

He identified four steps to effective thinking. The steps enable you to (1) *Take Notice* when you're not moving toward uncommon success, (2) *Pause* to reconsider your thoughts, (3) *Identify* right thoughts to replace wrong ones, and (4) *Choose* to make the switch.

Here's a third adjective — the word *possibility*. "Possibility Thinking" is espoused by Dr. Robert Schuller through *The New Possibility Thinkers Bible* and his many self-help books. It's a step-by-step process through which, with God's help, you can uplift yourself from failure to success, given that *anything* is possible. In other words:

> If you can dream it, you can do it.

To achieve a victorious life is to think *positively*. To achieve uncommon success is to think *effectively*. To reach the City of Joy in the State of Grace also is to think of the great *possibilities* for your life — then make your best day-to-day effort to be *productive* in what you think.

Here are what I call *Five Principles of Productive Thinking* to help you with the second set of <u>choices</u> — choosing how to think:

1. *Be wary of your perceptions.*

Perceptions do not always equal reality. Sometimes they don't even come close. Consider the viewpoints of people you respect when formulating your perceptions — especially people with demonstrated *wisdom*. Face up to important realities, but use them as starting points for further progress, not barriers to future success. People insensitive to how they develop their perceptions tend to *react* rather than *act*, thoughtfully and productively.

2. *Let your heart have faith, let your head have facts.*

Find a balance that works well for you and those around you. Blind facts are no better than blind faith when it comes to matters of this world. Learn when to be productively skeptical. But also learn *never* to be cynical.

3. *Control anger, fear, and greed.*

To live in anger is to accept self-destruction. To live in fear is to accept early death. To live a life of greed is to deny yourself a joyful life. As the Hindu saying goes: "There are three doors to the House of Sorrow — anger, fear, and greed."

4. *Love contentment, but don't let it end your journey.*

To be *totally* content about everything *all* of the time is to live a life of mediocrity in Malaisia. True *joy* in life comes from a productive blend of contentment and *dis*-contentment, especially when the latter focuses on ways to help others find success and happiness.

5. *Let your productive thinking show!*

To others, you are whom you *appear* to be. Make every day a great day for other people as well as yourself. Smile more. Laugh more. It's contagious. And it generates a cycle of thinking that becomes evermore productive.

These five principles should be of great help to you in choosing how to think, especially when blended with the principles of Positive Thinking, Effective Thinking, and Possibility Thinking.

You *choose* to program that on-board computer called your brain by how and what you choose to think. The pattern is like this:
- Your programming determines your attitude
- Your attitude determines your habits and priorities
- Your habits and priorities determine your actions and deeds
- Your actions and deeds determine your level of success.

3. What to Aspire To, What to Expect, and What to Feel Entitled To

Remember the three *Aspirations Factor* words? <u>Want</u>! <u>Way</u>! <u>Work</u>! You fulfill aspirations when you <u>want</u> them badly enough to find the best <u>way</u> to get them, then do the <u>work</u> that's required.

To feel *entitled* to your aspirations is to consign yourself to a life of unhappiness and frustration. People who see themselves as victims demand *entitlements* as offsets to failure. People who see themselves as victors develop strong *aspirations* as onsets to success.

To aspirate is to breathe. An aspiration is a breath of life and a *desire* for something better that is so strong that it *breathes life* into your efforts to achieve.

Big, positive aspirations not only are healthy, but are essential to a successful life's journey. These are the *dreams* which give a *reason* to reach for something better in life, and hold the *hope* of getting it.

As underscored earlier, many people today have given up hope of achieving their dreams. If you're one of them — if you have given up hope — consider this:

> Your greatest barrier to fulfilling big, positive aspirations is *not* the economy or the glut of college graduates or the re-engineering of corporations or any other external factor. It's how little you expect of yourself compared to how much you expect of other people.

You realize aspirations through what you expect and what you *demand* of yourself. You *kill* your aspirations by what you expect others to do *for* you.

People in America and many other nations have institutionalized what they expect of others. Such expectations have created central governments that are much too big and a success rate in other institutions — marriage, for instance — that is much too small.

Reduced to a simple diagram, here's the problem:

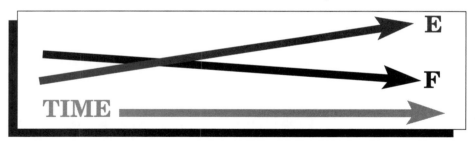

Over Time (T), people have come to Expect (E) far more of the institutions of society than the institutions are able to Fulfill (F).

The gap between Fulfillment and Expectations not only creates political turmoil but undermines the bedrock of American power — self-reliance and personal involvement in the care of others.

Think about it. Where do you or people you know turn when things go wrong? Too often, people turn toward the *wrong source*.

> When the going gets tough, the weak get going — to demand that somebody else *do* something about it.

Where *should* you turn? When the performance bar of success is raised, should you aspire to get over the bar *anyway* by expecting *more* of yourself? Should you down-size your aspirations so you don't have to expect more of yourself? Should you demand the government, your boss, etc. *lower* the bar so it's easier to get over?

What *are* you entitled to? A good job? Free health care? Four weeks of vacation a year? Wealth without work?

People often point wrongly to the three entitlements in the U.S. Declaration of Independence as "life, liberty, and happiness." Happiness? The declaration only guarantees the *pursuit* of it.

> Too many Americans have twisted the sensible right to *pursue* happiness into the delusion that we are entitled to a *guarantee* of happiness. If we don't get exactly what we want, we assume someone must be violating our rights.
> Susan Jacoby
> *Woman's Day*

To close the gap between what is expected of institutions and the ability of institutions to provide fulfillment requires two steps:
1. <u>Work</u> harder and smarter at raising your fulfillment level
2. *Expect* less of institutions and more of yourself.

> While Jesus Christ was preaching, someone in the crowd asked whether to obey when a Roman solider ordered him to carry his military equipment one mile down the road — a common practice. The answer was as unpopular then as it is now. "No, you don't have to carry it *one* mile," Jesus said. "Carry it *two*."

But imagine what would happen if *everyone* went a second mile — as spouses, parents, employees, employers, students, etc.

I believe the divorce rate would drop to zero, productivity would go through the roof, and alcohol, illegal drugs, violent crime, and a host of other bad personal <u>choices</u> would disappear.

If you expect too much of institutions and other people, you are unlikely to fulfill big, positive aspirations. To wit:

> Blessed are they who expect nothing,
> for they are never disappointed.
> Alexander Pope

The *only* way to fulfill big, positive aspirations is to expect more of yourself. Where your own personal success is concerned, which of the following statements makes the most sense to you?

- If it's to be, it's up to a stronger economy.
- If it's to be, it's up to my employees.
- If it's to be, it's up to the federal government.
- If it's to be, it's up to my spouse.
- If it's to be, it's up to Lady Luck.
- If it's to be, it's up to *me*!

Later on, in answering the fourth question (how should you

Chart Your Course?), you'll develop a vision for your future and set the goals necessary to achieve it.

For now, though, simply jot down what you consider to be your biggest and most-inspiring aspirations for your life. Include all major dimensions of your life, such as career or business pursuits, lifestyle, relationships with other people, and spirituality.

Then identify the most important expectations of yourself and others.

Activity: Draft your aspirations on notepaper, prioritize them, and write them below. Do the same for what you expect of yourself and what you expect of others.

What You Aspire To

1. _____
2. _____
3. _____
4. _____
5. _____

What You Expect of Yourself

1. _____
2. _____
3. _____
4. _____
5. _____

What You Expect of Other People and of Institutions

1. _____
2. _____
3. _____
4. _____
5. _____

Review your lists. Can you fulfill your aspirations from what you expect of yourself and others?

For example, do you *aspire* to be financially independent while expecting of yourself average performance in your job? If your present job is your only significant source of income, and financial independence will require much *more* income, how will you fulfill your aspirations through your present job?

Viewed from the other direction, to what extent are the expectations of yourself up to the task of *fulfilling* your aspirations? For example, if you aspire to be happily married (and to the same person forever), what expectations of yourself assure you will do *more* than your share to make the relationship work well?

Are expectations of yourself compatible with your expectations of others? For example, do you expect of yourself great leadership qualities while expecting people you lead to do what they're told without question?

Finally, there's the risky business of entitlements.

Activity: On notepaper, make a list of the five biggest aspects of life you feel entitled to. Try to look at all aspects of life, including career, personal relationships, and being a citizen of your country. Then write them below.

What You Feel Entitled To

1. _____

2. _____

3. _____

4. _____

5. _____

Think hard about what you have listed. Do you lean on entitlements to fulfill your aspirations? Entitlements should *never* be the determining factors in whether you succeed or fail on your journey through life.

Are there any "government entitlement programs" on your list? If so, are you undermining the fulfillment of your aspirations? For example, does your aspiration for a happy retirement depend largely on an entitlement to monthly Social Security checks?

What *should* be on your list of entitlements?

• How about entitlement to being treated with respect based, among other things, on how much you treat others with respect?

• How about being entitled to clean air and water based on your own willingness to be a responsible steward of the environment?

• How about being entitled to the responsibility for raising your children based on your performance as a responsible parent?

• How about being entitled to fair compensation for a good day's work, along with the right to take your services elsewhere?

In your journey through life, what is potentially productive and what is potentially unproductive in sorting out aspirations, expectations and entitlements?

Here are four considerations:
1. Big, positive aspirations are productive
2. All but the most basic entitlements are unproductive
3. High expectations of yourself are productive
4. Inordinate expectations of others are unproductive

So far, you've examined three sets of _choices_ — whether to be a victim or victor, how to think, and how to sort out aspirations, expectations, and entitlements. The fourth set of _choices_ will determine the extent to which you will be _able_ to fulfill your aspirations:

4. Choosing How Far to Go

It's easy to have lofty aspirations and easy to do little or nothing with them. "Average" people have neither lofty aspirations nor a strong will to do whatever it takes to fulfill them. An extraordinary person not only has great aspirations but the will to _go all the way_.

When it comes to aspirations and the willingness to do whatever it takes, are you average? Above average? Extraordinary?

If you're average, studies show, you consider yourself _above average_ in assessing your capabilities. But you also will be among the people who admit they are _not_ performing to their full potential!

Remember, once again, those three important "W" words — _Want_! _Way_! _Work_! If you _want_ more out of life, how _badly_ do you _want_ it? If you've found a good _way_ to get it, are you willing to do the _work_ — no matter how hard it gets or how long it takes?

> I knew it wouldn't be easy to become a doctor, but it was something I wanted more than anything else in my life. I wanted to help people and I wanted the prestige and the income that comes with the profession. I also knew that the only way to become a doctor would be to graduate from medical school and that would take a lot of hard work. By the end of my second year in medical school, I was exhausted. Many years of school, internship, and residency still lay ahead. Now I've fallen in love with someone I have too little time to be with, and I've decided to quit medical school and settle for some other field where I can enjoy life _now_ and still make some use of what I've learned so far.

Do you _really_ aspire to be a winner — a _victor_ in life? If so, never quit! Keep _at it_ and _at it_ and _at it_ until you get what you _want_.

That still leaves the question of changing aspirations — what you want to _win at_. When should you decide to try winning at something else? When is it okay to make a shift in your career pursuit or some other aspiration in life? When is it _not_ okay to give up trying?

How far _should you go_ in chasing your dream?

Only *you* can answer. But here are five guidelines that I hope will help:

1. Make sure you carefully *think through* what you <u>want</u> out of life — then *write it down*

2. Understand that you may have to try more than one <u>way</u> to get what you <u>want</u>

3. Set out determined to *succeed* at any <u>way</u> you try

4. Once you've chosen the best <u>way</u> to get what you <u>want</u>, be willing to do the <u>work</u> by *learning to love it*

5. If, after your *best effort* at doing the <u>work</u>, you see no way you'll *ever* be able to learn to love it, try another <u>way</u> or change what you <u>want</u>

When pursuing a <u>way</u> to get what you <u>want</u>, I believe there are four conditions or "stages" of the effort:

ISAT. *I'll Succeed at This!* ISAT is the starting point for any effort. No one should set out to fail, only to succeed at anything that's worth pursuing. It's where the <u>work</u> begins after the <u>want</u> and the <u>way</u> are chosen.

> If you're one of those people who would rather "go with the flow" than do whatever it takes to reach your destination, think of the fish. The successful ones overcome all obstacles to fulfill their destinies upstream. The ones that "go with the flow" — downstream — are *dead*!

ITTA. *I Tried That Already.* How many times have you set out to succeed at something only to quit and try something else? By planning your <u>want</u> and <u>way</u> carefully, there should be few — *if any* — times when you give up on a major pursuit. The biggest reason many people quit is not to find a better <u>way</u>, but because they let other people talk them out of what they <u>want</u> or the <u>way</u> they chose to get it.

> The grass is always greener on the other side of the fence. That's because you're looking over the fence instead of handling all the crap it will take to make *your own* grass greener!

IDTA. *I've Done That Already.* You reach this state when you let yourself believe nothing more can be accomplished — that you've achieved all the success you can achieve and, therefore, the best strategy is to quit and try something else. You're bored, telling yourself: "Been there, done that." While there are times it makes sense to declare IDTA, go back to ISAT and try something else, too often an IDTA decision is made on an excuse called burnout.

> There are *two* ways to change jobs — change employers or change yourself!

ILTE. *I Love This Experience!* What could be better to make sure the <u>*way*</u> you chose will get you what you <u>*want*</u> than learning to love the <u>*work*</u>? Even in the *worst* of workplaces and private business situations, there are people who *love it* no matter how hard or how unpleasant the tasks and responsibilities.

If work is what you're doing when you'd rather be doing something else, learn to love the work and watch how quickly "something else" begins to pale by comparison.

Here's a diagram of the four conditions or stages of effort involved in pursuing a <u>*way*</u> to get what you <u>*want*</u>.

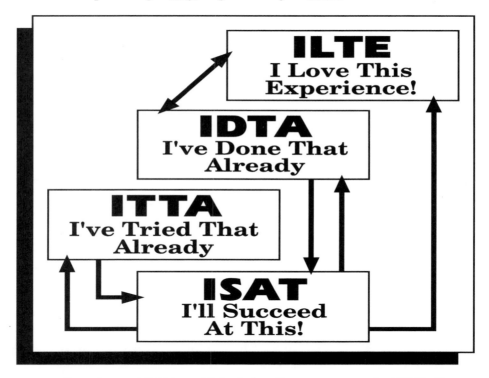

Starting at ISAT, you'll find the closest stage to be ITTA. If you find yourself going back and forth between ISAT and ITTA, you're not alone. Sadly, there are *all too many* people in these unfocused, instant-gratification, TV-oriented times who ride that shuttle often, never trying all that hard at anything and yet expecting success.

IDTA also lies above ISAT. It is reached when you think you've gone as far as you can go with a <u>*way*</u> to get what you <u>*want*</u>. You can keep plugging away at it until declaring burnout, or you can push on to ILTE — either confident that what you love will eventually get you what you *want*, or deciding to adjust what you *want* to accommodate the *way* you have come to love.

Loving the experience is the highest level. If you love what you do, you will find ongoing excitement and are most likely to have found the *way* to get what you *want*.

Even so, there may come a time when the pursuit no longer is the *way* to get what you *want*. Then it's time to declare IDTA, go back to ISAT, and get going again.

In a state of ILTE, you may or may not achieve mastery of what you're doing. But by loving the experience, the *pursuit* of mastery should be ongoing and satisfying.

You may or may not have chosen to go *far enough* in what you've tried (ITTA), what you've done (IDTA), or what you've learned to love (ILTE). Here's your chance to find out.

ITTA - I Tried That Already

Activity: Take a hard look at the two most important things you tried to do but gave up on. Consider pursuits related to career, *education*, sports, hobbies, relationships, etc. Circle the number that indicates how far you went based on your efforts with "5" meaning you went as far as *anyone* could have gone in trying to succeed, "1" meaning you tried hardly at all, and "4", "3", or "2" in between. Describe why you quit. Then, circle words to indicate whether you could have succeeded if you had tried harder, and whether you're glad that you tried.

1. What I tried:_____

_____

How far I went: (All the way!)   5   4   3   2   1   (Not very far)

Why I quit: _____

_____

Could I have succeeded?   Yes   No   Maybe

Am I glad I tried?   Yes   No   Maybe

2. What I tried:_____

_____

How far I went: (All the way!)   5   4   3   2   1   (Not very far)

Why I quit: _____

_____

Could I have succeeded?   Yes   No   Maybe

Am I glad I tried?   Yes   No   Maybe

IDTA - I've Done That Already

Activity: Now take a hard look at the two most important pursuits in which you had much or at least some success, but you decided (or are in the process of deciding) not to continue. How far did you *really* go in the pursuit? Circle a number as before. Then explain why you decided not to continue. To what extent was it burnout? To what extent was it changed *circumstances* over which you had no control at all? If you could have controlled the *circumstances*, why didn't you? Indicate whether you could have gone further, whether you are glad you did it, and whether quitting led to something better.

1. What I've done: _____

_____

How far I went: (All the way!)   5   4   3   2   1   (Not very far)

Why I quit: _____

_____

Could I have gone farther?	Yes	No	Maybe
Am I glad I did it?	Yes	No	Maybe
Did it lead to something better?	Yes	No	Maybe

2. What I've done: _____

_____

How far I went: (All the way!)   5   4   3   2   1   (Not very far)

Why I quit: _____

_____

Could I have gone farther?	Yes	No	Maybe
Am I glad I did it?	Yes	No	Maybe
Did it lead to something better?	Yes	No	Maybe

ILTE - I Love This Experience!

Activity: Finally, look at two present pursuits in which you don't love the experience at all, or don't love it as much as you'd like to. Identify the payoffs for *learning* to love each pursuit. Identify the three most important *circumstances* it would take to love each pursuit, circling words to show whether creating the *circumstances* would be mainly up to you or up to other people.

1. Pursuit: _____

_____

Payoff for learning to love it: _____

_____

What it would take
 for me to love it:

Which would be
 mainly up to:

• _____ Me   Others

• _____ Me   Others

• _____ Me   Others

2. Pursuit: _____

_____

Payoff for learning to love it: _____

_____

What it would take
 for me to love it:

Which would be
 mainly up to:

• _____ Me   Others

• _____ Me   Others

• _____ Me   Others

Review your self-examinations of what you've tried (ITTA), what you have done (IDTA), and what you love to do or could learn to love (ILTE). What can you discover about yourself?

How *far* have you gone each time you set out to succeed at something (ISAT)? For the pursuits you've tried, how far *could* you have gone if you had tried harder and kept going? What <u>outcomes</u> could have resulted?

Did you stop short of achieving your full potential? If so, why? What could have happened if you *did* achieve full potential?

How many times did you circle *Others* instead of *Me* in assessing what it would take to love a pursuit? Why? Could you take ownership of those items instead of ascribing them to others?

Every calling is great when greatly pursued.
Oliver Wendell Holmes

5. Choosing How to Define Yourself in the Future

Before embarking on the five sets of *choices*, you drew a pie chart showing how you've defined yourself up to this point in your life. You apportioned three slices in accordance with how much importance you put on material wealth (*Having* things), work and other activities (*Doing* things), and relationships (the essence of *Being* human).

Whom you choose to be for life's journey from this point on requires a new pie chart, called *This Pie Will Be "I"*.

To do a good job drawing that pie requires careful reflection upon what insights you have gained from this book so far, especially:

• That successful *outcomes* in life are personal *choices*, not just good *circumstances*.

• That *continuous white water* in life can be overcome and relative *stability* can be achieved.

• That success requires knowing what you *want* out of life, finding the best *way* to get it, and being willing to do the *work* well.

• That reaching your destination on the map (Question 1) begins with choosing whom you will be for the journey (Question 2).

But now, in preparation for putting pen to pie, *do this*:

Activity: Here are three simplified maps of the five "cities." Place a dot on each showing where you would be in life as of now when you consider *only* the aspect of life noted at the top of each map.

WHERE I'D BE BASED SOLELY ON:

MATERIAL WEALTH	WORK / ACTIVITIES	RELATIONSHIPS
City of Joy	City of Joy	City of Joy
Fat City	Fat City	Fat City
Malaisia	Malaisia	Malaisia
Purgatoria	Purgatoria	Purgatoria
Hades Gulch	Hades Gulch	Hades Gulch

Looked at *that* way, what implications are there for your *new* pie chart? For example: If you are in Fat City where material wealth is concerned but Hades Gulch for relationships, should you apportion less of a pie slice for material wealth and more for relationships? If so, how much of a shift should you make?

No matter where you placed your three dots and what your original pie chart looks like, there are two traps to avoid when drawing your new pie chart:

Trap No. 1: Trying to *balance* the three slices. As emphasized earlier, to choose three *equal* slices is to choose a life of mediocrity. To make progress in any area, your slices will have to be at least somewhat *out of balance.*

Trap No. 2: Carving out a single slice so big that one or both of the other slices is crowded out or eliminated. All three slices must have importance if you are to reach the City of Joy or even Fat City.

To illustrate the two traps, consider that either extreme of all three slices can be destructive:

A BALANCED LIFE?

GREED
HAVING
DESTITUTION

WORKAHOLISM
DOING
INDOLENCE

CO-DEPENDENCY
BEING
MISANTHROPY

Finally, ask yourself: What does *success* really mean to me? What does *true happiness* really mean to me?

Ralph Waldo Emerson, the famous 19th century American essayist and poet, wrote what many consider to be the *ultimate* definition of success. You may agree with all of it, part of it, or none of it.

How you relate to it, however, can make a big difference in how you draw your new pie chart.

Where Do You Stand on the 'Emerson Scale'?

Activity: Here is Emerson's definition broken into 10 parts and turned into "The Emerson Scale." Circle a number next to each part to indicate whether the words fit you completely (5), don't fit you at all (1), or fit you somewhere in between (4, 3, or 2).

"To laugh often...	5	4	3	2	1
...and to have loved much...	5	4	3	2	1
...to win the respect of intelligent persons...	5	4	3	2	1
...and the affection of children...	5	4	3	2	1
...to appreciate beauty...	5	4	3	2	1
...to find the best in others...	5	4	3	2	1
...to give of one's self...	5	4	3	2	1
...to leave the world a little better, whether by a healthy child, a garden patch or a redeemed social condition...	5	4	3	2	1
...to have played and laughed with enthusiasm and sung with exultation...	5	4	3	2	1
...to know even one life has breathed easier because I have lived."	5	4	3	2	1

Add up the numbers you circled, divide by 10, and circle the number closest to your score: 5   4   3   2   1

How did you do?

If you agree with Emerson's definition and your score was low, what should you do about the size of the *Being* slice of your new pie? What new priorities should you set?

If you put more emphasis on the *Doing* and *Having* slices of life, can you do so in a way that reflects Emerson's perspective?

Activity: Reconsider what's important in your life by deciding relatively how much emphasis you should put on each of the three slices. On the next page, check a space beside each of the three slices to indicate more, less, or the same emphasis. Then, referring to the Needs and Wants you listed earlier, determine your trade-offs.

How I Will Redeploy My Priorities

	More Emphasis	Less Emphasis	Same As Now
Material Wealth	_____	_____	_____
Work/Other Activities	_____	_____	_____
Relationships	_____	_____	_____

Here Are My Top 5 Trade-offs

More Emphasis on:	Less Emphasis on:
_____	_____
_____	_____
_____	_____
_____	_____
_____	_____

Activity: Now draw your new pie chart.

THIS PIE WILL BE "I"

MATERIAL WEALTH
_____ %

WORK / ACTIVITIES
_____ %

RELATIONSHIPS
_____ %

Question 2 most likely will be the toughest of the five questions. You've answered it thoroughly and *positively* and are ready to get *full value* out of Question 3 if you can check "Yes" for each of the following statements:

	Yes	No
• I've clearly defined who I have been up to now	___	___
• I've decided to be, or continue to be, a *Victor*	___	___
• I've improved the nature of how I think	___	___
• I've clarified aspirations, expectations, entitlements	___	___
• I've chosen to *go all the way* and love what I do	___	___
• I've clearly defined who I will be from now on	___	___

If you checked "No" on any of the above statements, go back and work on those areas — or, at the least, proceed to Question 3 fully aware there are one or more voids that need to be filled.

If I am what I *have* and what I have is lost, who then am I?
Erich Fromm

Which is the same as saying:
If I am what I *do* and what I do is lost, who then am I?

And should lead you to believe that:
If I am what I should *be*, then I should know who I am.

Chapter 8

The Third Question:

What Will It Take to Reach Your Destination?

- **The MECCA Matrix**
  - **Motivation** to Mobilize Your *Will* to Win
  - **Education** to Develop Your *Skill* to Win
  - **Concentration** to Focus *Will* & *Skill* on a *Way* to Win
  - **Communication** to Earn the *Right* to Win
  - **Achievement** to Win *Certain Success*
- **And the Secret Is...**

Question Three:

It's probably the question you were itching to get at in the chapter before last when you looked at the road map and put the dot where you are now and the star where you want to be.

If you're like I was when I started working on this process, you may literally have stood on a plain and looked at the top of a mountain and declared: "Okay, I'm at the foot of a mountain now and I want to be at the top, so just tell me what it will take to get there as quickly and as easily as possible.

Or maybe you already are *very* aware of what it took me a couple of years to figure out — that making it to the top (of a mountain, in this case) is best accomplished by first defining yourself as a successful mountain climber, then *choosing* to embrace all the winning attitudes and attributes that go with it.

The Full Power of All 11 Words

This chapter is where you can become firmly fastened to the full power of *all 11* words for winning.

- You've decided to make better personal _choices_, no matter what your _circumstances_, so you can enjoy better _outcomes_ in life.
- You have a firm fix on what you _want_ out of life, the best _way_ to get it, and are willing to do the _work_ and do it well.
- *Now* it's time to harness what I call *the five imperatives* for getting the _work_ done well and for succeeding in anything.

Insights Into the Imperatives

Remembering what the five imperatives *are* is easy, thanks to the acronymn MECCA. Understanding how they work and how to apply them involves a process I call *Meccanize!®*

Begin the process with a few insights:

• The five imperatives are *sequential* and *cumulative*. Without the *M* there will be no *E*. Without the *M* and *E* there is no substance for the first *C*. Without the *M, E, C*, there is nothing for the second *C* to put forth. Without the *M, E, C, C*, there will be no *A*.

• Each of the imperatives has five very important *personal attributes* underlying it. One out of each set of five attributes is of paramount importance, and I call that one the *core attribute*.

• Each attribute also relates to an imperative, resulting in what I call *The MECCA Matrix*. After 18 months of noodling and doodling — and 119 drafts — it came out looking like this:

THE **MECCA** MATRIX

	MOTIVATION	EDUCATION	CONCENTRATION	COMMUNICATION	ACHIEVEMENT
MOTIVATION You Need...	1 Self-Esteem	6 Aptitude	11 Judgment	16 Association	21 Opportunity
EDUCATION You Learn...	2 Purpose	7 Self-Development	12 Organization	17 Interaction	22 Expertise
CONCENTRATION You Develop...	3 A Plan	8 Creativity	13 Self-Discipline	18 Relationships	23 Influence
COMMUNICATION You Show...	4 Enthusiasm	9 Interest	14 Perspective	19 Self-Confidence	24 Character
ACHIEVEMENT You Can Attain...	5 Resilience	10 Knowledge	15 Focus	20 Recognition	25 Self-Fulfillment
	COMMITMENT				SUCCESS

Study the matrix carefully. Refer to it often as you examine each element and use it to answer the third question — *what will it take to reach your destination?*

Following are 10-page mini-chapters, one for each of the five imperatives. In each mini-chapter, you'll find material that:

1. Explains the imperative and its five personal attributes.
2. Identifies your strengths and needs for improvement.
3. Helps you strengthen every imperative and attribute.

Motivation
Mobilizes Your Will to Win
<u>Self-Esteem</u> • Purpose • A Plan • Enthusiasm • Resilience

---

Every journey does *not* begin with a single step. Every journey begins with *mustering the will* to begin the journey!

<u>*Motivation*</u> is what causes you to do something, whether it's your passion for running a marathon, or your spouse's threat of bodily harm if you don't get off the sofa and take out the trash.

> Motivation is an inner force compelling behavior. It may be stimulated by external potential for positive consequences such as reward or recognition. Or, it may stem from avoidance of negative consequences such as threat of harm.
>
> Dr. Denis Waitley
> *The Psychology of Human Motivation*

"Self-motivation" is redundant. All <u>*motivation*</u> is self-initiated — which means you can't motivate anyone else, and no one else can motivate you. Only *you* can motivate you.

Oh, sure, anyone can *create conditions* that cause you and others to become motivated. If, for example, a mean-looking guy stuck a huge handgun in your face and demanded your wallet, you might motivate yourself to hand it over, grab the gun, or talk fast.

So <u>*motivation*</u> takes you back to the *first* of the 11 words — <u>*choices*</u>. You are motivated when you make personal <u>*choices*</u> and act.

Now explore the five *personal attributes* that, as I see it, determine whether, to what extent, and in what ways you will be motivated. Start with the all-important *core attribute*:

★ Self-Esteem ★
The Motivation of Motivation

You will only *ever* be as good as you feel about yourself.

If you have low *self-esteem*, you bear a self-imposed burden that makes it hard to win, and puts a fulfilled life out of reach.

Don't confuse *self-esteem* with ego. If you have a big ego and think you're God's gift to humankind, it could be your way of covering up *low self-esteem*.

High *self-esteem* leads to humility, a big ego to arrogance. If you have a big ego, remember: There is a God and it isn't you.

> Jesus, Moses, and others tell us to love our neighbors *as we love ourselves*. How can we truly love our neighbors if we don't first truly love ourselves — in other words, have high *self-esteem*?

It's impossible to be a highly motivated person without high *self-esteem*. But it takes a lot more than feeling good about yourself to be highly motivated.

There's an educational element of *motivation* — something extremely important all of us have to learn. It's called:

Purpose
The Education of Motivation

No matter how high your *self-esteem*, you cannot be highly motivated until you've learned a *purpose* for your life.

Purpose is a moral or spiritual context for living. It's knowing your *mission* in life and having a big, positive vision for the future.

The *spiritual* dimension of your life is implicit in your *purpose*. If you have no belief in a power greater than yourself, finding and fulfilling a great *purpose* for your life will be difficult at best. As many theologians and philosophers have put it:

> We are not human beings having a spiritual experience.
> We are spiritual beings having a human experience.

People with high *self-esteem* tend to be people who can define themselves through a strong sense of *purpose*. A great, positive *purpose* comes hard to those who don't feel good about themselves.

Purpose is the garden of the mind in which dreams are planted, grow, and blossom. Dreams keep us growing and going. It's even been said that "you don't stop dreaming because you grow old, you grow old because you stop dreaming."

Motivation, however, *still* requires more. High *self-esteem* and a strong *purpose* won't fully unleash the power of *motivation* without:

A Plan
The Concentration of Motivation

Only about three percent of Americans have any specific, written goals for their lives, and only a fraction of those have a *plan* for their lives that's well-thought-out and written down.

And yet, scores of studies have *directly* linked written goals and effective planning to success and a fulfilled life.

> Having goals and not reaching them is not the greatest tragedy in life.
> The greatest tragedy is not having any great goals to reach for!

Having and fulfilling a *plan* helps you identify what it will take for you to achieve success. It also gives you a basis for measuring progress and a way to keep focused on what's important.

To be highly motivated begins with having high *self-esteem*, and requires learning a *purpose* for your life that can be concentrated through *a plan*. Those attributes are largely *within you*.

The fourth attribute shows your *motivation* to others:

Enthusiasm
The Communication of Motivation

Enthusiasm is the tip of an iceberg. It not only communicates your *motivation* to others, but gives you the *fervor* to live your *purpose*, carry out *a plan*, and make your dreams come true.

> Erudite people can make good livings.
> Enthusiastic people can make great fortunes.

Beneath the surface of *enthusiasm* lies the powers of mental and physical energy. The more your *enthusiasm* shines above the surface, the greater the mental and physical energy is stirred beneath the surface — *within you*!

Mental and physical energy is built on a foundation of health and wellness. The body is the temple of your mind and spirit, and how well you take care of yourself physically, mentally, and *spiritually* affects your energy level. *Enthusiasm*, by the way, comes from the Greek words *en theos*, meaning "in God."

But there's *still* more to *motivation*. How do you *stay* motivated? What keeps you going when the going gets rough? It's called:

Resilience
The Achievement of Motivation

If you're going through *continuous white water* in your life, *resilience* may be the most important of the *motivation* attributes.

> As a child of a great God, I am greater
> than anything that can happen to me.
> Norman Vincent Peale

Unless you are *resilient* in the face of whatever happens to you, how can you possibly maintain *enthusiasm*? Stick to *a plan*? Stay committed to a *purpose* in life? Maintain high *self-esteem*?

The tough people who get going when the going gets tough are the *resilient* people. They're the ones who turn *up* their energy levels and become *more* determined to *win no matter what*!

Resilience means persistence, determination, and bouncing back from adversity. It means doing *whatever it takes* to keep stress from sapping your energy, and turmoil from dashing your hopes.

Winston Churchill put it best when he said: "Success is going from failure to failure without loss of enthusiasm."

147

Motivation Self-Test

For each pair of statements, circle the 5 if the statement above the numbers fits you or the 4 if it mostly fits. Circle 1 if the statement below fits or 2 if it mostly fits. Circle 3 if either could apply.

★ Self-Esteem ★

I possess an inner peace and joy for living. I feel very good about myself all or nearly all of the time.

5   4   3   2   1

My life is filled with self-doubt and unhappiness. I rarely, if ever, feel good about myself.

Purpose

I have a clear, even "spiritual" understanding of my *purpose* in life, including what I <u>want</u> out of life.

5   4   3   2   1

There is no clear-cut *purpose* to my life. I mostly live from one day to the next.

A Plan

In line with my *purpose*, I have developed *a plan* that has specific goals and action steps, and that I am excited about.

5   4   3   2   1

My aims in life change from day to day. I have no well-developed plan to guide me in the months and years ahead.

Enthusiasm

I'm very excited about what I pursue and I find it easy to muster the energy to get things done.

5   4   3   2   1

I find little to be excited about and have a hard time mustering *enthusiasm* and energy to get things done.

Resilience

When the going gets tough, I'm one of those tough people who gets going. *Nothing* will keep me from succeeding!

5   4   3   2   1

I find myself devastated by major setbacks in my life and even little things "get to me" much of the time.

★ Self-Esteem ★

My self-test score (p. 148) is: For me, this attribute is mostly a
       5 4 3 2 1   ___ **Strength**   ___**Weakness**

Ways to Raise Self-Esteem

1. Make side-by-side, chronological lists of your successes and failures. Cross out all the failures that actually *contributed* to your growth and later successes. Feel *better* about yourself already?

2. Review your personal inventory on page 117 and your trade-offs on page 141. Which items contribute to your *self-esteem*? Which ones are simply ego-related?

3. Help other people. Lending a hand to others — especially those less fortunate — is one of the *best* ways to feel better about yourself.

4. Be honest, now: Do you tend to build yourself up by putting other people down? Whenever you do, you're probably lowering your *self-esteem* and fattening your ego. "Target" one or two people for deserved praise. *Be sincere!* Prove to yourself that simple acts of finding good in others helps you feel good about yourself.

5. If you have children, help *them* feel better about themselves and feel the positive effects it will have on you. Pick one of the many great children's books, games, videos, etc. designed to help children in different age groups raise their *self-esteem*.

6. Dress for success. Be well-groomed. Take pride in your personal appearance. The more you look and act as though you feel good about yourself, the more you will.

7. Accept compliments graciously. Never put yourself down.

8. Accept criticism objectively. Ask the critic for help, remembering what Abraham Lincoln said: "Who has the right to criticize has the heart to help."

9. If *self-esteem* is a serious weakness, seek professional help. Find a good counselor. Join a support group, if appropriate.

10. Write in 100 words or more why it's healthy for people to feel good about themselves. Then take your own advice.

Good Books to Read

The Six Pillars of Self-Esteem by Nathaniel Branden
Silver Boxes by Florence Littauer
Self Love by Robert H. Schuller

Improvements I Will Make

1. _____

2. _____

3._____

Purpose

My self-test score (p. 148) is: For me, this attribute is mostly a

5 4 3 2 1   ___ **Strength**   ___**Weakness**

Ways to Increase Your Sense of Purpose

1. Make a list of famous people you greatly admire. From their biographies, identify what you believe to be the guiding purposes in their lives. What can you learn from the people you admire?

2. Do a "values audit." Write down the principles you try to live by. Rate yourself on how you adhere to them. Revise the list to prioritize and underscore the principles you will live by in the future.

3. List some things you have done that will "leave the world a little better place." Consider people you have helped and causes you have supported. What can you learn from what you have identified? How and in what ways did they strengthen your sense of *purpose*.

4. Think about how you would like to be remembered. Read some obituaries in your local newspaper. Then pretend you're a reporter writing *your* obituary the way you would *like* it to be written someday. Did what you wrote reflect a person with a good *purpose*?

5. Take a hard look at the *spiritual* side of your life. Who is your higher power? In whom or in what do you believe? Find ways to strengthen your spirituality.

6. Turn to scripture. Attend worship services. Seek the counsel of clergy or other advisers in coming to grips with your beliefs.

7. Be selective when exploring "new-age" solutions to the age-old quest for *purpose* and meaning in life. There are some enlightened teachers and philosophers, but many hucksters and charlatans.

8. Stay away from cults and charismatic people who seek your obedience and money while getting you to serve *their* purposes.

9. Discuss *purpose* with loved ones. What you have trouble finding alone, you may find together.

10. Write in 10 words or less: The *purpose* of my life is to

_____ .

Good Books to Read

Hebrew Scriptures, The New Testament, The Koran...
Even Eagles Need a Push by David McNally
The Road Less Traveled by M. Scott Peck, M.D.

Improvements I Will Make

1. _____

2. _____

3. _____

A Plan

My self-test score (p. 148) is: For me, this attribute is mostly a
5 4 3 2 1   ___ **Strength**   ___**Weakness**

Ways to Be a Better Planner

1. How goal-oriented have you been? If you've set goals, have you *ever* put them in writing? Your answers should underscore the need to have *a plan* that's well-developed and written down.

2. Understand the difference between fantasies and dreams. Don't base your plan on fantasies, for they waste your energies on wishful thinking directed toward the unrealistic.

3. Develop big, positive *dreams* — things that you *are* willing and able to work for — to give direction to your plan. Stretch your dreams to the limits, remembering that virtually *anything* is possible if you *want* it badly enough and are willing to do the *work*.

4. Avoid the trap of trying to go in too many directions at once. Prioritize what you want to accomplish. Put less-important pursuits on hold in order that you can focus on what is of greater importance.

5. Use the goal-setting process explained in the next chapter. If you do a good job answering the fourth question — *how should I chart my course?* — you'll have *a plan* you can be proud of.

6. Always break your bigger goals into manageable pieces so you can achieve them one step at a time rather than let them overwhelm you.

7. Find the best way to hold yourself accountable for achieving your plan. At the outset, review your plan with your spouse or others you can trust. Keep them advised of your progress.

8. Strengthen your commitment by letting others know what you intend to do. You are *more accountable* when you do what you've already told other people you will do than you are when your goals are known only to yourself.

9. Attach rewards to ongoing *achievement*. Give up or deny yourself something of importance until a goal has been accomplished.

10. Celebrate successes and rejuvenate your planning process. The advent of a new year is an especially great time to do that.

Good Books to Read

The Magic of Believing, Claude M. Bristol
Who Stole the American Dream? by Burke Hedges
New Passages by Gail Sheehy

Improvements I Will Make

1. _____

2. _____

3._____

Enthusiasm

My self-test score (p. 148) is: For me, this attribute is mostly a
    5 4 3 2 1   ___ **Strength**   ___**Weakness**

Ways to Be More Enthusiastic

1. Identify the most enthusiastic people you've ever known. Find out how they *got* that way and *stayed* that way. *Learn* from them.

2. Assess your *enthusiasm* level by getting feedback from family, friends, associates, a good counselor, etc. What do *they* tell you? Are you usually upbeat or downcast?

3. Have yourself videotaped presenting an idea or trying to sell something you believe in. Watch yourself carefully. Does your *enthusiasm* show? Try it again, this time over-acting. You'll be surprised to see how much more *oompf* you project without *appearing* to overact.

4. Make two lists: one of the important things you are *most* enthusiastic about, and the other of things you are *least* enthusiastic about. Take one or two items from your "least" list and see what happens when you become demonstrably enthusiastic about them.

5. Take time out to "sharpen your saw." Unwind once in awhile. Get rejuvenated.

6. Keep physically fit through good diet and exercise. Reinforce yourself by joining a health club or by forming your own workout "team." Be sure to get a checkup before starting any kind of new diet or exercise program.

7. If weight is a problem, be wary of miracle drugs, crash diets, fads, etc. Think *long-term*. Keep a log of your daily weight. Heed sound advice.

8. Be a good sleep manager. Too little or too much sleep can reduce your level of *enthusiasm* considerably.

9. Smile more. Laugh more. Walk 20 percent faster. Put a *spring* in your step.

10. Never let a day go by without enthusiastically celebrating *something* — the end of an above-average day, a child getting a good grade, etc. Celebrations make *enthusiasm* habit-forming.

Good Books to Read

The Tough-Minded Optimist by Norman Vincent Peale
The Go-Getter by P.B. Kynes
The Sleep Management Plan by Dale Hanson Bourke

Improvements I Will Make

1. _____

2. _____

3._____

Resilience

My self-test score (p. 148) is: For me, this attribute is mostly a
5 4 3 2 1   ___ **Strength** ___**Weakness**

Ways to Be More Resilient

1. Tackle your toughest problems and goals first. Get anything out of the way that might dampen the energy and *enthusiasm* needed to fulfill your plan.

2. Think of change as life's No. 1 inevitability and No. 1 opportunity. Learn to identify and focus on the *positive* aspects of change.

3. When faced with sudden or major change, identify with "super-resilient" people like Thomas Edison who "never had any failures — only learning experiences."

4. Find constructive outlets for your frustrations, such as prayer, meditation or vigorous sports. Master the art of *letting off steam* in ways that help you and won't hurt others.

5. Write down two or three instances in your life when you were experiencing a lot of stress. Who created the stress and kept adding to it? If you look hard enough, you'll find that *you* did.

6. Take a stress management course. Community colleges and employer training departments usually offer them, and there are many good traveling seminars.

7. If you're facing nasty <u>circumstances</u> beyond your control, examine the *terms* under which you accept or reject related change. A positive attitude almost always overcomes the downsides of change.

8. Know your limitations in trying to control situations. If you *can't* control or influence <u>outcomes</u>, you *can* control your attitude.

9. Not all stress is bad. Learn the difference between "bad stress" (distress) and "good stress" (eustress), then work at eliminating the former and harnessing the latter.

10. Put life's defeats and challenges in a positive light. Remember: Babe Ruth became the home-run king by *striking out* 1,330 times. And God saved Daniel *in* the lion's den not *from* the lion's den.

Good Books to Read

How to Stop Worrying and Start Living by Dale Carnegie
When Bad Things Happen to Good People by Harold Kushner
Storms of Perfection (Vols. 1, 2, 3, 4) by Andy Andrews

Improvements I Will Make

1. _____
2. _____
3._____

The Motivation Imperative

My self-test scores are:
Self-Esteem ___
Purpose ___
A Plan ___
Enthusiasm ___
Resilence ___

Added together, the numbers = ___ divided by 5 = ____ for *motivation*. That overall score and how I rated *self-esteem* (the core attribute) indicates my *motivation* is mainly a:
___ **Strength** ___**Weakness**

Ways to Increase Motivation

1. Fear undermines your *motivation*. What are you afraid of? Make a list of the fears that stand between you and success. Prioritize them. For each, determine the best ways to overcome them.

2. Become fully aware of how many times you *initiate* action, rather than simply respond when *other people* initiate action. If necessary, keep a log of important activities you initiate and others initiate. Bottom line: work on being a better *self-starter*!

3. Examine your reading, listening, and viewing habits. A constant diet of negative news and "entertainment" is a big *de*-motivator. Read positive mental attitude books. Listen to positive tapes.

4. Take a motivational course. Check on local colleges, training centers, and traveling seminars to see what's available. Check with the training or human resources department where you work.

5. Do a daily affirmation and practice positive self-talk to keep yourself pumped up. In the back of this book, you'll find a powerful affirmation to help you make each *new* day a *great* day.

Good Books to Read

If It's Going to Be, It's Up to Me by Dr. Robert H. Schuller
The Courage to Live Your Dreams by Les Brown
Unstoppable by Cynthia Kersey

Improvements I Will Make

1. _____

2. _____

3. _____

Get Going! Keep Going!
**Even if you're on the right track,
you'll get run over if you just sit there.
Will Rogers**

Education
Develops Your Skill to Win
Aptitude • <u>Self-Development</u> • Creativity • Interest • Knowledge

Let's hear it for John Henri Fabre! He's a guy who demonstrated that *motivation* without *education* will get you nowhere.

Fabre was fascinated by processionary caterpillars, which march across forest floors in long trains coupled together head to, uh, *butt* — which means only the leader gets to enjoy a view.

The 19th Century entomologist put these strange creatures around the rim of a flower pot, forming a complete circle. Although the pot was filled with their favorite food, the caterpillars marched around and around for days, until they finally dropped off and died.

Well, at least they were *motivated*.

Anything Familiar Here?

Sadly, many people lead lives not too far from what Fabre observed. They just go around and around, from job to job, motivated to meet basic needs by following blindly a long line of others uneducated in life's vast expanse of blessings and opportunities.

So *motivation* is of no value without *education* and without being motivated, no one can become educated. What's more, a good education should result in increased *motivation*.

> An education which does not cultivate the will
> is an education that depraves the mind.
> Anatole France

Motivation is the imperative of the heart. *Education* is the imperative of the head. Strong heart, strong head. Faint heart, dead head. That's why I make the first of the five *education* attributes:

Aptitude
The Motivation of Education

Here is either a springboard for learning or a major barrier to becoming successful, which is why I tie it to *motivation*.

Aptitude is your natural ability to learn and to do. It becomes a barrier, though, when your *attitude* toward your capabilities is negative — maybe due to a low score on an aptitude test years ago, or because someone *told* you you're no good at something.

Walt Disney and Thomas Edison were both told they lacked imagination and wouldn't go far. Robert Schuller, the author of many best-selling books, was told by a teacher that he had no talent for writing. The aunt who raised the famous musician John Lennon told him he could never make money playing the guitar.

History is full of famous people motivated to overcome a perceived lack of *aptitude*. For many of them, being told they *couldn't do it* was all it took for them to go out and *do it anyway*.

God doesn't call the equipped, he equips the called.

With enough *motivation*, you can clear most any *aptitude* hurdle and do anything you can *believe* you can do. With plenty of talent, the sky's the limit. But in either case you'll need a lot of:

★ Self-Development ★
The Education of Education

You may think your peak years of *self-development* are the ones spent as a youth in the classroom. *Schooling*, however, is but a small and temporary part of developing yourself.

Self-development should *accelerate* after graduation day with the standard being *continuous improvement* and the operating principles being: (1) stay teachable, and (2) keep learning.

He who stops being better stops being good.
Oliver Cromwell

As the years go by, most people apply the brakes to *self-development*. They succumb to a "hardening of their mental arteries," doing the minimum necessary to get by. As a result, life is less fulfilling, and probably will be spent in the rut called *Malaisia*.

If you're staying teachable, it means you have made a *habit* of ongoing *self-development*. You look continuously for opportunities to sharpen skills and broaden your storehouse of information.

Expansion and renewal of the process comes best from a personal attribute that enriches the mind more than any other:

Creativity
The Concentration of Education

Don't ever convince yourself — or let anyone else convince you — that you're not creative. *Everyone* is creative! Everyone is blessed with some amount of imagination and the ability to look at things from more than one perspective.

"Right-brained people" are noted for being creative, but some of the most creative solutions to problems have come from engineers and some of the most incisive analyses from artists.

Creative activity could be described as a type of learning process where teacher and pupil are located in the same individual.
Arthur Koestler

By concentrating your creative powers, you will never be at a loss for new ways to grow. Without *creativity*, there can be no meaningful e*ducation*. *Motivation*, in turn, will be reduced to the plight of the caterpillars, going round and round, getting nowhere.

Creativity is making the new. It's also arranging the old in new ways. Its roots run deep into another personal attribute:

Interest
The Communication of Education

Interest is the basis for unending curiosity. It can be both the outgrowth of *creativity* and the onset of further *creativity*.

The breadth and depth of what you're interested in brings light into your life and communicates much about you to others. You become an *interesting person* to others when you also are interested in them and what *they* are interested in.

How do you *direct* your *interest*? Do you dwell on only those things *you* find interesting, or do you also extend your curiosity to what *other people* find interesting?

> The test of interesting people is that subject matter doesn't matter.
> Louis Kronenberger

Have you compressed your range of interests into a narrow comfort zone or are you constantly looking for new areas in which to learn and grow? Do your interests run shallow or deep, especially when related to fulfilling your *purpose* and reaching your destination?

Finally, there is the often-misunderstood attribute called:

Knowledge
The Achievement of Education

Knowledge is power — right? Wrong! It's *potential* power, for it is of no value unless acquired, applied, and shared.

> Knowledge is of two kinds: we know a subject ourselves, or we know where we can find information upon it... Mankind has a far greater need to be reminded than informed.
> Samuel Johnson

Your brain's capacity to store information is virtually unlimited, but the amount of information in the world keeps doubling every few years and, if you're like me, you're bombarded with tons of it every day — much of it conflicting and confusing.

So the greatest power of *knowledge* can come quickest to those who not only keep adding to their mental storehouse, but who also make the best use of what they already know.

Education Self-Test

For each pair of statements, circle the 5 if the statement above the numbers fits you or the 4 if it mostly fits. Circle 1 if the statement below fits or 2 if it mostly fits. Circle 3 if either could apply.

Aptitude

There is virtually nothing I can't do if I put my mind to it and decide to make it happen.

5   4   3   2   1

My lack of talent and ability puts severe limitations on what I can learn and do.

★ Self-Development ★

I am doing everything I can to develop my capabilities, expand my skills, and learn in areas important to my goals.

5   4   3   2   1

I am already sufficiently self-developed and don't see the need to do any more.

Creativity

I am an "idea person" with a vivid imagination who loves to create things and/or find new ways to solve problems.

5   4   3   2   1

I stick to the tried-and-true. Rarely, if ever, do I originate ideas or come up with new solutions to problems.

Interest

My curiosity is endless and I maintain a variety of interests, some of them unrelated to fulfilling my goals.

5   4   3   2   1

I have few interests, and what few I have are limited to what is necessary to get by.

Knowledge

I possess a rich storehouse of *knowledge*, most of it in the form of know-how needed to succeed in life.

5   4   3   2   1

I know all I need to know and there's little else I would be interested in knowing.

Aptitude

My self-test score (p. 158) is:　　For me, this attribute is mostly a
5　4　3　2　1　　　　　　___ **Strength**　　___**Weakness**

Ways to Handle Aptitude

1. Don't be influenced by *aptitude* test scores from years ago. Declare yourself *good* at what they said you're not, and move on.

2. If it's important to you, take a new *aptitude* test. The tests have gotten much better over the years and you may be pleasantly surprised when you compare results.

3. Think back to childhood. What were you told by parents, teachers, peers and others that you couldn't do or wouldn't be any good at? Did you believe them then? Do you *still* believe them?

4. Test scores and bad advice notwithstanding, make lists of what you *really believe* you're good at and not good at. For each item on both lists, describe your *attitude*. Ask yourself whether problem areas are more related to attitude than *aptitude*.

5. Use your lists to match desires and needs to skills and abilities. Focus on areas of highest desires and needs.

6. Distinguish between abilities and interests. Make sure you don't discount your potential because of likes and dislikes. Remember: Success depends on doing what's *necessary*, not what you *like* to do.

7. Never strengthen negative beliefs about yourself by confessing the inability to do anything. Use positive affirmations and self-talk to help you break down mental barriers.

8. Demonstrate to yourself the ability to overcome self-imposed limitations by doing or learning something you've always imagined to be beyond your capacity.

9. Constantly remind yourself that <u>motivation</u> comes before <u>education</u> and not being motivated enough can impose limits greater than a lack of intelligence, talent, or "natural ability."

10. *Aptitude* can be improved, and one good way is to help your children or others become stronger in areas in which you're weak. Teaching is a great way of learning.

Good Books to Read

Self-Scoring IQ Tests by Victor Serebriakoff
You're Smarter Than You Think by Linda P. Moore
The Elements of Human Potential by Nevill Drury

Improvements I Will Make

1. _____

2. _____

3. _____

★ Self-Development ★

My self-test score (p. 158) is: For me, this attribute is mostly a

5 4 3 2 1   ___ **Strength**   ___**Weakness**

Ways to Strengthen Self-Development

1. Make a list of everything you've done in the past year *at your initiative* to improve yourself. Include courses taken, self-help books read and seminars attended. How long is your list? How relevant to your plan are the items on the list? What *level of commitment* to your own *self-development* does the list reflect?

2. Examine your career-related goals, then research criteria for success in the areas represented. Support your plan with specific *self-development* steps.

3. Check employer-offered training opportunities that could help meet your development needs and help you achieve your goals.

4. Obtain continuing education catalogues from local colleges, your school district, etc. Attend courses that will help you fulfill your plan, whether job-related or not.

5. Visit your library and/or a good book store. Look for titles that would be of greatest help to you.

6. Review evaluations of your work. Look for opportunities to improve. Seek additional feedback from your boss, a mentor, et al.

7. Make a list of *self-development* priorities for the coming year. Decide which would be of greatest benefit, make a schedule, integrate them into your plan, and get going.

8. Develop networks of individuals who can share educational experiences with you. At work, look for ways to add new dimensions through job rotation, temporary assignments, etc.

9. Take courses with people you know. Inspire each other to learn and develop.

10. Join the professional association that is likely to be of greatest help in advancing your career. Attend meetings. Read the publications. Attend workshops and seminars. Seek and network with people who can help you grow personally and professionally.

Good Books to Read

Worklife Transitions by Paul Barton
Making a Living Without a Job by Barbara J. Winter
Growing Strong in the Seasons of Life by Charles Swindoll

Improvements I Will Make

1. _____

2. _____

3. _____

Creativity

My self-test score (p. 158) is: For me, this attribute is mostly a
5 4 3 2 1   ___ **Strength**   ___**Weakness**

Ways to Increase Creativity

1. Uncouple from the idea that some people are creative, others aren't. *Everyone* is creative, especially you! Jot down some creative things you've done in your life, just as a reminder.

2. In an age marked by the need for continuous improvement, get into the habit of looking at the conventional and asking "why?" Then, look at the unconventional and ask *"why not?"*

3. Make a list of <u>circumstances</u> that get in the way of your efforts to become more creative. Eliminate as many as you can — or find ways to work around them.

4. Have fun tinkering, but don't get obsessed by it. Identify the top priorities for change and apply your imagination. Learn how to strike a productive balance between deploying the tried-and-true and reinventing the wheel.

5. Enhance your *creativity* through the many workshops, tapes, books and mind-bending games that are readily available.

6. When faced with a problem, start the creative process by finding creative ways to restate the problem. Good solutions may emerge when you find a better way to define the problem.

7. Each day, write one fresh idea on each of three index cards. That's 21 ideas a week. Sort the cards into categories at the end of each week. Pick out the best ideas and act upon them.

8. Have *fun* being creative. Lighten up. The more serious the effort, the harder it is to fire the imagination. When you can, poke fun at the problem. Be irreverent. Pretend you're a stand-up comic doing a routine based on the problem. Then get serious and solve it.

9. Nurture *creativity* with a *creative environment*. Do your best ideas come in a hot shower? A hammock? While jogging?

10. Stop being judgmental. Every time you pass judgment on yourself or somebody else, you close a door to potential *creativity*.

Good Books to Read

A Whack on the Side of the Head by Roger von Oech
The Creative Edge by William C. Miller
Creativity in Business by Michael Ray & Rochelle Myers

Improvements I Will Make

1. _____
2. _____
3. _____

Interest

My self-test score (p. 158) is: For me, this attribute is mostly a
5 4 3 2 1   ___ **Strength**   ___**Weakness**

Ways to Broaden Interests

1. List interests beyond your obligations to career and family. Evaluate how each enriches or diminishes your life. Concentrate on what's enriching. Rethink what diminishes your span of interests.

2. Become an *avid reader*. Join a book club or literary circle. Subscribe to publications. Forage through the public library. Set annual, monthly, even weekly goals for what you read.

3. Keep track or make an honest estimate of how many hours a week you spend watching television. What sorts of programs are you watching? Do they expand your horizons or simply kill time? Should you cut TV hours and add hours for books, lectures, trips to museums, new hobbies and other *interest*-enhancing pursuits?

4. Think of *travel* as an opportunity to learn and become more "rounded." It need not be a costly trek to Tibet. Fascinating things are all around you. See something *new* on your next vacation.

5. Take lessons — music, art, dancing, whatever. Take them with your spouse or a friend to build *common* interests.

6. Think about *people* you find interesting. Isn't it true that you find them interesting because they are interested in interesting things? To what extent are you?

7. Have at least one hobby. Find something to unwind into — to help you *recharge your batteries*.

8. Declare war on boredom. People and things can't bore you, you *choose* to be bored by them. Jot down one or two things you find most boring. Pick one, over-do it and become *fascinated*.

9. Do occasional reality checks on your *level* and on your *range* of interests. Be sure to have a good balance between variety and intensity of interests.

10. Incorporate new interests into your personal plan. Prioritize opportunities to expand your horizons. Set goals accordingly.

Good Books to Read

1000 Great Lives by Jonathan Law
14,000 Things to be Happy About by Barbara Ann Kipfer
New World of Travel by Arthur Frommer

Improvements I Will Make

1. _____

2. _____

3. _____

Knowledge

My self-test score (p. 158) is: For me, this attribute is mostly a
5 4 3 2 1   ___ **Strength**   ___**Weakness**

Ways to Expand Knowledge

1. Remind yourself that *knowledge* is only *potential power.* Distinguish between your storehouse of information and your base of *knowledge* that is important *know-how.* Identify weak spots, especially in *applying* what you already know.

2. The vast majority of what you know now will be *forgotten* later. How do you *retain* what you've learned? Find ways to make good on-the-spot decisions as to what's important to remember, what should be stored for later use, and what can be forgotten.

3. If you don't have a computer, get one. Tap into databases. Phenomenal amounts of *knowledge* you could never store in your brain are readily available via modem.

4. Get to know your area's public and university library systems and the people who run them. Much information can be accessed by phone or fax or modem or in person.

5. Review your basic reference tools such as an almanac, encyclopedia, unabridged dictionary, etc. And remember: most of what fills whole bookshelves are now available on CD-ROMs.

6. Take a memory course. There are many good ones offered on tape, at seminars, or through local colleges.

7. Build *knowledge* through *involvement,* not just through books and by rote. The more involvement, the more understanding.

8. Play games that stretch your mind and increase your information base. There are plenty available and they can be fun for the whole family.

9. Be a good note-taker with a good system to retrieve and apply what you've written down.

10. Set up ready-reference files at home and at work. Establish categories for your notes and articles clipped from newspapers, magazines, etc. Refer to and review your files regularly.

Good Books to Read

Instant Recall by Jeff Budworth
Internet in Plain English by Bryan Pfaffenberger
An Incomplete Education by Judy Jones & William Wilson

Improvements I Will Make

1. _____
2. _____
3. _____

The <u>Education</u> Imperative

My self-test scores are:
    Aptitude   ___
    Self-Devel. ___
    Creativity   ___
    Interest   ___
    Knowledge ___

Added together, the numbers = ___
divided by 5 = _____ for *education*.
That overall score and how I rated
self-development (the core attribute)
indicates my *education* is mainly a:
   ___ **Strength**   ___**Weakness**

Ways to Expand <u>Education</u>

1. Assess how well-educated you are in three areas: (1) how to build good and lasting relationships, (2) how to perform well in your job or business, and (3) how to lead a fulfilling life; in other words, how you're equipped for *being*, *doing*, and *having* as explained in Chapter 7.

2. Consider your *formal <u>Education</u>*. In light of the three areas, decide whether additional courses, certificates, degrees, etc. would help you get to the "destination" you chose in Chapter 6.

3. How *motivated* are you to learn, grow, and apply what you've learned? There are times when being highly motivated is better than being highly educated. As someone once put it, "ignorance on fire will get you farther than *knowledge* on ice."

4. Make this resolution: "From now on, anything that looks or feels like failure I will chalk up to <u>Education</u>. Never again will I experience failures, only learning experiences."

5. Examine your habits. Which ones add to your efforts to become better educated, which ones detract from it? Make whatever changes are needed so that learning becomes a constructive *habit*.

Good Books to Read

Learning to Use What You Already Know by Stumpf & DeLuca
Make the Most of Your Mind by Tony Buzan
Zapp! in Education by William C. Byham

Improvements I Will Make

1. _____
2. _____
3. _____

If you think education is expensive, try ignorance.
Derek Bok

Concentration
Focuses Will & Skill on a <u>Way</u> to Win
Judgment • Organization • <u>Self-Discipline</u> • Perspective • Focus

<u>*Motivation*</u> without <u>*Education*</u> is wasted motion. <u>*Education*</u> without <u>*Motivation*</u> is motion wasted. <u>*Motivation*</u> with <u>*Education*</u> is ready to be channeled into a worthwhile pursuit.

Juggling apples, oranges, pie plates and flaming shish kebabs makes a great circus act but is no way to live. Determine what's important, be sure you know all you need to know, and *concentrate* your efforts.

Remember Curley in the movie *City Slickers*? He was the old cowboy (played by Jack Palance) who shared his secret of life by holding up a finger and proclaiming: *"One Thing."*
"What's the one thing?" asked the city slicker (Billy Crystal) who had gone on a cattle drive to escape his hum-drum urban life.
"That's for *you* to decide," the old cowboy replied wryly.
If you're like me, boiling life down to "one thing" is out of the question. There are too *many* things to enjoy and to take advantage of. That said, it's also a fact that most people have unlimited things to do, but a limited number of things they can do *well*.
<u>*Concentration*</u> begins with deciding what to concentrate on and do well. That takes a personal attribute called:

Judgment
The Motivation of Concentration
Decisions, decisions, decisions.
When to say "yes"? When to say "no"? Which of two or more courses of action would be best?
Judgment is the process through which you discern options and make the best <u>*choices*</u>. It's a decision-making process requiring a strong blend of wisdom and common sense.
Remember: Personal <u>*choices*</u> determine nearly all <u>*outcomes*</u>.

We may fail of our happiness, strive we ever so bravely; but we are less likely to fail if we measure with judgment our chances and our capabilities.

Agnes Repplier

Everything you need for good *judgment* can be found within the attributes of <u>*motivation*</u> and <u>*education*</u>. If you have high *self-esteem*, you are more likely to make good judgments than if you think poorly of yourself.

You also will tend to make good judgments if you are strong in the attributes that follow: a clear *purpose* for your life, A *plan* to guide you, *enthusiasm* to get you going and *resilience* to keep you going, plus the attributes of _education_, especially *self-development*.

Life is a melange of day-to-day decisions, minor judgment calls, and major _choices_. Inevitably, a significant decision in one area of your life will have an effect on decisions to be made in other areas.

Having good _outcomes_ from making those wide-ranging and day-to-day decisions requires an attribute many — especially me — find an ongoing challenge:

Organization
The Education of Concentration

How well-organized are you? How well do you use your time? Are you constantly wasting time due to a lack of *organization*?

> Time is a paradox stated thus:
> No one has enough time,
> but everyone has all there is.

Even if you possess the *judgment* of Solomon, you can't harness the power of _concentration_ without being well-organized.

It took me *years* to reach the point where, it seems, I spend more time *doing* stuff than *looking for* stuff. One study claims the average CEO spends *six weeks* each year just trying to find things.

If you're one of those gifted people who can keep everything sorted out in your head, God bless you! For me, it's a matter of figuring out — and using — organizational *systems*.

Now, for one thing, I can't *imagine* how I could live productively (and happily) without the day-planner I've used every day for the past 10 years. Is it a burden being chained to a day-planner? Nope. It's just a stress-reducing *habit*.

Learning how to be organized is one thing. Doing it consistently, along with handling well the many other tasks and responsibilities at hand, requires the core attribute of _concentration_:

★ Self-Discipline ★
The Concentration of Concentration

Resilient people can keep going but people with a great deal of *self-discipline* go on to *win*!

Self-discipline means controlling your life and not letting the demands of life control you. It's the power within you to defeat the greatest obstacle on the roadway to a better place — procrastination.

> In your journey through life, you'll pay one of two prices — the price of *self-discipline* or the price of regret. That's because if you don't *discipline yourself*, someone else *will discipline you*.

If you aren't self-disciplined and are inclined to stay that way, it may dawn on you some day that the pain of *self-discipline* is *nothing* compared to the painful <u>outcomes</u> of an undisciplined life.

But being self-disciplined, well-organized, and good at making decisions requires another important personal attribute:

Perspective
The Communication of Concentration

It's easy for *perspective* to get out of whack — not seeing the forest due to the trees while setting records for conclusion-jumping.

> Every man takes the limits of his own
> field of vision for the limits of the world.
> Arthur Schopenhauer

Perspective is keeping a healthy amount of balance in your life, especially when your life must be somewhat out of balance to fulfill your *purpose* and achieve your goals.

People lacking *perspective* have a *deviated spectrum*. Without doubt, the worst deviations in your spectrum are taking yourself too seriously and denying yourself the joys of a good sense of humor.

Nancy enjoys my *perspective* on our marriage, by the way: "I rejected *three billion women* in the world, honey, to marry *you!*"

Without *perspective*, the <u>concentration</u> imperative can turn you into a workaholic rather than a peak performer. It's the essential buffer between *self-discipline* and the bottom-line attribute called:

Focus
The Achievement of Concentration

With *focus* you can fully deploy your <u>motivation</u>, <u>education</u>, and <u>concentration</u>. It also lets you become productively single-minded, when that's in your best interests.

> First be well-rounded, then be sharply pointed.

Rooted in *self-discipline*, a strong sense of *focus* will help you avoid letting what seems to be urgent block out what you know to be more important. And by having good *perspective*, you are protected from the fate of military pilots who become *so* focused that, instead of bombing or strafing the target, they fly into it.

Trying to be focused on everything at once creates a blur, not to mention migraine headaches. Effectively focusing means having the *self-discipline* and *organization* to concentrate 100 percent on what good *perspective* and *judgment* tells you is most important.

Focus enables you to get done what needs to be done, when it needs to be done, and how it needs to be done.

Concentration Self-Test

For each pair of statements, circle the 5 if the statement above the numbers fits you or the 4 if it mostly fits. Circle 1 if the statement below fits or 2 if it mostly fits. Circle 3 if either could apply.

Judgment

I'm an excellent decision-maker. I am very good at "calling the shots right" and deciding what is and isn't important.

5   4   3   2   1

I am a poor decision-maker. I find it hard to make up my mind, and/or frequently make bad judgments.

Organization

I'm a highly organized person. I manage my time very effectively, allocating sufficient time to handle what is most important.

5   4   3   2   1

Day-to-day living tends to be chaos and confusion. I *never* can seem to get organized.

★ Self-Discipline ★

I have the kind of strong willpower that enables me to break bad habits and stick to things until they're done.

5   4   3   2   1

I have little self-control. I can't break habits on my own and find it hard to adhere to schedules and work regimens.

Perspective

My great strengths include being able to look at things in a broad context and keeping important matters in balance.

5   4   3   2   1

It's very hard for me to get a handle on the "big picture." I often lose sight of what's most important.

Focus

Once I decide on the right thing to do, almost nothing distracts me. I get the job done.

5   4   3   2   1

My attention span is very short. I tend to drift from one thing to the next.

Judgment

My self-test score (p. 168) is: For me, this attribute is mostly a
5 4 3 2 1   ___ **Strength** ___**Weakness**

Ways to Strengthen Judgment

1. Make a list of the most important decisions you've made over the past two or three years. Critique the results. What can you learn in order to make better decisions in the future?

2. Consider *how* you make decisions. Do you follow formulas? Flip coins? Do you assemble data and weigh alternatives? Do you get advice from others? Identify the methods that work best for you.

3. Always weigh both *means* and *ends* when making a decision. Be careful when trying to use ends to justify means. There's no *right way* to do what's *wrong*!

4. Distinguish between *judgment* and being judgmental. Are you *open-minded* when making decisions? Do you jump to conclusions, *then* decide?

5. Err on the side of the long-term. Decisions often are made with insufficient attention to what will happen down the road.

6. Explore decision-making models and processes. Find one that works well for you. Use it whenever it makes sense, but only as a guide. Never trust a formula to make a decision for you. Your *well-tested instincts* are at least as good as someone else's magic formula.

7. For each alternative, develop the best and worst possible <u>outcomes</u> as well as the most likely outcome.

8. Do a *sanity check* before finalizing major decisions. Does your intended course of action make sense? Find a devil's advocate — someone who will provide an outsider's view of your alternatives.

9. Who are the best decision-makers you know — the people who always seem to exercise good *judgment*? Seek them out. Learn from them.

10. Watch the movie *Command Decision*. What does the World War II classic demonstrate about decision-making and good *judgment*. What would you have done if you were the commander?

Good Books to Read

Choices by Shad Helmstetter
Secrets of Executive Success by Rodale Press
Taking Charge by Perry Smith

Improvements I Will Make

1. _____

2. _____

3. _____

Organization

My self-test score (p. 168) is: For me, this attribute is mostly a
5 4 3 2 1   ___ **Strength**   ___**Weakness**

Ways to Be Better Organized

1. Be a *systems person*. Have a place for everything and keep everything in its place. Stop wasting time looking for things!

2. Pick a good time-management system (Franklin-Covey, Day-Timer, etc.) or develop your own. Take a time-management course. *Make time-management an integral part of your life.*

3. When handling paperwork, handle each paper *once*. Take the time to *complete* action on it rather than put it aside and have to start all over again with it later.

4. Scan magazines and newspapers from front to back. Read what's important, clip items of long-term value and put them in your reference files for easy retrieval. Throw the rest out — *now*.

5. Organize your work so *you* manage it, rather than letting it manage you. Break large projects down into series of small tasks. Set priorities. Mark items on the daily task list in your day-planner.

6. When practical, get hard things done first, then tackle the easier ones when you may have less physical and mental energy.

7. If you're handy with a computer, use contact management software, electronic calendars and the like to help you stay on track. If you're a Komputer Klutz, you might as well start learning now.

8. Take a time management course. There are lots of good seminars, most community colleges offer them, and your employer may even spring for the bill.

9. If you're a manager, get your people "paper-trained." Cut the *amount* of paper with *electronic* mail and by other means. *Talk* to each other. Remember: "Memo" is a four-letter word.

10. Faithfully allot time at the start of each day to *organize* your day. Begin by rating yourself on how well you accomplished what you had set out to do on the previous day — and how well you handled the inevitable challenges and changes that came along.

Good Books to Read

Getting Organized by Stephanie Winston
Time Management Made Easy by Peter A. Turla
Time Tactics of Very Successful People by B. Eugene Griessman

Improvements I Will Make

1. _____

2. _____

3. _____

★ Self-Discipline ★

My self-test score (p. 168) is: For me, this attribute is mostly a
5 4 3 2 1   ___ **Strength**   ___**Weakness**

Ways to Strengthen Self-Discipline

1. Understand the relationship among the first three core attributes — *self-esteem, self-development,* and *self-discipline.* The better you *feel* about yourself, and the more you *develop* yourself, the more you will be willing to *impose discipline* on yourself.

2. The key to *self-discipline* is self-control. To what extent do you keep control of yourself in stressful situations? Keep reminding yourself that composure under pressure is *vital* to your success. And "never let them see you sweat!"

3. Find *positive outlets* that will help you relieve pressure. Jog. Meditate. Engage in sports. Racquet ball after a bad day at work is better than arriving home grumpy. Watch the movie *Ghandi.* What can you learn from the late-great leader of India?

4. Divide your day into segments. When it's time to work, work. When it's time to relax, forget work and *relax!*

5. Understand that the opposite of *self-discipline* is self-indulgence. Again: if *you* don't discipline yourself, *someone else will* — and you'll end up with even *less* opportunity to indulge yourself.

6. *Self-discipline* is the practice of delayed gratification. To be more successful in your pursuits, make this vow: *"I will do today what others won't, so I can do tomorrow what others can't."*

7. *Believe* in your plan. Be *driven* by it. Review it, update it, and constantly renew your commitment to it.

8. Defeat habits and practices not in your best interests. You have the power *within you* to stop or start almost anything. Demonstrate to yourself and others that you can *overcome* bad habits.

9. Work with others, holding one another accountable for establishing or reinforcing good habits and eliminating bad ones.

10. Use charts on the refrigerator, diary entries, notations in your planner, or other visible means to help reinforce your resolve.

Good Books to Read

Managing Yourself by Alfred Goodloe et al
Doing It Now by Edwin Bliss
Do It! Let's Get Off Our Buts by John-Roger & McWilliams

Improvements I Will Make

1. _____

2. _____

3. _____

Perspective

My self-test score (p. 168) is: For me, this attribute is mostly a

5 4 3 2 1   ___ **Strength**   ___**Weakness**

Ways to Keep Things in Perspective

1. Take time out to laugh — at yourself, at what you're doing, at life around you. Others will take you *more* seriously when they see you taking yourself *less* seriously, and vice versa.

2. Enjoy comedy — the *positive* kind, not the off-color, in-your-face, put-down sort of stuff so prevalent today, but the sort of comedy that makes you feel good about yourself and others.

3. Be wary of obsessions. Take a careful look at the *risks* as well as the rewards of trying to do *too much* of anything. Always know the price as well as the payback of what you're seeking.

4. Concentrate on the spiritual dimensions of life. Spend more time counting your blessings than counting your possessions.

5. Avoid turning leisure activities into chores, especially if you are engaged in high-pressure work. Your diversions should be enjoyable, not add to on-the-job stress.

6. Are you a perfectionist? If so, you're not leading a *constructive* lifestyle. Strive for *excellence,* but don't expect to be perfect in all that you do. Only God is perfect, and you're not Him!

7. Ask these three questions before taking on new goals, tasks or responsibilities: (1) Will this add value to my life and, if not, should I do this at all? (2) If it *will* add value, how can I accomplish it in order to achieve *maximum* value? (3) What price must I pay to achieve this; is it worth it and, if so, and how can I handle it?

8. Watch the movie *Citizen Kane.* What does the Orson Wells classic teach you about putting money and power into *perspective*?

9. Go back to page 140. Review the *perspective* you revealed in rating yourself on "The Emerson Scale."

10. Treat yourself to 15-seconds of loud, raucous laughter at least once every day. This will release *endorphins* in your brain — powerful proteins that make you feel better and even can improve your health. Encourage others to join you. *Have fun!*

Good Books to Read

Don't Sweat the Small Stuff by Richard Carlson, Ph.D
Success Trap by Dr. Stan J. Katz & Aimee E. Liu
The Laughter Prescription by Peter Dana

Improvements I Will Make

1. _____
2. _____
3. _____

Focus

My self-test score (p. 168) is: For me, this attribute is mostly a
5 4 3 2 1 ___ **Strength** ___**Weakness**

Ways to Be More Focused

1. Plan your work, then work your plan. Each time you set out to do something, decide on a logical sequence for your actions. Set realistic deadlines and meet them consistently.

2. Examine the *environment* in which you're trying to *focus* your efforts. Will it support or detract from your efforts to concentrate on what needs to be done?

3. Limit your accessibility. Set aside times for people to see you, for answering the telephone, etc. The fewer the distractions, the better the *focus* on the task at hand.

4. Based on your over-all plan and a good inventory of your capabilities, set *specific goals*, measurements, and deadlines.

5. Prepare for setbacks. Reinforce your energy and *enthusiasm*. When faced with roadblocks, ask yourself whether the problem is within you. Are you deciding "I can't" or simply "I don't want to."

6. Banish procrastination. Eliminate the word "later." For example, instead of saying "I'll do this later," say "I'll have this done by 9 a.m. tomorrow." Then *hold yourself* to the deadline.

7. Be *passionate* about what you're doing. If you believe in what you're doing and are enthusiastic about it, you will accomplish it well, *enjoy* getting it done, and feel it add value to your life.

8. If focusing is a problem, weigh it against other <u>concentration</u> attributes. Is there a shortfall in *judgment*? Do you need to be better organized or self-disciplined. Are things out of *perspective*?

9. Consider going on a retreat — alone or with associates. Whether a cabin in the woods or a motel room across town, a few days "away from it all" can help get things into sharp *focus*.

10. Use a visual aid to map out what you want to achieve. Hang it up so even staring at the wall can help you stay focused!

Good Books to Read

First Things First by Stephen R. Covey
Getting Unstuck by Sidney B. Simon
The Power of Focused Thinking by Edward de Bono

Improvements I Will Make

1. _____

2. _____

3. _____

The Concentration Imperative

My self-test scores are:
Judgment ___
Organization ___
Self-Discipline ___
Perspective ___
Focus ___

Added together, the numbers = ___
divided by 5 = _____ for *concentration*.
That overall score and how I rated *self-discipline* (the core attribute) indicates that *concentration* for me is a:
___ **Strength** ___**Weakness**

Ways to Strengthen Concentration

1. Review how the imperatives and attributes fit together. *Motivation* drives *education* which, if you're highly motivated, can leave you awash in *knowledge*. It is through *concentration* that you give value to what you know and are willing to do.

2. Effective *concentration* reduces wasted effort in your life. Rate yourself on how well or how poorly you pursue what is *truly important*. How have you done so far in making the most of what you have and in pursuing what you want?

3. Habits are made and broken within the *concentration* attributes. Make a list of your habits. Which ones help you succeed and should be reinforced? Which ones hold you back and should be eliminated?

Good Books to Read

The 7 Habits of Highly Effective People by Stephen R. Covey
Concentration! How to Focus for Success by Sam Horn
Message to Garcia by Elbert Hubbard

Improvements I Will Make

1. _____
2. _____
3. _____

It is not book learning young men need, nor instruction about this and that, but a stiffening of the vertebrae which will cause them to be loyal to a trust, to act promptly, concentrate their energies, do a thing — "carry a message to Garcia."
Elbert Hubbard
Message to Garcia

Communication
Earns Your Right to Win
Association • Interaction • Relationships • Self-Confidence • Recognition

---

Okay, so you're motivated and educated. So you've taken all that ambition and know-how and concentrated it on something. Without *communication*, it's all for nought. It means *nothing*. You will go *nowhere*.

Life is a journey that *can't* be taken alone. In a variety of ways, you need the *permission* of others to win at anything. And no one will give you permission unless you communicate with them.

That said, let me point out a huge difference between two words: *commmunication* and communications — the same word, but with an "s" on the end.

People send and receive many *thousands* of communications every day. These are the *messages* competing for attention. They involve *senders* of messages and, they hope, *receivers* of messages.

When a sender gets a message through to a receiver and achieves some sort of mutual understanding, there is *communication* (no "s"). The result may be positive, negative, or neutral.

Communications are constant and, out of that daily deluge of messages, some amount of *communication* — for better or worse — is inevitable. *Lack* of this imperative is a ticket to failure .

> The vacuum created by a failure to communicate will quickly be filled with rumor, misrepresentation, drivel and poison.
> C. Northcote Parkinson's Final Law

The bottom line? Be a good communicator — both as sender and receiver of communications. Unless you are, no amount of *motivation*, *education*, and *concentration* will get you very far.

There are five *personal attributes* underlying the fourth imperative, the first three of them are very closely related.

Association
The Motivation of Communication

If you find it hard to be in contact with people — *to associate* — you'll also find it hard to succeed in life. Joy of living? Impossible!

Deciding who to associate with is your choice. Being a winner or a loser in life will depend on who you hang around with.

> He who walks with wise men becomes wise, but the companion of fools will suffer harm.
> Proverbs 13:20

Establishing *new* associations with people is a skill you can develop with practice and good training. An important part of that skill is learning to be likable and approachable — to be a magnet that attracts other people, leading *them* to want to associate with *you*.

Your *association* skills are high when you are good at striking up conversations in person or on the phone, making a good first impression on people, and finding it easy to make acquaintances.

There's much to learn if you are to be good at associating with people. Closely related to *association* is the attribute which may pose the biggest learning challenge:

Interaction
The Education of Communication

Meeting and getting to know people is one thing. Dealing with them *productively* is something else!

How well you interact depends on your care and concern for others as well as your skills as a communicator. The single most important aspect is understanding yourself and other people.

> If you do not understand a man you cannot crush him. If you do understand him, very probably you will not.
> G.K. Chesterton

Knowing how *you* think and why *you* think that way isn't enough. You must gain understanding of how *other people* think and why *they* think that way.

There are other specific habits and skills to develop, too:

Become a good listener. *Hear* what is being *said*. Master the art of conversation. Learn how to present your views persuasively. Be a good negotiator. Control your temper. Focus on win-win <u>outcomes</u>.

Underlying all of those things, you'll find the need to speak and write the language effectively, be a good reader, store and retrieve information efficiently, and consistently use the right communications *media* to send the right *messages* to the right people.

Association leads to *interaction*, and the better you interact the better you can associate. *Interaction*, in turn, should lead to:

Relationships
The Concentration of Communication

I find it hard to imagine life without love, family, friendships, mentors, and other forms of positive *relationships*.

> If a man could mount to Heaven and survey the mighty universe, his admiration of its beauties would be much diminished unless he had someone to share in his pleasure.
> Cicero

How important are *relationships*?

An in-depth study of why a small town in the eastern U.S. had fewer fatal heart attacks than a town nearby traced the sole reason to cohesive, supportive *relationships* through families and friends.

How strong and positive are the *relationships* in *your* life? If you're married, how strong are your bonds to each other? How many true friends do you have? Do you have a career mentor — someone ahead of you professionally who advises you and helps you advance?

Be very good at *association, interaction*, and enduring *relationships* and you will radiate the core attribute of <u>*communication*</u>:

★ Self-Confidence ★
The Communication of Communication

You do not have to become *fearless* to be self-confident, only *courageous*. To be *fully fearless* is to be a fool. To be courageous is to overcome your fears, including those that always will be with you.

> They can do all because they think they can.
> Virgil

Self-confidence is what you communicate to yourself and the rest of world. It not only helps you overcome your fears, but underscores belief in yourself. And by radiating belief in yourself, other people are likely to believe in you.

When you're in search of a job or seeking a promotion, the decisionmakers are likely to consider your level of *self-confidence*. If they sense you have none, they'll probably choose someone who does.

That brings us to:

Recognition
The Achievement of Communication

A wall full of plaques is the *least* important part of *recognition*. Being recognized after the fact for what you've done is not nearly as important as being recognized before-the-fact for what you *can* do.

In this context, *recognition* comes in two forms:

1. Your ability to recognize your own capabilities and the opportunities that lie before you, and

2. Being recognized by others for having great potential and being *worthy* of opportunities.

The more others become aware of who you are and what you can do, the more you will be able to fulfill your dreams and goals.

> It is far more important that one's life should be perceived than that it should be transformed; for no sooner has it been perceived, than it transforms itself of its own accord.
> Maurice Maeterlinck

Communication Self-Test

For each pair of statements, circle the 5 if the statement above the numbers fits you or the 4 if it mostly fits. Circle 1 if the statement below fits or 2 if it mostly fits. Circle 3 if either could apply.

Association

I find it easy to meet people. Making new contacts and getting into new groups is one of my strong points.

5   4   3   2   1

It's hard for me to meet people. I'm not comfortable in dealing with others and would rather keep to myself.

Interaction

I am highly skilled in interpersonal *communication*. I am a good listener and do well in establishing rapport.

5   4   3   2   1

My interpersonal *communication* skills are weak. I need much improvement in such areas as listening and establishing rapport.

Relationships

I have many friends and associates I can trust and I enjoy building good — especially loving — *relationships* with people.

5   4   3   2   1

I have few friends and/or family members I am close to. I find it very hard to build good—especially loving—*relationships*.

★ Self-Confidence ★

I have total faith in my capabilities and believe I can succeed in whatever I choose to do.

5   4   3   2   1

I have strong doubts about my capabilities. It is very hard for me to muster *self-confidence* because of doubts about myself.

Recognition

I am well-recognized for what I do and who I am and it is of equal or even greater pleasure for me to give *recognition* to others.

5   4   3   2   1

I feel left by the wayside many times. I find it hard to attract the attention of others and/or compliment and praise other people.

Association

My self-test score (p. 178) is: For me, this attribute is mostly a
    5 4 3 2 1   ___ **Strength** ___**Weakness**

Ways to Associate Better

1. Stop depending on others to associate with *you*. Reach out to associate with *them*. Research shows nearly 70 percent of people are uncomfortable in making initial contact.

2. If you think you're shy, take a hard look at Personal Attribute No. 1 — *self-esteem*. The better you feel about yourself, the easier it will be to establish contact with others.

3. Think of yourself as *a product going to market*. How do you *appear* to the people who would "buy" your product — you?

4. List people and organizations whose support is most important. Find the best ways to make or widen those contacts.

5. Connect with others through volunteer activities, professional organizations, special projects and the like. *Practice* associating in settings where mistakes won't be costly.

6. Develop and *practice* a good, *brief* self-introduction. Include a clear description of who you are and what you do.

7. Always wear a name tag high and on the right side so it's easy to read when shaking hands. When you print your own name tag, make big, bold block letters that can be read from a distance.

8. Your personal appearance is important! How you *look* usually means more than what you *say* when you make a first impression. Get feedback and good advice on dress and grooming.

9. When meeting people, concentrate more on getting them to feel *they're impressing you* than in trying to get them to feel that you're impressing them. *Association* with others should set the stage for developing rapport and good *relationships*.

10. Prepare for meetings and social events. Bone up on subject matter likely to be discussed or suitable for conversation. Be well-versed and knowledgable, but never come off as a know-it-all.

Good Books to Read

The 100 Best Ways to Meet People by Ben White
Instant Rapport by Michael Brooks
Great Connections by Anne Baber & Lynne Waymon

Improvements I Will Make

1. _____

2. _____

3. _____

Interaction

My self-test score (p. 178) is: For me, this attribute is mostly a
5 4 3 2 1   ___ **Strength**   ___**Weakness**

Ways to Interact More Effectively

1. Assess your listening skills. A good communicator is, first, *a good listener.* Get family and friends to give you candid feedback.

2. Take an interpersonal communication course to improve your skills. Most colleges offer them, and good workshops abound.

3. Learn the importance of the verbal, vocal and visual aspects of communicating, noting the enormous importance of the *visual* dimension. Unless you are in a cultural setting where it's considered impolite, maintain *good eye contact* when conversing.

4. Remember people's names. *Use their names* when talking with them. Set up a file of business cards or other means to help you keep track of where you met, common interests, etc.

5. Keep your communications positive. Translate anger into concern. Translate concern into genuine caring for other people and their viewpoints. Remember: *People don't care how much you know until they know how much you care.*

6. Don't be a whiner. The quickest way to lose the ability to interact effectively is to be a constant complainer and critic.

7. Work on body language. Do you use facial expressions or gestures that may interfere with your efforts to relate well?

8. Be a *good listener.* Make the people with whom you are trying to communicate feel *important.* Whenever applicable, let the *other person* speak first, and work toward establishing rapport by genuinely being interested and asking good questions.

9. Learn to be a *good negotiator.* Take a course or turn to books and tapes to develop your skills. Learn the *principles* of good negotiations, especially how to work toward *win-win outcomes.*

10. Honor the language. How you use it makes a *strong statement about you,* good or bad. *Speak* it well and *write* it well, and it will *serve* you well. Communicate as a *professional.*

Good Books to Read

The Art of Talking So That People Will Listen by Paul W. Swets
Getting What You Want by Kare Anderson
Nasty People by Jay Carter

Improvements I Will Make

1. _____

2. _____

3. _____

Relationships

My self-test score (p. 178) is: For me, this attribute is mostly a
5   4   3   2   1   ___ **Strength**   ___**Weakness**

Ways to Strengthen Relationships

1. Make lists of people with whom your *relationships* are best and worst. Find ways to shift people from the negative list to the positive list. Set a goal to get everyone *off* the negative list.

2. Always try to contribute *more* to a relationship than you expect to receive from it. Identify situations in which that isn't the case. Work hard at making changes for the better.

3. Recognizing that *people like people who are like themselves*, try to find ways you can strengthen personal ties by actively pursuing common behaviors and areas of common interest.

4. When trying to resolve conflicts, challenge the issues or situations, *don't attack the people*. Try to resolve such situations with rapport or, at least, mutual respect.

5. Find joy in the achievements of others. Build rapport by making people feel they are successful in your eyes. Reallocate your pronouns, using less "I" and much more "you" and "we."

6. Put your highest priority on strong bonds *within your family*. Doing so helps build strong bonds outside the family as well.

7. Know when to seek professional help when family *relationships* are at risk. There are many good counselors, clergymen, and programs available. When there's an impasse, consider the good offices of a third party skilled in the art of mediation.

8. Have a mentor and be a mentor to strengthen career pursuits. Mentorships are professional *relationships* at their best.

9. If you're in a hopelessly "toxic" relationship, find the best way to end it. Don't let fear of rejection or codependency keep you attached to someone who constantly pulls you down.

10. To get the best picture of *relationships*, the picture to see is the movie *Brian's Song*. It's the true story of a dying football player — and a reminder that the balance between power and love is neither powerless love nor loveless power, but *powerful love*.

Good Books to Read

Personality Plus by Florence Littauer
The Mentor's Spirit by Marsha Sinetar
Living Beautifully Together by Alexandra Stoddard

Improvements I Will Make

1. _____

2. _____

3. _____

★ Self-Confidence ★

My self-test score (p. 178) is: For me, this attribute is mostly a

5 4 3 2 1   ___ **Strength**   ___**Weakness**

Ways to Bolster Self-Confidence

1. Make a list of your successes. Think of positive feelings you had or still have. Harness them to move forward confidently.

2. Seek feedback. Take satisfaction in the positive and treat the negatives as opportunities to learn and to change for the better.

3. Update your resume or prepare a new one, even if you're well-satisfied with your current job. Getting your qualities on paper can help reinforce your levels of *self-esteem* and *self-confidence*.

4. Build upon your *relationships* — at home, in the work-place, through professional and civic associations, and anywhere else where your positive qualities can be practiced and reinforced.

5. Think of the two or three most self-confident people you know of. Were they *always* that way? What are their "secrets" to becoming more self-confident?

6. Stop worrying about things you *can't control*. Concentrate your mental energies on making a positive difference in the things you *can* control.

7. When facing a challenging situation, imagine it being handled by the most capable and confident person you can think of. Cloak yourself in the same imagery. Envision yourself in that person's shoes — handling the situation, enjoying success.

8. Learn to be a good presenter. Prepare well, practice well. Videotape rehearsals and have others help critique your perfor-mance. Role play before a key negotiation, discussion or debate.

9. Don't bottle up your worries. Talk them out with friends. Remember: *you will not fail!* You'll succeed or have a *learning exper-ience*. Either way, you *win!*

10. Consider taking a "ropes course" or other programs that can increase your *self-confidence* by teaching teamwork in physical or mental settings outside your comfort zone.

Good Books to Read

Total Self-Confidence by Dr. Robert Anthony
Stand Up, Speak Out, Talk Back by Alberti & Emmons
The Confidence Quotient by Meryle Gellman

Improvements I Will Make

1. _____

2. _____

3. _____

Recognition

My self-test score (p. 178) is: For me, this attribute is mostly a
5   4   3   2   1   ___ **Strength**   ___**Weakness**

Ways to Recognize & Be Recognized

1. Be assertive, not aggressive. Assertive people can earn positive *recognition* that will lead to success. Aggressive people bring out anger in themselves and others, weakening or destroying *relationships* and creating *roadblocks* to success.

2. Write down two or three important areas in which you could earn the positive attention of others. Identify barriers and develop strategies to overcome them.

3. Put your efforts to be recognized in the context of your principles and the best interests of *everyone* involved. Getting people to acclaim you at any cost exacts a price too high to pay.

4. Arrive at meetings early to meet people and strengthen *relationships*. Introduce yourself to the hosts and offer to help with any last-minute challenges. Build rapport. Be a team player.

5. Speak in public. Volunteer to give speeches or presentations for your employer or on behalf of non-profit organizations. Teach. Offer to help train others in your organization.

6. Pattern your manner of dress, speech, and mannerisms after people recognized for their integrity, leadership, and success.

7. Develop a personal marketing strategy. Get specific about exactly what must be done by when and through whom in order to achieve deserved *recognition*.

8. Never deflect a compliment. Accept praise graciously and be gracious in praising others. Edify and you will be edified.

9. Remember that *recognition* also involves *your* ability to recognize *opportunity*, which is the first step to *achievement*. Is your ladder to success leaning against the right building?

10. Build a network of people who recognize opportunities. Learn from them. Share ideas with them. Put more into your network than you expect to get out. The rewards will be even greater.

Good Books to Read

You Are the Message by Roger Ailes
Developing Positive Assertiveness by Sam R. Lloyd
Balcony People by Joyce Heathersley

Improvements I Will Make

1. _____

2. _____

3. _____

The Communication Imperative

My self-test scores are:

Association	___
Interaction	___
Relationships	___
Self-Confidence	___
Recognition	___

Added together, the numbers = ___
divided by 5 = ___ for *communication*.
That overall score and how I rated *self-confidence* (the core attribute) indicates that *communication* for me is a:

___ **Strength**   ___**Weakness**

Ways to Strengthen Communication

1. Rate yourself as a communicator. Are you in the top 10 percent of the people you know? The top half? Be honest — and careful! About 25 percent of the people asked that question "modestly" put themselves in the *top one percent*! Your biggest barrier to *communication* may be your assumption that you're good at it.

2. Get feedback from people who are willing to be candid. Ask them what you could do to be more effective as a communicator. Set improvement goals.

3. Study great communicators back through time — Winston Churchill, Abraham Lincoln, Jesus Christ, et al. *Learn* from them.

4. Start honing your skills at home. If you're married, you and your spouse should set the example for your children. And if you communicate well with *children*, you should be able to communicate well with just about *anyone*!

5. Remember: what people *see* when you communicate can be even more important than the words or the way they're heard. Look sharp, smile a lot and, as someone once said with great tongue-in-cheek humor: "Always be sincere, even when you don't mean it."

Good Books to Read

How to Win Friends and Influence People by Dale Carnegie
Skills With People by Les Giblin.
50 One Minute Tips to Better Communications by Phillip Bozek

Improvements I Will Make

1. _____

2. _____

3. _____

The great illusion about communication is that it has been accomplished.

George Bernard Shaw

Achievement
Wins Certain Success

Opportunity • Expertise • Influence • Character • Self-Fulfillment

It's fundamental in life that productive people tend to win and unproductive people tend to lose. That was true when God created humankind, and it's true today in spite of government interventions.

Productivity produces *achievement*. And the secrets of being supremely productive are found in the first four imperatives — *motivation*, *education*, *concentration*, and *communication*.

As to the fifth imperative, the rewards go far beyond money, power, and ever-greater acclaim.

> The highest reward for man's toil is not what he gets for it, but what he becomes by it.
>
> John Ruskin

Like the other four imperatives, the fifth one has five important personal attributes. The first unlocks the door to *achievement*:

Opportunity
The Motivation of Achievement

Recognition and *Opportunity* form a bridge between the last two of the five imperatives. To be recognized by others as worthy of *opportunity* is at the *communication* end of the bridge and being able to recognize a chance to move forward in life is at the *achievement* end.

Simply being recognized won't get you across the bridge and on to great *achievement*. If you have trouble believing that, take a look at the British Royal Family. Today's young royals were *born* to be recognized the world over, but seem to have a lot of trouble recognizing the rights and wrongs of the opportunities at hand.

If you're waiting for *opportunity* to knock, you're sitting at one end of the bridge waiting for someone to carry you across.

> If opportunity doesn't knock, build a door.
>
> Milton Berle

Opportunity is your chance to make the *most* out of life and achieve certain success, no matter how uncertain the world may be. Making the most of opportunities to be found everywhere nowadays requires the *best* of your full range of personal attributes, especially the core attributes of *self-esteem*, *self-development*, *self-discipline*, and *self-confidence*.

It also requires harnessing the power of the first six words for winning — making good personal *choices*, whatever your *circumstances*, so you can produce good *outcomes*; then, knowing what you *want* out of life, finding the best *way* to get it, and doing the *work* involved and learning to do it well.

All of which leads to the second attribute of *achievement*:

Expertise
The Education of Achievement

If you are a person who has developed *expertise* that is of value to others, you have grasped the educational aspect of *achievement*. What I'm *really* talking about here, of course, is *excellence*:

> The quality of a person's life is in direct proportion to their commitment to excellence — no matter what their field of endeavor.
> Vince Lombardi

Being an expert on something trivial can be fun, so long as you recognize it as trivial and fun. That said, it's also true that seemingly trivial *expertise* can be amazingly profitable, given the right *opportunity*. Just look at all the collectors of rare and unusual things who have turned one person's trash into another's treasure!

Being an expert on something *important* can be fulfilling, so long as you stay current and think ahead. How about being the leading expert on making 8-track tape decks for automobiles? Or building drive-in theaters? Or manufacturing asbestos insulation?

The closest you'll ever come to being indispensible to someone else is when you know more about something of importance than anyone, stay ahead of changes, and share what you know productively.

In other words, you're able to apply positive:

Influence
The Concentration of Achievement

While *knowledge* is defined as only potential power, *influence* can be viewed as your power *potential*. The greater your *influence*, the greater your power to achieve.

Opportunity, expertise, influence. Here are two examples of how these three attributes fit together:

• Grasping an *opportunity* for fame and fortune, people with *expertise* came under the *influence* of those who told them what they wanted to hear, built the *Titanic*, and brought about disaster.

• Thanks to accepting the *influence* of God, Noah and his family — all of whom lacked *expertise* in weather forecasting and shipbuilding — took full advantage of their *opportunity* to survive.

Influence may or may not involve leadership. Not everyone can or should become a leader. And yet there are many cases where success — or even survival — depends on most anyone's *influence*.

Sociologists say even the *shyest* person will have some sort of influence over about 10,000 people in a lifetime.

Bo Short, author of
The Foundation of Leadership

The *principles* of good leadership, however, apply to *influence*, whether you're a leader or not. Such principles also are the basis for:

Character
The Communication of Achievement

The four <u>communication</u>-related attributes of the first four imperatives — *enthusiasm, interest, perspective,* and *self-confidence,* — all reflect your personality, or who you *appear* to be.

Other attributes, such as *interaction, relationships, expertise,* and *influence,* reflect your reputation, or who people *think* you are.

It is *character* that represents to yourself and others who you *really* are. Your values are implicit in your *character.* If you are of good *character,* it means you have learned the practical as well as the moral value of doing what is right.

If *influence* will give you power, *character* will test how well you *handle* that power.

Nearly all men can stand adversity, but if you want to test a man's character, give him power.

Abraham Lincoln

Character is the doorstep of the most important attribute of all:

★ Self-Fulfillment ★
The Achievement of Achievement

This last of the 25 attributes reflects your location among the five "cities" on the road map. To be self-fulfilled *is* to experience joy of living and to be all you can be.

To be what we are, and to become what we are
capable of becoming, is the only end in life.

Life is like electricity. It can neither be collected nor stored. If you *thought* electricity could be "stored" in a battery, go back and review basic physics. A battery *manufactures* electricity.

And so it is with life. You can *store* certain properties in your brain and your biceps and other parts of your body. And, through the grace of God and proper maintenance, you can *extend* life for a long time. But you can't *collect life* and you *can't store life*!

Life is for you to *live*! To live a life of *self-fulfillment,* you must constantly recharge yourself, rejuvenating and extending the capacity of *all* your attributes and the qualities they represent.

Achievement Self-Test

For each pair of statements, circle the 5 if the statement above the numbers fits you or the 4 if it mostly fits. Circle 1 if the statement below fits or 2 if it mostly fits. Circle 3 if either could apply.

Opportunity

Many opportunities are and have been open to me. I recognize them and make the most of them.

5   4   3   2   1

Doors seem mostly closed to me. I rarely get the breaks I deserve and even if I did, I'm unlikely to take full advantage of them.

Expertise

I have turned *knowledge* and experience into *expertise* that is valued by others and helps me be successful.

5   4   3   2   1

There's not a lot that I'm good at. I know a little about some things, but there are few if any things of importance I excel at.

Influence

People continually turn to me for advice, guidance, or leadership in areas important to my goals or for helping them reach their goals.

5   4   3   2   1

For the most part, nobody pays much attention to me. Rarely if ever do people look to me for advice, guidance, or leadership.

Character

I have a clear, organized and articulated set of values, live by them consistently and am *recognized* for living by them.

5   4   3   2   1

My values are unclear and I often find them shifting to fit the situation at hand.

★ Self-Fulfillment ★

I experience great satisfaction, even *joy* in the results of my efforts. I feel successful in the best sense of the word.

5   4   3   2   1

There's little satisfaction and joy in my life and what I do usually leads to mediocrity, boredom or failure.

Opportunity

My self-test score (p. 188) is: For me, this attribute is mostly a
5 4 3 2 1   ___ **Strength**   ___**Weakness**

Ways to Take Advantage of Opportunities

1. Purge from your thinking any notion of *the good old days.* If you think there were greater opportunities in times past, you will find it harder to recognize the opportunities before you *now.* These *are* the good old days — if you are determined to make them so!

2. Gauge opportunities by the motivational attributes. Ask whether each *opportunity* would help fulfill your plan or deviate from it. Do you have the *enthusiasm, resilience,* etc. it will take?

3. Check opportunities against your values — especially in matters with potential impacts on family and other aspects of your life. If your basic values will be compromised, don't do it.

4. Beware of anything that sounds too good to be true. Assemble facts. Sleep on it. Pray. Weigh it carefully. Then decide.

5. Cherish luck but don't depend on it. While some people may seem to be luckier than you are, most often it's a lot of *hard work* that preceded the "luck."

6. Capitalize on setbacks and adversity. There are opportunities hidden within *everything* that goes wrong. Search the lessons learned carefully, and you will find them.

7. Never give up the pursuit of an *opportunity* too soon. There are countless cases of people throwing opportunities away, stopping just short of success. Before ending a pursuit, be certain that *every* avenue has been totally checked and discounted.

8. Get advice. Find good sounding boards, especially among people who can view a venture from different perspectives.

9. Make sure an *opportunity* "feels right" before pursuing it. Have faith, but don't plunge ahead on *blind* faith.

10. Conquer fear. There are few rewards without risk and few opportunities without risk-*taking.* Fear is the biggest barrier you can place across your pathway to certain success.

Good Books to Read

Think and Grow Rich by Napoleon Hill
You Can't Steal Second With Your Foot on First by Burke Hedges
101 Best Businesses to Start by Kahn & Lief

Improvements I Will Make

1. _____

2. _____

3. _____

Expertise

My self-test score (p. 188) is: For me, this attribute is mostly a
5 4 3 2 1   ___ **Strength** ___**Weakness**

Ways to Strengthen Expertise

1. Identify your main areas of *Expertise*. Considering the people you work with, what of importance can you offer more than anyone else? In what areas are you considered the *resident expert?*

2. Identify several areas where your know-how and experience points *toward* becoming an expert. Set priorities and goals to concentrate on in those areas that are most worth pursuing.

3. Find out who the leading experts are in the fields in which you want to develop your own *expertise*. How did they become experts? What could you do to emulate them?

4. Read. Set aside time each day and set goals to read books, journals, papers, etc. that will help you grow in *expertise*.

5. Teach. There's no better way to build a body of *knowledge* and *expertise*. You not only learn to teach but *learn* as you teach.

6. Publish. Whether it's an article in your company's publication or a whole series of books, the research and discipline of writing will help build your *expertise*. It also will provide an excellent means of gaining *recognition* and *influence*, on the job and beyond.

7. Speak. Prepare a 20-minute talk on an area you know a lot about. Offer it to your employer, professional association, service club — wherever you can find a good audience.

8. Assess the market value of your *expertise* in the arena in which it is being applied. Are you earning a satisfactory return on the investment in acquiring it? If not, weigh your alternatives.

9. Keep your resume up-to-date as an inventory of your *expertise* and achievements. Use the MECCA Matrix as a guide to the strengths you have to offer.

10. Review your plan and your *focus*. With mastery of specific areas comes the need to make a decision. Should you optimize what you have or build *expertise* in new areas?

Good Books to Read

Being the Best by Denis Waitley
The Executive Resume Book by Loretta D. Foxman
Skills for Success: The Experts Show the Way by Soundview

Improvements I Will Make

1. _____

2. _____

3. _____

Influence

My self-test score (p. 188) is: For me, this attribute is mostly a
     5 4 3 2 1   ___ **Strength** ___**Weakness**

Ways to Increase Your Influence

1. Consider carefully whether you prefer to assert *influence* mainly as a subject-matter expert or as a leader. Both avenues offer power, but the risks and the rewards are much different. Not all influential people make good leaders, and not everyone *needs* to become a leader to be a great person of *influence*.

2. If you seek leadership, re-examine your areas of *expertise*. The transition from subject-matter expert to leader brings a need to shift *focus*, especially in how you relate to people.

3. If you *want* to lead, *get good training*. While you may be an honor graduate from the "School of Hard Knocks," you can still gain much from good leadership development programs.

4. In whatever capacity you seek to *influence*, concentrate on style. Go through an assessment center or other program to identify your personality type and related strengths and weaknesses.

5. Experiment with various leadership styles and learned personality traits. Get good feedback. Make adjustments.

6. Build *influence* by heeding organizational culture. Find ways to work within the culture, strengthening and nurturing it for positive change.

7. Become a leader or resource for your professional association. It can easily translate into power and *influence* in your work.

8. Accept responsibility for *everything* over which you have control. Your *influence* will be diluted or enhanced in proportion to the amount of responsibility you are *willing* to accept.

9. Show appreciation for the work of others. The more you do, the more they'll appreciate (and be influenced by) you.

10. Help *other people* succeed. It's the primary responsibility of every leader and person of positive *influence*. Be a champion of your boss's career, for example, and you'll be an asset, not a threat.

Good Books to Read

Everyone's a Coach by Don Shula and Ken Blanchard
Bringing Out the Best in People by Alan Loy McGinnis
Developing the Leader Within You by John C. Maxwell

Improvements I Will Make

1. _____

2. _____

3. _____

Character

My self-test score (p. 188) is: For me, this attribute is mostly a
5 4 3 2 1   ___ **Strength** ___**Weakness**

Ways to Strengthen Your Character

1. How you handle *influence* is a much bigger test of your *character* than how you handle the lack of it. Write down and adhere to *basic principles* you will follow when asserting *influence*.

2. Another true test of your *character* is *adversity*. How do you handle situations that go awry? With power? With grace? With integrity? Assess your handling of important things that have gone wrong in your life. What would you do differently today?

3. The more power you gain and assert, the harder it is to get good feedback. Don't be an *emperor* who shoots messengers, be an *empowerer* who gets, heeds, and appreciates honest advice

4. Ask (or re-ask): "Who *really* is my higher power?" Yourself? Your boss? "The Almighty Dollar"? God? People with the greatest *character* tend to be people with strongest spiritual commitment.

5. Are you a *humble person* or are you "extremely proud of your humility"? Very self-centered people tend to lack charisma. Charisma conveys *influence*, and *influence* conveys *character*.

6. Do a "values audit." Where do you *draw the line* with your integrity? At what point do you refuse to compromise your principles, no matter *what* the consequences?

7. Develop a personal crisis strategy. What are the toughest tests of integrity you might face? How will you handle them?

8. Shun the trappings of power. The more power you gain and the less you try to distinguish yourself *from* others, the *more distinguished* you are likely to become *among* others.

9. Develop *expertise* in the *ethics* of your chosen field. Write articles. Teach. Be the person turned to for ethical advice.

10. Write your own code of ethics, standards of integrity, or personal credo. Frame it and hang it on the wall. Follow it!

Good Books to Read

Principle-Centered Leadership by Stephen R. Covey
The Power of Ethical Management by Blanchard & Peale
How Could You Do That? by Dr. Laura Schlessinger

Improvements I Will Make

1. _____

2. _____

3. _____

★ Self-Fulfillment ★

My self-test score (p. 188) is: For me, this attribute is mostly a
5   4   3   2   1   ___ **Strength**   ___**Weakness**

Ways to Increase Self-Fulfillment

1. Look again at the five "cities" on the road map (page 108). If *City of Joy* is where you want to be for your life's journey and you're not there yet, list key areas in which you're not self-fulfilled.

2. For each item on your list, identify specific ways to be self-fulfilled. Turn those ways into goals and include them in your plan.

3. Review the Emerson exercise on page 140. Each of the 10 components is a seed that could help you become more self-fulfilled. Which seeds would help you most? How should you grow them?

4. Be wary when using numbers to assess your achievements. Count your blessings, not just your money.

5. Increase *self-fulfillment* by sharing the *secrets* of your success with others. The more you help others, the better you should feel about yourself.

6. Find joy in life's *little things*. You'll be more self-fulfilled and you'll be less affected when some of the *big* things fall apart.

7. Constantly strive for excellence in all that you do, maintaining a realistic and healthy mix of *material wealth, satisfying work, and good relationships* (Have-Do-Be).

8. Make *time* for joyful living. There's no *self-fulfillment* without joy — only self-satisfaction at best. There's no joy when no time is allowed for it.

9. Look at your self-test score for *purpose* (page 148). If it's less than a 5, you can raise your score when you are able to achieve greater *self-fulfillment*. You'll have a good *opportunity* to work on that in the next chapter when you develop personal mission and vision statements.

10. Be more self-fulfilled in just 130 minutes. Watch the classic movie *It's a Wonderful Life*. If that old Jimmy Stewart flick doesn't help you, what on earth will?

Good Books to Read

Experiencing God by Henry T. Blackaby & Claude V. King
When All You've Ever Wanted Isn't Enough by Harold Kushner
Effective Thinking for Uncommon Success by Gerald Kushel

Improvements I Will Make

1. _____

2. _____

3. _____

The Achievement Imperative

My self-test scores are:

Opportunity	___
Expertise	___
Influence	___
Character	___
Self-Fulfillment	___

Added together, the numbers = ___
divided by 5 = _____ for *achievement*.
That overall score and how I rated *self-fulfillment* (the core attribute) indicates that *achievement* for me is a:

___ **Strength**   ___ **Weakness**

Ways to Strengthen **Achievement**

1. Big achievers are big agents of positive change. Look back at your pursuits. Were you a good change agent? Were you *resistant* to positive change? What resulted? What should you change now?

2. Based on how you see what's ahead, write down ways you can do *better* as an agent of positive change. Make the effort part of your *self-development* and of your goals.

3. If you're like most people, you'll judge your achievements by your best intentions, most noble acts, and most virtuous habits. But others will judge you more by the last bad thing you are perceived as having done. Safeguard *achievement* and build upon it by having and *living by* a strong personal credo.

4. Just as important, don't be ruled by a *"committee of they."* Do what's right, not just what might score well in opinion polls.

5. To be a high achiever, accept the four disciplines espoused by basketball coach Bobby Knight: (1) do what *needs* to be done, (2) do it *when* it needs to be done, (3) do it the *best* that it *can* be done, and (4) do it that way *every time you do it*.

Good Books to Read

Courage Is Contagious by John Kasich
Psycho-Cybernetics by Maxwell Maltz, M.D.
Live Your Dreams by Les Brown

Improvements I Will Make

1. _____

2. _____

3. _____

> **Let us, then, be up and doing,**
> **With a heart for any fate;**
> **Still achieving, still pursuing.**
> **Learn to labour and to wait.**
> **Longfellow**

And the Secret Is...*Commitment*!

Go back to page 144 for a moment and take another look at *The MECCA Matrix*. You'll find two words underlying the five imperatives and their respective personal attributes.

Did you find them? Great!

The foundation word for the first four imperatives is *commitment*. That's the "secret" of doing what it takes to become more motivated, better educated, more effectively concentrated on dreams and goals, and better able to communicate effectively.

But don't take my word for it:

Motivation

Until one is committed, there is hesitency, the chance to draw back, always ineffectiveness. ...the moment one definitely commits oneself, then Providence moves, too.

W.H. Murray, mountain climber

Education

...one of the goals of American education is to start students on a road toward the feelings of success and achievment that comes from commitment, ownership, and responsibility for their own educational progress.

William C. Byham
Zapp! in Education

Concentration

Sacrifice, discipline, commitment and perseverance are vital to those who want to fulfill dreams and overcome challenges and crises.

Pat Mesiti
Dreamers Never Sleep

Communication

Ordinary people become extraordinary communicators when they are fired up with commitment.

Roger Ailes
You Are the Message

The payoff for being committed to the first four imperatives is Imperative No. 5 — *Achievement*.

Which Comes First?

The second underlying word is *success*, which is the bottom line for *achievement* and its five personal attributes.

It took me a while to figure out that *success* should follow, not precede, *achievement*'s core attribute — *self-fulfillment* — for reasons well beyond making the five core attributes line up in a neat diagonal row on the matrix.

Must you be self-fulfilled before you can be successful? Or must you be successful before you can be self-fulfilled?

The answer lies in how you define *success*.

If you believe it to be Rolls-Royces and Rollexes and residences on the Riviera, without which there will be no joy or even much happiness in your life, by all means turn back to the matrix, take a thick felt-tip pen and put *success* ahead of *self-fulfillment*.

But if you believe Ralph Waldo Emerson got it right and high scores on the "Emerson Scale" (page 140) portray a person who is *truly* successful, then leave the order as is.

Maxing out all 10 parts of Emerson's definition reflect a life that's *totally* self-fulfilled, in my opinion. And who besides an abject materialist could argue that such a person isn't successful, whether wealthy or not?

Success as a Continuum

Another great definition underscores *success* as a continuum rather than an outcome.

Success is the progressive realization of a worthy ideal.
Earl Nightingale

Put in terms of life's journey and what it will take to reach your destination, Earl Nightingale's wonderful insight suggests that *Success* doesn't begin *on arrival*, but in making steady progress on attaining it throughout the journey.

What's the answer to Question 3? — *what will it take to reach your destination*? It's all five MECCA imperatives, built on a foundation of *commitment* and resulting in progressive *success*.

Without *motivation*, there is little or no *education*. Without *motivation* and *education*, there is no substance for *concentration*. Without *motivation*, *education*, and *concentration*, there is little basis for *communication*. And without *motivation*, *education*, *concentration*, and *communication*, there can be no *achievement* — and no *certain success*.

Chapter 9

The Fourth Question:

How Should You Chart Your Course?

- **Begin With Your Aspirations**
- **Chart Your Course in 5 Steps**
    1. *Write a Personal Mission Statement*
    2. *Create a Vision for Your Future*
    3. *Determine Your Key Objectives*
    4. *Divide Key Objectives Into Personal Goals*
    5. *Break Goals Into "Do-It!s"*
- **Put Your Plan Into Action**

Question Four:

It's the question asked by a traveler who knows the destination and knows what's required for the travel being planned, but is missing a very important ingredient for a successful trip.

What's missing, of course, are directions — a process, really, for charting the *best* course to reach your destination.

In the context of life and of this book, it's a process in which you've already determined where you are and where you want to be (Chapter 6), whom you will be for the journey (Chapter 7), and what it will take to reach your destination (Chapter 8).

But, you ask: "How should I chart my course?"

Curious Traveler: "Does it matter which road I take to Urbania?"
Crusty Local: "Not to me it don't!"

You're about to learn a career and life planning process that has worked very well for me and for many others. As to whether you choose to put it to work in your life — well, at the risk of sounding like the Crusty Local, it doesn't matter to me.

What *does* matter is having a planning process that works well for *you*, and there are a lot of good ones out there. Use the one taught here or pick another, but *have* a process and *use* it!

"Life is a series of personal *choices*." Remember? Well, this chapter will challenge you to make a *major* choice.

- Will you choose to be among the 85 percent of the population with *no* goals for their lives?
- Or will you choose to be among the 12 percent who *say* they have goals, but who haven't bothered to write them down?
- Or will you choose to be among the 3 percent who actually *have* written goals?
- Or will you choose to join the *elite few* among the 3 percent who have a well-thought-out, well-written career and life *plan*?

To re-re-re-quote the bodacious bromide:

People don't plan to fail, they fail to plan.

How much razor-sharp planning have you done so far in life?

If you're a typical American adult, you learned relatively little about planning since pulling a pot of hot soup from a stove top to discover a link between *choices* and *outcomes*.

Who *taught* you how to plan? Have you ever taken a course on planning? What, besides ill-fated new year's resolutions, have you committed to — in writing or by barefaced braggadocio?

You may have gone through phases of life and learned *nothing* about how to plan strategically, tactically, thoughtfully, and thoroughly. Or, you may have had some very *good* lessons and experiences during those phases of life up to now.

How much, if any, of the following personal history fits you?

Childhood & the Teen Years

Initially, planning was done *for* you — mostly by parents and teachers. In school, most everything was determined by requirements based on what *other people* thought you might need or be good at.

If you were a typical teenager, conflict and upheaval probably made good planning a near-impossibility.

You may have had *big dreams* of great success — and little or no thought about *how* to fulfill them. You probably clashed with parents, teachers, and peers over what you wanted to be when you grew up, whether and how to buy a car, the clothes you wore, the people you associated with, your hair style, a nose ring — whatever.

Planning among you and your peers was so haphazard that having any two or three teenagers show up at the right time and right place was a near miracle. You probably timed homework and other activities around the TV schedule.

The College Years

If college was part of the picture, you may have gotten caught up in course options, living arrangements, Greek-letter groups, sports, dating, protest marches, anguish over changing majors, parents at a distance with advice that sounded antediluvian, some good professors and some who couldn't make a living in the areas they were teaching if their lives depended on it — and, near the end, *fear of not finding a good job.*

Perhaps you even took a good-study-habits course, got an "A" in it and, with a big exam looming, *still* put it off to the last minute and stayed up all night on a desperate exam-cramming coffee binge.

Was a course in planning even *offered*? If so, did it teach you how to plan your *life*? Or, was it a business course that taught you how to develop a production schedule for a mythical company?

The Career Years

If you went to work for a well-run organization, you finally may have learned a little about planning.

Your employer may have given you a copy of the company *mission statement* to help you understand your job in a larger context. And you may have attended briefings and received booklets explaining a strategic vision, guiding principles, key objectives, and goals.

If you became a manager, you probably found yourself *responsible* for a piece of the organization's plan and learned a thing or two about time management.

While some bits and pieces of on-the-job planning may have crept into the *rest* of your life, the odds are that you *still* haven't done much to harness the power of effective career and personal planning.

Marriage & Family

If you're married, consider whether your *wedding* was your greatest single planning feat up to now. Dates had to be set, places nailed down, bridesmaids color-coordinated, menus selected, rings and gifts chosen, and everyone had to show up at the right place at the right time in the right attire.

If you had a *big* wedding, the planning may have rivaled the Normandy invasion. The nervous family of the bride may have hired a bridal consultant complete with jack boots, clipboard, two-way radio, police whistle, and a degree in behavioral psychology.

In your wedding vows, you accepted a divine *plan* to love, honor, cherish, and care for one another until the very end. And *that,* no doubt, became your biggest-ever long-term *planned* commitment.

A marriage is a collision of two histories.

More than half the marriages in the United States end in divorce. Why? Often, it's because of poor or virtually non-existent planning. What planning *does* take place sometimes is so focused on creating an impressive marriage *ceremony* that little attention is paid to planning an enduring *marriage.*

If you're a *typical* married person in the career years, there are two careers with attendant work pressures to endure, along with an array of other challenges, especially when children come along.

When you fell in love, you probably didn't think of falling into a good his-and-her career and personal planning process. Without such a process, your odds of staying together get worse. *With* one, such as the process offered here, the odds get much better.

If you're *not yet* married, share the process with your partner-to-be *before* you tie the knot. Develop your plans *together*.

The process will help you reconcile differences *together*. And if your differences are irreconcilable, the process will help you identify them and part as friends *before* solemn vows are exchanged.

> ...for better or for worse, richer or poorer, in sickness and in health, until *death* — not irreconcilable differences — do us part.

Begin With Your Aspirations

Remember the three "W" words from Chapter 5 and the questions they pose? I call it *The Aspirations Factor*:

1. What do you *want* out of life?
2. What's the best *way* to get it?
3. What's the *work* involved and to what extent are you willing to do it and learn how to do it well?

Effective career and life planning is *impossible* without good answers to those three questions.

If you've cut back on what you *want,* is it because you can't find the right *way* to get it? Is it that you have a *way* but are unwilling (or believe you're unable) to do the *work* that's required?

You *rated* yourself on the three "W"questions on pages 82-83. Go back and review your ratings. Also go back to Chapter 6 and review how you answered Question No. 2 — whom do you choose to be for the journey? Pay close attention to the aspirations you identified on page 130 and the pie chart you drew on page 141.

Activity: List in order of importance three to five of your greatest aspirations for an abundant and fulfilling life. Assume you already have identified a *way* to get whatever time, money and security would be needed. Then describe why you would find each aspiration so desirable.

What I *Want* — If I Had a *Way* to Get It

1. _____

     Why? _____

2. _____

     Why? _____

3. _____

   Why? _____

4. _____

   Why? _____

5. _____

   Why? _____

Now ask yourself how much of what you _want_ could be achieved through the primary _way_ (or ways) you're currently engaged in to get from *where you are now* to *where you want to be.*

Activity: In the blank next to each number, write a key word or two to identify the three to five aspirations you just identified. Then, for each, check one of the three choices to indicate whether you have or could find a _way_ to fulfill the aspiration. If you check "maybe" or "yes," note by when you could reasonably expect it to happen. Then describe the _work_ you would have to do.

Will My Current _Way_ Get Me What I _Want_?

1. _____ : No _____ | Maybe _____ Yes _____

by _____ if I would_____

_____

2. _____ : No _____ | Maybe _____ Yes _____

by _____ if I would_____

_____

3. _____ : No _____ | Maybe _____ Yes _____

by _____ if I would_____

_____

4. _____ : No _____ | Maybe _____ Yes _____

by _____ if I would_____

_____

5. _____ : No _____ | Maybe _____ Yes _____

by _____ if I would_____

_____

Did you check "no" to any of your aspirations? If so, you'll need to find a new *way* to get what you *want* — at least in those areas. Identifying new vehicles to fulfill your aspirations should be a top priority as you plunge into your planning process.

Ah, yes — planning *process*.

There's a big distinction to be made between plans and the planning process, and the best attention-grabber I've seen on the subject is this one:

> *Plans* are worthless, but the *planning process* is priceless!
> General Dwight D. Eisenhower

Ike was one of history's greatest planners and what he said helped me learn an important lesson back in my corporate career.

The lesson? Simply that the fat, impressive-looking binder marked "Strategic Plan" I had placed *strategically* behind my desk, to impress people with the fact that that I *had* a copy, didn't mean diddleysquat. Yes, it contained some important stuff, but most of it was obsolete by the time it was printed.

The *real* value was in the *process* and how much it helped me stay *on course* through all the day-to-day bumps and grinds.

That said, here's how to:

Chart Your Course in 5 Steps

Now that you've given further thought to aspirations, here is an overview of the five-step process through which you can do what very few others are willing to do — develop a *written* career and personal plan that is easy to assemble, follow, and revise.

• *Step 1:* **Write a Personal Mission Statement**

This is the essential starting point if you are to *fulfill* your answer to the first crucial question — *where are you now and where do you want to be?*

Your personal mission should reflect your *purpose* in life which, you'll recall from the MECCA Matrix, was the educational attribute of *motivation*.

• *Step 2:* **Create a Vision for Your Future**

Your vision for the future should paint a vivid word picture of the life you *want* and are willing to *work* for.

A vision for the future should be *evolutionary*, not set in concrete. As the *universe* of your career and personal plan, it should continue to expand and be charted, never leaving you at the dead-end of having done everything with nothing left to do.

While many organizational planners like to start with the

vision and *then* develop a mission, I believe that in life planning it should be the other way around. What sort of future could you envision without first determining your mission or *purpose* in life?

Could fulfilling your vision lead to changing your mission? Of course. And if that happens, the need for — and direction of — such a change will be apparent.

• *Step 3:* **Determine Your Key Objectives**

What are the *major pursuits* in your life that, when accomplished, will enable you to *realize* your vision?

Key Objectives are your highest priorities. They may involve career pursuits, educational achievements, marriage and family, a new hobby — any great pursuit in line with your mission and vision.

• *Step 4:* **Divide Key Objectives Into Personal Goals**

Breaking a major pursuit into manageable pieces is essential to *any* planning, be it in business, in sports, in a church, or in *life.*

Like key objectives, you should prioritize your goals. Which goal is most important? Which ones should be put on hold until which other ones are achieved?

• *Step 5:* **Break Goals Down Into *Do-It!s***

You may need to divide some or all of your goals into even *smaller* pieces if you are to make the most of your planning process.

In doing this, methodology is more important than terminology. You can call them projects or tasks or sub-goals or jobs or activities or whatever you want.

I call these small steps *Do-It!s.* Want to achieve a personal goal? Break it into small pieces and *Do-It! Do-It! Do-It!*

It's Like Assembling Puzzles

To offer a simple example, if you devoted your life to little more than assembling jig-saw puzzles, your five-step planning process could include something like this:

Personal Mission: Enjoy assembling jig-saw puzzles.

Vision for the Future: Five years from now, be recognized as the greatest jig-saw puzzle assembler the world has ever known.

Key Objective No. 1: Assemble the 10,000-piece Rubens "Apotheosis of Henry IV" by the end of this year (starting with...)

Personal Goal No. 1: Make an an initial sort of the pieces by the end of this month (starting with...)

***Do-It!* No. 1**: Find all the edge pieces by the end of this week.

The five planning steps *answer* the fourth crucial question — *how should you chart your course?* The five steps give you a personal planning process that looks like this:

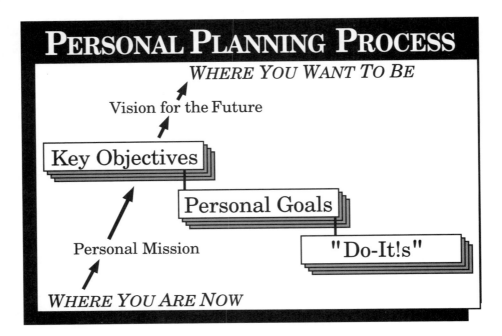

Now take a much closer look at each of the five steps and, one step at a time, develop your plan.

1. Write a Personal Mission Statement

***Words that give direction to your journey through life
in keeping with whom you've chosen to be.***

You'd have a hard time finding a company, non-profit organization or government agency that *didn't* have a mission statement. It may be long or short, simple or incomprehensible, written down or in the founder's head, well-communicated or kept under lock and key — but it's there *somewhere*.

Trying to run an organization without a mission is like trying to drive a car without a steering wheel. The best organizations tend to have the best mission statements — short, powerful, and widely understood both inside and outside the organization.

Organizations need a sense of direction. So do I and so do you. A well-managed organization identifies and communicates direction through a well-developed mission statement. And so should we.

As a child, direction was set *for* you (or *should* have been!). As an adult, you may have found a new direction or may continue according to the direction given to you as a child. Or, you may be among the many who *lack* direction, wandering from one pursuit to another, unable to figure out what they should *make* of their lives.

One of the best reasons for developing a personal mission statement can be found in a great book that has helped *millions* become more successful:

> People can't live with change if there's not a changeless core inside them. The key to the ability to change is a changeless sense of who you are, what you are about and what you value... With a mission statement, we can flow with changes.
>
> Stephen R. Covey
> *The 7 Habits of Highly Effective People*

Covey goes on to say that a mission statement is like your personal constitution. His urging that you develop a personal mission comes as part of a habit he identifies as *Beginning With the End in Mind*. That's where *personal mission* is located in this planning process — at the *beginning*.

A personal mission statement, then, consists of words that give direction at the *beginning* of your personal planning process. It stands as No. 1 in the five-step process, helping to make sense of the other four steps.

Here's another example of how to distinguish among the five steps. Let's pretend you're a team in the National Football League:

1. Team Mission	Win football games
2. Vision for the Future	Win the Super Bowl next season
3. Key Objective No. 1	Get in this season's playoffs
4. Goal No. 1	Win the season's opening game
5. *DO-IT!* No. 1	Score a touchdown on the first drive

The mission identifies what the team is all about. It reminds everyone of what is important and needs to be done on an ongoing basis. The mission need never change.

The vision is what the team realistically could accomplish by a specific time in the future, given maximum attention to the mission.

The other three elements represent the well-organized, step-by-step process to achieve the vision by fulfilling the mission *well*.

Coming up with an effective personal mission statement may not be easy, especially if you haven't given much thought to what your life is (or should be) all about.

Develop a Good First Draft

In my workshops, participants develop a good first *draft* of their missions. I urge them to give their mission statements much more thought before finalizing them.

If you're starting from scratch in this process, don't expect to come up with your mission in life in a few minutes or even a few hours. Take your time. Get it right. Feel good about it. Commit to fulfilling it.

Your mission should be firmly linked to the five personal attributes of the *motivation* imperative:

• **Self-esteem.** Your mission will be greatly influenced by how you feel about yourself and your own potential.

• **Purpose.** Your mission is the *embodiment* of your *purpose* in life. It should reflect why you believe you were placed on this earth.

• *A plan.* You can't develop an effective career and personal plan without first determining your mission.

• *Enthusiasm.* You should be *excited* about fulfilling your mission, and the mere fact of having *identified* a clear mission for your life should raise your overall *enthusiasm* level considerably.

• *Resilience.* Your best defense against the changes and setbacks that are inevitable in life is the *"changeless core within you"* that comes from commitment to a good personal mission. The better the mission and the stronger your commitment to it, the greater your *resilience*.

The Other Core Attributes

Your mission also should relate well to the four other core attributes in the matrix:

• *Self-development.* This is the educational aspect of fulfilling your mission. What you set out to *learn* should be *driven* by your personal mission.

• *Self-discipline.* Your mission probably won't be *easy*. Your level of *self-discipline* will be your primary strength in sticking with your mission and plan, then attaining your vision for the future.

• *Self-confidence.* The higher your *self-esteem, self-development* and *self-discipline*, the greater your level of *self-confidence*. When you *know* you can fulfill your mission, you will fulfill it.

• *Self-fulfillment.* Each day you believe that you are fulfilling your mission in life you are *raising* your over-all level of *self-fulfillment*. The same is true of carrying out your personal plan and working toward your vision for the future.

Characteristics of a Good Mission Statement

What are the characteristics of a good personal mission statement? For the most part, they are the same characteristics found in a good *organizational* mission statement: relevance, succinctness, realism, and emotion.

As employees may be "smitten" by an especially good company mission statement, so it is that you should become *smitten* by your own well-developed personal mission. Accordingly, your mission should be:

S *Short.* Twenty words at most, 15 or less if you can. The shorter it is, the easier it will be to remember.

M *Meaningful.* No empty words. You should be able to know when you're on track and when you stray from your mission.

I *Inspirational.* You should be invigorated by your Personal Mission, maybe even raising a few good goose bumps.

T *Timeless.* You may change it someday, but it should be written as though it will go on forever.

E *Empowering.* Your mission should leave you license to grow and room to grow.

Here are five *drafts* of personal mission statements. How would you rate them? How would you characterize the people who wrote them, based on the "SMITE" guidelines?

Could you improve upon the statements? If so, put pencil to paper and give it a try.

> Instill love, independence and compassion in family and friends so that their lives will also be enriched as they strive for their own missions and goals.

> Assist others in becoming all they are willing to become.

> Lead a life I love by loving myself and others as the human beings they are, achieving fulfillment by encouraging others to realize all the joy that life can provide.

> Just enjoy life.

> Run the family businesses in a way that assures maximum profits and, as a result, the largest possible inheritances for all those entitled to share in the estate.

You may have found one or more of them outrageous, amusing, hollow, uplifting, not all that good, or not all that bad. What's important, though, is to see where five people *started* their efforts and what you might learn as a result.

Here are five mission statements that, after one or more drafts and a lot of reflection, emerged in *final* form. By no means should you consider them "model" statements. They illustrate some careful selection of words and a lot of emphasis on the priorities identified in that all-important second crucial question — *whom do you choose to be for the journey?*:

Emphasis on Having
Attain great wealth in order to enjoy life to its fullest.

Emphasis on Having & Doing
Build my professional practice so I can enjoy a lifestyle commensurate with a seven-figure income.

Emphasis on Doing
Experience the happiness that comes with being the best in all that I do.

Emphasis on Doing & Being
Experience joy and achievement by helping others become successful.

Emphasis on Being
Live a life of love, beauty, joy and laughter with family, friends, and community.

What can you learn from these mission statements? Do they offer some ideas for you? Are you ready to develop your own personal mission statement?

Should you develop a personal mission that embraces all three slices of life—relationships (*Being*), work and other activities (*Doing*), and material wealth (*Having*)? Two of the slices? One slice?

Activity: Using a separate sheet of paper, develop rough drafts of your personal mission statement. When you have checked it against the SMITE Scale and other factors, edit it into a good final draft and write it below:

_____

_____

_____

_____

2. Create a Vision for Your Future

A description of life as you want it to be by a future date, based upon ongoing fulfillment of your personal mission.

For your personal mission to be of value, it must *lead* somewhere. Of what value is a mission unless you see worthwhile results from pursuing it?

Pity those who might identify their mission in life with a single word — *work*. Unless the labor results in something fulfilling or at least meaningful, life's journey is made in Malaisia or somewhere near the bottom of the road map, around Purgatoria or Hades Gulch.

By developing a written statement of your vision for the future, you add *value* and specific *meaning* to your personal mission.

Another term for vision is *dream-building*. Use the full power of such personal attributes as *creativity, interest, judgment, perspective,* and *opportunity* to paint a vivid picture of life as you <u>want</u> it to be, as it *can* be, and as you're willing to *make* it be.

Distinguish between big, realistic dreams and pure fantasies. If you're a person of modest means and average ambition whose mission is simply to enjoy life, your vision for the future should not depict *Lifestyles of the Rich and Famous.* Owning a nice car might fit your vision, but owning a twin-jet private aircraft? Pure fantasy.

On the other hand, if you're *driven* by a willingness to do *whatever it takes* to fulfill your vision, the bigger the dreams the better.

As with the SMITE qualities of a good mission, here are five qualities of a good vision. Create a vision that is GRAND:

G *Growth-oriented.* A vision for your life as it is today is no vision. If you're not growing, you're dying. Envision growth. See *more* in life. *Stretch* yourself!

R *Realistic.* Envision the achievable and, in stretching yourself, what is *conceivable.* Be guided by belief in yourself, not by what others say you can't do.

A *Assessable.* You should be able to measure progress toward the realization of your vision. To be rich isn't enough. Rich in what? *How* rich?

N *Noble.* If the City of Joy is where you desire to be, your vision for the future should reflect the excellence and high ideals that are associated with residency there.

D *Date-specific.* While your mission is timeless, your vision should have a date attached to it, preferably long-term (two years or more into the future).

Vision and Mission in Harmony

Make sure your vision is in *harmony* with your mission. If your mission is simply to make money and have fun, your vision for the future should paint a vivid picture of *how much* wealth you will have accumulated and *what kinds* of fun you will be having by a date two or more years hence.

If your mission is to experience a joy of living by serving God and humankind, your vision is *out of synch* if it depicts wild romps across the beaches of the world.

Here are examples of vision statements based on the *Have-Do-Be* criteria. Note that unlike your mission, there is no need to keep your vision for the future short and, therefore, easy to memorize.

Emphasis on Having

By (date), I will be living in a million-dollar-plus home in an elegant, gated community. My home will have white columns in front and a large, screened pool on expansive grounds adjoining a private lake. I will have developed an income that will enable me to buy an island in the St. Lawrence River as a summer retreat and, for winter, I will have a 60-foot Hatteras motoryacht with twin turbodiesels, full electronics, and custom furnishings, professionally maintained at a private yacht club in the Florida Keys.

Emphasis on Doing

By July 1, (year), I will have completed work on my masters degree and will have become the manager of my department. I will have joined at least two more non-profit boards of directors and will have reduced my golf handicap by at least half. I will have purchased and restored a 1965-67 Ford Mustang convertible and will have all the equipment needed to start a woodcrafting hobby in a shop I will have built next to my garage.

Emphasis on Being

By mid-(year), I will have met and married the right person, settled into a comfortable home near our families and have at least two children, hopefully a boy and a girl. I will have made great progress on the spiritual dimension of my life, including the completion of a major study course on scripture and will have become a teacher in the primary department of our place of worship. I also will have made at least one overseas trip to the Holy Land and, if possible, with my new spouse. Surrounded by many new friends, my spouse and I will have become very focused on helping others live lives that are joyful and productive.

Your vision for the future is more likely to incorporate some elements of all three have-do-be slices. Here's another example of a vision for the future, this one bringing together all three slices:

Emphasis on Having, Doing & Being

By the beginning of (year), I will have earned a masters degree and an executive position with a major company. The income from my new position, combined with my prior savings, will enable me to settle down and start a family. I will find the right person to become my partner in life, possibly by expanding my activities in my place of worship and as a community volunteer. By the time we are ready to marry, I will have the resources for an extended honeymoon as well as a substantial down payment on a home in a good neighborhood where we can raise children.

If you have trouble coming up with a good vision statement,

you're not alone. Many people in these frenetic times find it hard to envision a bright future, achieving great things, or a grace-filled life in the City of Joy. But an old adage (which I've modified to fit) expresses the importance of having both a mission *and* a vision:

> A mission without a vision is drudgery;
> A vision without a mission is sheer fantasy;
> A mission *with* a vision is the road to victory.

Activity: Review your personal mission. Then, using a separate sheet of paper, develop a first draft of your vision for the future. Check it against the GRAND Scale and the other factors just described, then edit it into a final draft and write it here:

_____

_____

_____

_____

_____

_____

_____

_____

_____

_____

Developing a Shared Mission and Vision

Harmony between your personal mission and your vision for the future is important. But harmony is *crucial* between you and a personal planning partner such as a spouse or fiance.

Disharmony in the missions and visions of two people in a marriage is a major reason marriages fail. As I pointed out earlier, the partners undoubtedly never identified *before* the marriage their own missions and visions — then, having made some adjustments to accommodate each others' needs and interests, developed *shared* mission and vision statements.

If you are already married, whether for the first, second, third, etc. time, would it be helpful for you and your spouse to go through this process *together*?

Synchronize Your Life Plans

You may be deeply in love today, but your relationship may become one more divorce statistic if you are unable to synchronize your *life plans*, starting with a *shared* mission and a *shared* vision.

It's quite possible for two people with greatly different missions in life to stay married to each other, perhaps even *happily* married.

For example, one partner may be devoted to acquiring wealth and the other, because of the wealth, may be able to fulfill a mission of helping others. Or, there could be harmony between a homebody who loves to be alone and a person who loves to make a living by traveling all over the world.

Despite accommodation or even harmony between two very different missions, serious problems in a marriage may arise if visions are out of synch.

His Vision	Her Vision
By (date), I will be enjoying life as a socially active New Yorker, living in a luxury penthouse overlooking Central Park...	By (date), I will be enjoying life as a cattle rancher in the Australian Outback totally isolated from the chaos of New York...

Unless, of course:

Our Shared Vision for the Future

By (date), we will lead exciting lives of contrasts, enjoying six months each year in a luxury New York penthouse apartment during the theater season, and the other six months totally "away from it all" as cattle ranchers in the Australian Outback...

Share this process with your planning partner, if you have one. Map out your personal missions and visions, then develop a compatible shared mission statement and a shared vision for the future.

3. Determine Your Key Objectives

Major life pursuits in support of your personal mission and vision, usually requiring months or years of effort.

So far, you've charted your course by developing a personal mission statement that gives direction to your journey through life in keeping with whom you've chosen to be. And, you've anchored your long-term outlook with a vision for the future that describes life as you *want* it to be in keeping with your personal mission.

As illustrated by the personal planning process on page 204, fulfilling your vision requires determining and prioritizing major life pursuits, for which I use the term "key objectives."

Distinguish carefully among your mission, vision and key objectives. For example, let's say you're young and totally focused on a career as a concert pianist.

Experiencing the joy of sharing your gift of music with others is *not* a key objective. Nor is becoming the *world's greatest* concert pianist. Rather, the foundation of your personal plan might look something like this:

Personal Mission
Experience fully the joy of music by sharing with others my gifts as a concert pianist.

Vision for the Future
By 2025, I will be recognized as the world's greatest living concert pianist, having...(describe crowning achievements)

Key Objectives
1. Graduate with highest honors from Julliard by (date).
2. Complete my first national concert tour by (date).
3. Be principal soloist with a leading symphony orchestra by (date).

Many key objectives, evolving over time, would be needed to fulfill the budding pianist's big, long-term vision to be the greatest in the world. Although it's *possible* to map out every objective from now until fulfillment of such a vision, it's better to identify and achieve *nearer-term* objectives — especially those that represent progress toward the vision in the coming year or so.

Hanging target dates on a years-long string of milestones may not be very productive when so many opportunities and setbacks are almost certain to force big changes in direction along the way.

Are You One Dimensional?

In the example, the concert pianist is "one-dimensional" with a personal plan that also has a single dimension. The mission, vision, and key ojectives all center on one thing — music.

That's not the *best* way to live a joyful, fulfilled life, although many of the world's biggest achievers won fame and fortune by being *obsessed* with a single aspect of life.

If you're like me, you'll set key objectives on two or more areas of life. And if you're like I was at one point, you may even succumb to the temptation of setting key objectives in *too many* areas — in other words, going off in too many directions at once.

I agree with those who believe goals should be set in specific areas, even though a single area may be dominant. Consider at least one key objective to help you grow in each of these areas:

1. *Self-improvement* to strengthen your potential for success.
2. *Relationships* with God, family, friends, associates, etc.
3. *Professional* for success in career, business, finances, etc.

Other areas can be added, such as sports and hobbies, but I believe those three to be paramount and in the order listed. Self-improvement (1) paves the way for better relationships (2) and both pave the way for professional success (3).

Consider carefully these three areas in setting your key objectives. Keep in mind, though, that everyone starts a process like this from a different place, some requiring more self-improvement and relationship-building than others.

If your career and life skills already are well-honed and you enjoy very good relationships in all aspects of life, by all means put at the top of your list the key objectives related to professional success and, perhaps, areas such as sports and hobbies.

Always Room for Improvement

But I believe *continuous improvement* should be an important aspect of life and that everyone should have a Key Objective such as *"be a better me"* — whether it's No. 1 or No. 6.

While you may have key objectives not covered specifically by your mission or your vision, none should be *in conflict* with your mission and vision.

Always put key objectives in their order of importance, not the order in which they are to be accomplished. Some objectives may have specific target dates and some may be of an ongoing nature. Example:

Personal Mission

Enjoy a life of professional success and good relationships with family and friends.

Vision for the Future

By (date), I will have at least doubled the size of my professional practice. I will be proud of my role as a loving spouse and parent, and will have helped our sons and daughters get college educations. With the children grown and gone, I will concentrate more on golf, tennis and other recreational pursuits with family and friends. I also will have developed and will be implementing a comprehensive financial plan that will help assure me a secure retirement.

Key Objectives
(For a calendar year)

1. Be a better me.
2. Spend more quality time with my family.
3. Increase net income from my practice by at least 20 percent.
4. Help achieve the next major bonus level in our network marketing business by July 15.
5. Prepare and implement a comprehensive financial plan by May 1.

In this example, the first two key objectives have no target dates for completion. Since key objectives are listed in order of importance, they've been given top ranking and are *ongoing*. They may be carried over year after year.

The third objective is to be achieved by year's end, since the example is based on a calendar year. Specific dates were set for the other two.

Setting key objectives annually is a good way to plan. I like to roll out a fresh set on New Year's Day in place of those traditional resolutions that tend to be widely touted and quickly forgotten.

How Many Key Objectives Should You Have?

If you come up with more than four or five — six at the very most — you're having one or more of these problems:

• *You're getting key objectives confused with personal goals.* Let's say that in addition to (1) make a big career move, (2) get my daughter married off in grand style, (3) finish my doctoral thesis, and (4) be a better me, you also set as your key objectives for the coming year or so to (5) kick my smoking habit, (6) reduce my weight to a monthly average of 20 pounds less than it is today, and (7) develop and stick to a vigorous exercise regimen.

That's *seven* key objectives. The last three are related to your health and would fit nicely as personal goals under a key objective to *improve your health.* Now you have *five,* not seven, objectives.

You could cut the key objectives to *four,* if you put the three health-related goals under "be a better me," since they relate to the <u>motivation</u> and <u>concentration</u> imperatives in the matrix, along with such personal attributes as *self-esteem, enthusiasm* (the umbrella covering energy, health, and wellness), and *self-discipline.*

To go even further, you could cut key objectives to only *three* by also putting completion of your doctoral thesis under "be a better me" since it relates well to strengthening the <u>education</u> imperative.

• *You're trying to go in too many directions at once.* Let's say your key objectives for the new year involve (1) break the all-time sales record where I work, (2) earn an associate degree from a community college, (3) double the net income from my sideline business, (4) help my son become an Eagle Scout, (5) be a better me (you'll need *plenty* of that!), and (6) write a book.

Unless you're super-human, or already have a couple of those objectives nearly achieved, you're going in too many directions at once.

Use the process to set priorities and allow time to assure that you can *achieve* each key objective. Which ones *must* be done this year? Should the book wait until next year? If you're going to have to work a lot of nights and weekends to break the sales record, which is the more important use of remaining time and energy — getting the associate degree or helping your son become an Eagle Scout?

• *Trying to plan too much, too far ahead.*

If you are a 23-year-old newlywed with dreams of an idyllic professional and family life within the next 25 years, avoid the temptation to develop such key objectives as: (1) find a better job in a bigger company by the end of the year, (2) earn a masters degree in biochemistry within five years of joining the bigger company, (3) have at least three children by age 35, etc.

The first objective is the only one that, for the coming year, can be divided into personal goals and pursued effectively.

How could you *plan* for the masters degree that far ahead? By the time you'd be ready to even *start* on the program, you might find biochemistry irrelevant to your career. And how could you *possibly* divide three children into personal goals 12 years in advance?

Use your vision for the future to paint as vivid a picture as possible of future family life and professional achievements, then set key objectives that will get you headed in the direction of your vision. As you update your plan, adjust both the vision and your objectives to stay on course and *keep moving forward.*

Additional Guidelines for Key Objectives

• Aim high to stretch your abilities but not so high that you become overwhelmed. Be sure you are *willing and able* to accomplish whatever you set out to do.

• Make each key objective a single subject. Be wary of the word "and," for a key objective with an "and" in it probably contains more than one major pursuit.

• Set realistic deadlines. Prioritize. Back off deadlines for the key objectives of least importance so you can *tighten* deadlines for those of greatest importance.

• Make sure each key objective has the strongest, most appropriate action verb. *Earn* a masters degree... *Become* a deacon... *Enjoy* a world cruise... *Exceed* last year's sales record...

• State key objectives in *positive* terms — for example, "improve my outlook on life," not "stop having a rotten attitude."

• Make key objectives *measurable.* There must be a clear sense of when and with what degree of success each key objective is accomplished. Either achievement is implicit in the language of the key objective itself, or the key objective is achieved when every one of its goals are accomplished.

• Use clear language. The clearer, more precise the language, the easier it will be to stay on course and carry out your plan.

• Assemble objectives and goals logically. List key objectives in order of importance. List goals under each objective chronologically.

Activity: Review your mission and vision as well as other decisions you've made so far. Then, following the guidelines, draft your key objectives on a separate sheet of paper. *Try to end up with no more than four,* including "be a better me." Edit them carefully, then put them in order of importance and write them in the spaces on the next page.

1. _____

   _____

2. _____

   _____

3. _____

   _____

4. _____

   _____

5. _____

   _____

6. _____

   _____

4. Divide Key Objectives Into Personal Goals

Specific activities which, when accomplished, will result in achievement of your key objectives.

Key objectives can be overwhelming. What may *seem* so desirable and attainable when you draft your personal plan can become a major source of discouragement if you try to achieve it in its entirety all at once. Too easily, you may get the feeling that *"it can't be done,"* so you quit.

Divide each key objective into personal goals. Not only will you make key objectives achievable, but you create a step-by-step process to chart progress. You also should be reinforcing your <u>motivation</u> each time you achieve a personal goal.

How do you eat an elephant? One bite at a time.

Let's say it's the beginning of a new year and you decide to start a part-time business that, within two years, will be producing $2,000 a month in net income.

This will require two key objectives. The first objective, which you can map out right away, will be to find the right business opportunity. The second objective, to build the business, can be stated now but must be developed later in line with the nature of the business you find.

You don't want to grab the first "opportunity" that comes along, but you *do* want to move methodically and quickly, making the best decision in the shortest time.

217

Here's how you might state your key objective and divide it into personal goals:

Key Objective
By May 1, launch a part-time business with high long-term income potential that will net at least $2,000 per month within two years.

Personal Goals
1. Determine and commit to writing exactly *why* I want to have the business and what I wish to gain from it. By Jan. 15.
2. Decide the maximum amount of time and money I would be able to invest in the business. By Feb. 1.
3. Develop a list of business opportunities that could meet my criteria. By March 15.
4. Select the best business opportunity based on a thorough examination of the options. By April 15.
5. Launch the business. By May 1.

You have set the basic criteria for your business venture by *clearly wording* the key objective. You're looking for something that is part-time, has good long-term income potential and should produce at least $2,000 a month in net income by the end of its first year.

Your key objective? *Launch* the business by May 1. You've divided the effort into five manageable personal goals.

Your first goal is a starting point too-often overlooked when planning. You're asking yourself, loud and clear, a very *powerful* question: *"why should I do this?"* Lack of a strong reason is an underlying cause of failure in many business ventures.

Apply the 3 'W' Words
Remember the three most important words in planning anything? Of the *11 Words for Winning*, they're the "W" words that pose three questions — (1) what do I _want_? (2) what's the best _way_ to get it? (3) what's the _work_ involved and to what extent am I willing to do it and do it well?

In this example, your *reason* to put time, money, and effort into something *has* to be based on something you _want._ Decide the *why*, then decide the *how* — the best _way_ to get what you _want_ and the _work_ that will be required.

Your second personal goal brings you face-to-face with additional criteria for your key objective. You want $2,000 a month by the end of the second year. Fair enough. But what are the *outer limits* of the time and money you could invest?

If you're nearly flat broke and have bad credit, it's obvious that buying a $250,000 franchise is not an option. And if you're already working 70 hours a week, "part-time" should be closer to 10 to 15 hours a week than 25 to 30.

Developing a good list of opportunities fitting your criteria (the third goal) is no easy task. Nor is making a final selection based on having thoroughly investigated the two or three choices that appear to be the best (the fourth goal).

So, you have developed five personal goals in chronological order and will focus on them one at a time, doing your best to meet or beat the deadlines you have set for yourself.

The fifth goal is due for completion on the same day as your key objective. In this case, when the last of your personal goals is accomplished, you've also achieved your key objective.

Activity: Practice the process by choosing one of the key objectives you wrote on page 217. Use a separate sheet of paper to draft up to five personal goals to achieve it. When you're satisfied, write the key objective and the goals that support it in the spaces below. Be sure to put the goals in order of their due dates (By ____). In this exercise, the due date on the last personal goal should once again be the same as the due date on the key objective.

Key Objective # _____ : _____

_____ By _____

Personal Goals

1. _____

_____ By_____

2. _____

_____ By_____

3. _____

_____ By_____

4. _____

_____ By_____

5. _____

_____ By_____

5. Break Personal Goals Down Into *Do-It!s*

Specific day-to-day tasks that will result in achievement of your personal goals.

A quick recap:

You determined what you _want_ out of life by answering the

crucial questions and developing your personal mission and vision for the future. You outlined the _way_ to get what you _want_ by identifying major life pursuits called key objectives. And, you learned how to manage key objectives by breaking them down into personal goals.

With the _want_ and the _way_ identified, all that remains is the make-or-break tough part — the _work_. No matter what or how much you _want_ and no matter how good may be the _way_ you found to get it, you _will not succeed_ without doing the _work_!

Like everyone, you don't plan to fail. And, surely now, having come this far, you're not failing to plan!

The important first step in doing the _work_ is to complete your personal plan by reducing each personal goal to the small, bite-size pieces I call _Do-It!s_.

It is those small, day-to-day tasks that will determine whether you achieve your personal goals and key objectives and, ultimately, whether you fulfill your personal mission and make your vision for the future a reality.

The more you break your plan into small, manageable pieces, the less likely it is that you will become overwhelmed, discouraged and give up on the pursuit.

> Nothing is particularly hard if you divide it into small jobs.
> Henry Ford

Suppose, for example, that what you _want_ more than anything else in life is warm, loving companionship. The _way_ to have it, you decide, is to get married.

The problem is that you know of no one you would want to marry — and all your life you've been very shy around members of the opposite sex.

So you might line up your first key objective and personal goals something like this:

Key Objective
1. Get married by (date)

Personal Goals
1. Develop a prioritized list of specific qualities to look for in a spouse. By (date).
2. Overcome my shyness, becoming good at meeting people. By (date).
3. Identify and prioritize specific places, events, and people through which I could meet prospects with the qualities I'm looking for. By (date).
4. Meet prospective marriage partners and begin dating regularly by working my list of places, events, and people. By (date).
5, 6, 7, etc.

Well, I won't attempt to identify Personal Goals 5, 6, 7, etc. because, at this late stage, I don't want to turn *11 Words for Winning* into a romance novel. But let's take a look at the first four goals and see whether or how they could be broken into bite-sized *Do-It!s*.

• *Goal No. 1.* Listing the qualities of a prospective marriage partner could be done in a single step with no *Do-It!s* required. Or, it could involve steps such as getting advice from shy people who now are happily married, interviewing marriage counselors, etc.

• *Goal No. 2.* There are many ways to overcome shyness and this goal could be broken down into many *Do-It!s*, including books, tapes, courses, counseling, joining Toastmasters — whatever.

• *Goal No. 3.* This one's ripe for research from a variety of sources or getting some single and married friends together and brainstorming a list in a single sitting.

• *Goal No. 4.* A separate *Do-It* for each place, event, or person to talk to probably would work best. The *Do-It!s* should be lined up and tackled in priority order.

It's the 'Little' Things

If you're pursuing a "get married" key objective, have put together a good plan, and *still are single* 10 years later, is it because your _want_ (key objective) was "bad" or that your _way_ (personal goals) was all wrong? No, it's probably because you never did the _work_ as identified through those all-important *Do-It!s*.

Maybe there was a book you were supposed to read but you didn't *Do-It!*. Maybe there was a great singles group you were supposed to join but you didn't *Do-It!*. Maybe you signed up for a public speaking course to help overcome shyness, attended a session or two and "chickened out" — so you really didn't *Do-It!*.

Failure to attend to the *little* things can undermine even the greatest of plans.

A little neglect may breed mischief: For want of a nail the shoe was lost, for want of a shoe the horse was lost; and for want of a horse the rider was lost.

Benjamin Franklin
Maxims, *Poor Richard's Almanac*

You can achieve *anything that's possible* if you plan it in small, *Do-It!*-able pieces; then, apply to each piece your full powers of the five MECCA imperatives and *just go out there and Do-It!*.

Do-It!s will make or break your entire personal planning process. As words on paper, your plan is of little value. But your planning process will be of *tremendous* value when you continually improve it, consistently act upon it, and constantly accomplish those little *Do-It!s*.

Let's use self-improvement efforts as an example of how to

organize a key objective into personal goals, then into *Do-It!s*. The time frame is a calendar year. Each goal relates to a personal attribute from the MECCA Matrix, and is shown in parentheses.

Key Objective # ____ : Be a better me.

> **Goal # 1:** (*Organization*): Implement a system that will help me make much better use of time. By May 15.
> > ***Do-It! # 1:*** List at least 10 payoffs for making better use of my time. By Jan. 21.
> > ***Do-It! # 2:*** Find the best seminar, course or other program to increase my time-management skills. By Feb. 1.
> > ***Do-It! # 3:*** Complete the training program. By April 1.
> > ***Do-It! # 4:*** Implement the process in a way that will work best for me. By May 1.
> > ***Do-It! # 5:*** Get feedback from peers to confirm that I am managing time better. By May 15.
>
> **Goal # 2:** (*Knowledge*): Expand my access to information that is important to my career. By Sept. 15.
> > ***Do-It! # 1:*** Join a professional association. By Feb. 1.
> > ***Do-It! # 2:*** Attend the association's trade fair. On March 26.
> > ***Do-It! # 3:*** Buy a computer modem. By Aug. 15.
> > ***Do-It! # 4:*** Select the best on-line network and subscribe to it. By Sept. 15.
>
> **Goal # 3:** (*Self-Esteem*): Reduce weight to a monthly daily average of no more than 150 pounds by June 30 and hold weight to 150 or less for the rest of the year.
> > ***Do-It! # 1:*** Average 160 or less. By Jan. 31.
> > ***Do-It! # 2:*** Average 158 or less. By Feb. 28.
> > ***Do-It! # 3:*** Average 156 or less. By March 31.
> > ***Do-It! # 4:*** Average 154 or less. By April 30.
> > ***Do-It! # 5:*** Average 152 or less. By May 31.
> > ***Do-It! # 6:*** Average 150 or less. By June 30.
> > (Keep it off with monthly *Do-It!s* to be at 150 or less)
> > ***Do-It! # 12:*** Average 150 or less. By Dec. 31.

Note the due dates. Always list *Do-It!s* in chronological order. Under each personal goal, try to achieve one *Do-It!* before tackling the next *Do-It!*.

In other words, achieve each personal goal *one step at a time*.

Activity: Choose one of the personal goals you wrote on page 219. Use separate paper to break it into *Do-It!s*. When you're satisfied, write them on the next page as an example. Be sure the due date on the last *Do-It!* is the same as the due date on the personal goal.

Goal # _____ : _____

_____ By_____

Do-It!s

1. _____

_____ By_____

2. _____

_____ By_____

3. _____

_____ By_____

4. _____

_____ By_____

5. _____

_____ By_____

If you're a very organized, highly detail-oriented person, you may feel the urge to break a *Do-It!* into even *smaller* pieces. If so, simply call them "tasks" and organize them in due-date order. And if that's *still* not enough detail, break tasks into "sub-tasks."

Put Your Personal Plan Into Action

Are you involved in *organizational* planning? If so, you know that the only thing worse than not having a plan is having a *good* plan that's sitting on a shelf someplace gathering dust.

Whether its an organization's plan or your personal plan, a plan will be of no value unless it's put into action and kept fresh and dynamic through an action-oriented *planning process*.

Here are five steps to putting your personal plan into action:

• *Step 1:* **Finish developing your plan**

You've written a personal mission, vision for the future, and key objectives. And you've learned how to break each key objective into personal goals and each personal goal into bite-size, one-step-at-a-time *Do-It!s*. Now finish drafting your plan.

• *Step 2:* **Choose a Format**

Many good planning formats and systems are available, but a specially designed personal planner is available in the format you are working with in this chapter. It enables you to simply copy your plan directly onto pre-punched pages that fit in popular mid-size planners such as FranklinCovey and DayTimer. Information on how to order one can be found in the back of this book.

• *Step 3:* **Coordinate Systems & Eliminate Duplication**
Your personal plan will be broader and longer-term than the daily, weekly and monthly goal-setting tools found in most day-planners or pocket calendars. Keep the elements of your plan together, but use your calendar or day-planner to remind you of your personal plan's due dates as well as for day-to-day appointments and the like.

• *Step 4:* **Stick With the Process!**
You gain the most from your personal plan when you make the *process* a habit. Harness such personal attributes as *enthusiasm, resilience, creativity, self-discipline* and *focus*. Reward yourself when you achieve key objectives, goals, etc. Reset them when you don't.

• *Step 5:* **Update Your Plan Regularly**
Review your personal mission, vision for the future, and key objectives at least quarterly with a major update at least annually. *Continually* update everything else. When a barrier is insurmountable, re-do that part of the plan. Reset priorities to accommodate opportunities. Keep the process dynamic and *flexible*!

> It is a bad plan that admits no modification.
> Publilius Syrus
> *Maxim 469*

And...when all is said and done, there's nothing left to say or do — except the *work*!

Activity: Complete your personal plan. Put it into action. Focus the full force of the MECCA imperatives on your personal mission and vision for the future, and each key objective and personal goal. Then *Do-It! Do-It! Do-It!*

Plan ahead. It wasn't raining when Noah built the ark.

Chapter 10

The Fifth Question:

When Will You Know You've Arrived?

- **5 Measurements to Make —** *Later*
  1. *You're the Person You've Chosen to Be*
  2. *Your Personal Power Is in High Gear*
  3. *You've Charted Your Course Well*
  4. *You're Following Through on a Well-Crafted Plan*
  5. *You're Applying All 11 Words for Winning*
- **Ongoing Support to Engage —** *Now*

Question Five:

It's *not* a question you can fully answer right now. You should come back to it in a few weeks, months, or even years to determine how well you've answered the other four crucial questions and have applied to your life the *11 Words for Winning*.

So I urge you to put your pen or pencil down, read this chapter carefully and pick a date when you'll return to it and rate yourself on whether or to what extent you've "arrived."

Knowing you've arrived is easy when the journey is to visit a loving relative. You know you've reached your destination because of the hugs and kisses, perhaps even tears of joy.

You may have a strong sense of arrival in your career when you're handed the proverbial keys to the executive washroom, or get to drive a company car with leather seats. If you own your own business, arrival may mean the day you're able to turn day-to-day management over to someone you trust.

A *'Spiritual'* Sense of Well-Being

But knowing when you've arrived on *this* journey may not be so easy. The City of Joy, where you live life in a state of grace and be all you can be, defies traditional measurements.

It involves a deep and spiritual sense of well-being rather than a physical sense of reaching a spot on a map or the psychological sense of accomplishing a series of key objectives and personal goals.

"Arrival" means an *enduring* sense of destination — a better place from which you can *continue* life's journey. It means a positive *outlook* on life. It means a new set of attitudes that take you far beyond brief periods of joy and fulfillment.

It means you have developed a powerfully positive attitude that carries you all the way to joy of living and a new zest for life. And, it means life's inevitable periods in Purgatoria and even Hades Gulch will be short-lived, enabling you to return quickly to your "home" at the top of the map.

If the City of Joy *is* your destination of choice, arrival need not wait until all or most elements of your personal plan are accomplished. Like success, joy of living should come as much from *pursuing* worthwhile dreams and goals as *achieving* them.

Avoid a trap that many fall into. Don't use fulfillment of your key objectives or even realization of your vision for the future as a license to stop growing. Develop even *grander* dreams and set even *bigger* key objectives to make your dreams come true.

Keep going! Keep growing!

Like the other questions, No. 5 has five parts, starting with:

1. You're the Person You've Chosen to Be

As you no doubt discovered, the second question (whom do you choose to be for the journey?) is the toughest of the five. But answering it well is very important if you are to develop a strong *internal context* for life's journey — and a firm *basis* for success now and in the future.

As I suggested early on, determining *who* you are now and *who* you want to be isn't a silly navel contemplation exercise. It's just as important as the No. 1 question that establishes *where* you are now and *where* you want to be.

A good self-definition points to how you can *live* your life instead of just working your way past one milestone after another.

> First I was dying to finish high school and start college.
> Then I was dying to finish college and start working.
> Then I was dying to marry and have children.
> Then I was dying for my children to grow up.
> Then I was dying to retire.
> And now I *am* dying and suddenly realize I forgot to live!

Here's a checklist you can come back to later. It will help you determine whether you have answered and applied Question No.2. When you can check all five in the affirmative, you *are* the person you've chosen to be:

_____ Revisiting the victim/victor assessment (page 121), there's no doubt I'm now and will continue to be programmed as a victor.

_____ I have incorporated the five principles of productive thinking into my life (pages 126-127) and have come to believe that my personal happiness depends totally on how I choose to think.

_____ My choices of aspirations, expectations, and entitlements (pages 130-131) not only are realistic, but are heavily weighted *toward* positive and achievable aspirations and *away from* a pervasive thirst for entitlements.

_____ After carefully charting and analyzing my track record on how far I chose to go in the past (page 135-137), I am now able to *love the experience* as well as strive for mastery in my major pursuits.

_____ I have charted my priorities among material wealth (*having*), work and other activities (*doing*), and relationships (*being*), and I am living my life in harmony with those priorities (page 141).

2. Your Personal Power Is in High Gear

The five imperatives easily remembered by the acronym MECCA can help you along every foot of your journey. Use the five to test your capabilities in making career decisions, in strengthening relationships, in achieving your key objectives, and in handling other elements of your personal plan.

Your "personal power" is in high gear when you have eliminated every weakness you identified on your self-assessment (Chapter 8). "High gear" is having every one of those personal attributes on the MECCA Matrix (page 144) identified as a *strength*.

Reinforcing *all* the imperatives and personal attributes on the matrix should be an ongoing, life-long process.

There are some personal attributes in which you have inherent strengths. For example, you may be an outgoing person to whom *association* comes naturally and never has been a problem. It is a strength and always will be.

On the other hand, you are very likely to have some attributes subject to back-sliding. These are attributes that *once were* weaknesses, but that you've now turned into strengths.

Example: Let's say you've been disorganized most of your life but now, thanks to a new system, you see *organization* as a strength. Without ongoing reinforcement, how long will it be until bad habits start creeping back and you become disorganized again?

Keeping your personal power in high gear is important. Identify attributes that could slip back into becoming impediments to your progress.

After you've turned all or most of the attributes into strengths, come back to this page and circle the ones you'll want to pay ongoing special attention to:

Motivation

Self-Esteem   Purpose   A Plan   Enthusiasm   Resilience

Education

Aptitude   **Self-Development**   Creativity   Interest   Knowledge

Concentration

Judgment   Organization   **Self-Discipline**   Perspective   Focus

Communication

Association   Interaction   Relationships   **Self-Confidence**   Recognition

Achievement

Opportunity   Expertise   Influence   Character   **Self-Fulfillment**

3. You've Charted Your Course Well

Your personal planning process (Chapter 9) is the key to turning good intentions into terrific outcomes. Its five elements convert the first three crucial questions into clear direction and specific actions.

One more piece of evidence that you've "arrived" (or are well on your way) is when you can come back and check off each of those first three questions as having been answered well:

1. Where Are You Now and Where Do You Want to Be?

_____ Referring to where I put the dot and the star on the map (page 108), I have crafted my statements of personal mission and vision for the future in ways that have taken me to my star.

_____ I have arrived where I want to be and am living my life in a way *that will help me remain there.*

2. Whom Do You Choose to Be for the Journey

_____ Throughout the development of my personal plan, I have been guided by the five personal choices (Chapter 7) and nothing that I have planned is in conflict with those choices.

3. What Will It Take to Reach Your Destination

_____ The five MECCA imperatives serve me well as a constant reminder of what I need in order to succeed in any pursuit.

_____ Through effective goal-setting and ongoing reinforcement, all 25 personal attributes are now strengths.

4. You're Following Through on a Well-Crafted Plan

Writing and tracking your personal plan on notepaper or the backs of brown paper bags makes tracking, updating, and following through a lot harder than it needs to be.

Select and stick to a well-formatted planning tool, preferably one that can be linked to a good day-planner. Yes, you can develop your own format, but you can save time and headaches by using one that has been well-designed and tested.

The *11 Words for Winning Personal Planner* follows exactly the process shown in Chapter 9. You'll find information about, along with how to obtain a copy, in the back of this book.

Here's a checklist to confirm that you have established and are following a well-crafted plan:

_____ My personal plan has been organized into a good format and is kept up to date.

_____ I have printed my personal mission and key objectives on a wallet card (included in the *11 Words for Winning Personal Planner*). I carry it with me, and I refer to it regularly to help me stay focused on what's most important.

_____ If my personal plan includes *shared* statements of mission and vision, I am working closely with my planning partner for mutual support.

_____ My key objectives are clearly identified, with each divided into personal goals that I am accomplishing persistently and and consistently.

_____ I am making good use of the *Do-It!* process, breaking each of my personal goals, when practical, into manageable pieces and keeping each *Do-It!* before me until completed.

_____ I work on elements of my personal plan day-by-day, review the over-all plan regularly, and do a major update at least annually.

_____ Once each month, or at least quarterly, I assess where I am on the road map, posting a new dot to note a change.

5. You're Applying All 11 Words for Winning

Here's one final checklist. When you can check all 11 items on it, there's no question that you are on a winning course in life and are achieving certain success in our uncertain world.

How many of the 11 can you check now? What changes will you have to make in order to check the others? By when might you be able to come back to the list and check them all?

_____ *Choices*. I make good personal *choices* in all aspects of my life.

_____ *Circumstances*. Good or bad, the *circumstances* that surround me do not deter me in my quest for certain success.

_____ *Outcomes*. I accept full responsibility for handling *outcomes* in my life, never using *circumstances* as excuses for bad ones.

_____ *Want*. I know exactly what I *want* out of life.

_____ *Way*. I have found the best *way(s)* to get what I *want*.

_____ *Work*. I am doing the *work* well and seek ways to do it better.

_____ *Motivation*. I am highly motivated and *stay* that way.

_____ *Education*. I believe in and pursue life-long learning.

_____ *Concentration*. I stay focused on what's most important in life.

_____ *Communication*. I am recognized as a first-rate communicator.

_____ *Achievement*. I am a self-fulfilled achiever who *dreams big*.

Ongoing Support to Engage — *Now*

Life is a journey you cannot make successfully alone. Similarly, a personal planning process is an activity that, at best, would be *very difficult* to undertake alone.

Whether it's the advice of a trusted friend or the active participation of your spouse, putting one or more additional minds to work on your behalf vastly improves your chances of success in your pursuits as well as in your willingness to stick with the planning process and make the most of it.

Getting advice is easy.

> Nothing is given so profusely as advice.
> Rochefoucauld

Getting *sound* advice is another matter.

> Never trust the advice of a person in difficulties.
> Aesop

The key to getting *sound* advice is turning to successful people. Just as you wouldn't seek an important medical opinion from someone who flunked out of medical school, so it is you shouldn't rely on financial advice from someone who is broke, career advice from someone who couldn't hold a job, or marital advice from someone who couldn't make a marriage work.

Even *professional* advisors should be considered with caution. How successful are they *personally* in the fields in which they are advising?

Seek the advice of people who have *done it*. Get second and third opinions when there's any doubt at all. Have a list of people you can turn to for good advice in various areas of your life.

For *ongoing* support of your personal planning process, turn first to the personal involvement of:

A Planning Partner

Your spouse or a trusted relative, friend or business associate actively supporting your planning process.

The best partnerships are between people united in marriage who have an abiding love-based interest in each other's success.

Partnerships also can be very productive outside a marriage, even if the partnership — by design or by circumstance — isn't long-term. What's important is *commitment* to the planning process and that *both* partners gain from it, even if the support given is one-way.

You have established a productive planning partnership when you can check all of the following:

_____ You are comfortable sharing ideas and feelings in an atmosphere of mutual respect and positive reinforcement.

_____ Mutual support between the partners is based on use of a common planning process, avoiding the distractions of having to understand and adapt to different systems.

_____ You hold each other accountable for achieving results from your planning process in a climate of confidentiality and constructive activity. Accountability includes mutually agreeing to specific deadlines for achieving key objectives, personal goals and *Do-It!s*, with praise and celebration for achievements and positive reinforcement for shortfalls.

_____ When support is intended to be a two-way street, you give and receive support in generally equal portions, but with each partner providing extra measures of help when the other has a great need.

_____ You devote the time necessary to making the partnership productive, typically dedicating larger amounts of time to assure development of sound plans — then setting aside shorter periods regularly to fine-tune and track progress.

_____ You help each other find and take full advantage of opportunities and experiences that will result in achieving key objectives and personal goals.

Partnership with one individual can be extended to a *team* of people. In the *11 Words for Winning* process, this is called an:

Empowerment Team

*A mutually supportive partnership of people genuinely interested
in each others' success and willing to help each other
develop and carry out their personal plans.*

You may have close friends who, having similar interests and needs, quite easily could become an empowerment team (E.T.). Or, if you're married, you may know another couple who also could benefit from this process.

Businesses use teams to develop and carry out *organizational* plans. The advantages of individuals doing likewise are:

• Positive peer pressure that comes when a *group* of people hold each other accountable for results.

• A greater diversity of opinions and advisers available to support the planning process.

• Stronger positive reinforcement when elements of a personal plan are achieved and celebrated.

Here are five guidelines for setting up an E.T. and operating it successfully:

1. Keep it small, keep it confidential.
Consider four as the minimum for a good team. Fewer than four denies diversity of viewpoints. Consider 12 to be the maximum. More than 12 spreads individual support too thin and may result in *too many* different viewpoints.

If others like what you're doing and want to join, consider going over 12 until the new people get started, then split into two teams. While the two teams would operate separately, they could get together now and then — especially when successes can be celebrated.

Agree at the outset that what is shared through the process is strictly confidential. What is said in meetings should stay in meetings.

2. Organize it.
Decide who should lead the initial meeting of the team, then develop a clear mission statement. Use this book's definition of an empowerment team as your guide.

Decide how often to meet, when, where and who should be responsible for leading meetings. Consider rotating locations and leadership, giving everyone a turn.

3. Bring planners and other materials to meetings.
Initially, you probably will be helping each other develop plans. Later, the E.T.'s activities will focus on tracking, updating, advising, encouraging, and celebrating success.

Everyone should bring their written plans, day-planners, meeting notes and other helpful materials. Use this book as your primary reference, not only as a guide to the process, but to help spawn ideas and overcome individual problems.

4. Establish a meeting format and stick to it.

Consider these guidelines:

• Members, including the discussion leader, should sit on chairs arranged in a circle or, when possible, at a round table. Everyone should have "equal" seating. Planning partners should sit next to each other.

• Besides the discussion leader, someone *other than* the discussion leader's planning partner should be designated as the meeting's recorder. The recorder's job is to keep track of individual and team commitments, reporting them for followup at the next meeting.

• Establish E.T. traditions such as opening and closing prayers, "high-fives" at adjournment, special recognition for the person who accomplishes the greatest number of *Do-It!s,* a humorous "penalty" for arriving late, forgetting a planner, etc.

• Be consistent with the meeting format. Have each individual or pair of planning partners report progress made and problems encountered since the previous meeting. Achievement of objectives, personal goals and *Do-It!s* should be reported, along with where members are on their road maps.

• Consider using the same seating arrangement at each meeting and rotating the order of who starts the reports.

• Agree to a time limit on reports and strictly observe it. The discussion leader should keep track of time, letting the person speaking know when a minute or two remains and when time is up.

• Include in the meeting format a process I call "SAGA" (Special Accountability for Goals and Attributes). Each person identifies the most important personal goal to be achieved by the next meeting as well as the most important imperative or personal attribute on the MECCA Matrix to be worked on.

• Include results achieved on SAGA items in the opening round of reports at each meeting. Just before adjourning, everyone should make new commitments to report on at the start of the next meeting.

• Between the opening round of reports and the closing round of SAGA commitments, allow time to give extra support for people with special needs, discussion of a specific topic, an audiocassette or videotape, verbal book reviews or, simply, open discussion.

5. Reinvigorate, rejuvenate, renew.

An E.T. should be a dedicated group of people who not only work hard to help each other, but enjoy the process *and* each other's company. Although an E.T. can go on productively and enjoyably for years, there probably will be times when new life needs to be pumped into the team.

Vary the format, help others form a team, get together with other teams, bring in speakers, do whatever is necessary to help people *grow, grow, grow*!

Onward!

I hope you have come up with your own best answers to the first four questions, and will be able to come back soon to this chapter and Question No. 5, answering it with big, bold check marks in every single space.

Then you'll know you've *arrived*, but only in the best place for your joyful journey through life to *continue*.

The only thing greater than the
joy and significance of knowing
***where you are* in life is the**
joy and significance of knowing
***where you're going* in life.**

Conclusion

Keep Going!
Keep Growing!

Closing thoughts:

Winston Churchill is widely misquoted on what is said to be the shortest speech ever given by a major public figure.

Near the end of his illustrious life, Britain's great war-time leader delivered to raptly attentive students at his boyhood school, Harrow, words that are a legacy for generations of winners to follow. Sadly, though, only *half* of what Churchill said is usually quoted.

The aged orator rose with some difficulty, walked slowly to the lectern, adjusted his glasses and intoned brusquely:

Never give in! Never give in! Never! Never! Never! Never!

And then he sat down, the story goes — end of speech.

Well, it *wasn't* the end of the speech, and Churchill's blunt enjoinder has been taken grossly out of context, over and over. What Churchill *really* said was:

Never give in! Never give in! Never! Never! Never! Never — in anything great or small, large or petty — never give in *except to convictions of honor and good sense* (emphasis added).

He was telling us to overcome obstacles and *keep going*, but he also was telling us to *keep growing* and to do what's *right*.

How sad that the *rest* of Sir Winston's famous speech has been lost on so many people. Without considering *convictions of honor and good sense*, Churchill would be telling us to keep doing whatever will enable us to win, even if it's *wrong*.

Honor? Good Sense?

Whatever happened to *honor*? To what extent are even the *greatest* among us today *honorable* people who use *good sense*?

What's happened to *honor and good sense* in the years between Churchill's immortal words and Bill Clinton's immoral deeds?

What did it mean when the President of the United States had yet another in a long line of extra-marital sexual encounters, this time in the Oval Office, looked the world in the eye and lied about it, then refused to resign even after irrefutable DNA evidence?

What did it mean when the president's moral outrage itself was considered "a private matter," impeachment focused on hair-splitting over what constitutes sex, lying, and abuse of power, and the president was acquitted — thanks to *100 percent* of the senators in his own political party saying the charges didn't merit removal?

What did it mean when polls show most Americans wanted the president retained because *"he's doing a good job"* and favored weakening a process by which a president can be held accountable?

To what extent are *anyone's* values and character important any more? Is "right" whatever we can get away with? Are we wrong only when we're caught? Should we be judged not by our *deeds* but by the slippery ingenuity of our *excuses*?

I took it because I needed it.
I took it because I wanted it and couldn't afford it.
I took it because even though I *could* afford it, I wanted to use my money for something *else* I wanted.
I took it because everybody else is taking stuff.

Keep Going & Growing in Values

This book is about winning in life — but not winning by any means and at any cost. It's about winning by *doing what's right.*

Who should we trust to tell us what's right? God. It says so right on every U.S. coin and greenback — *In God We Trust.*

God gave us *The 10 Commandments*, not "The 10 Options Subject to the Latest Spin on Situational Ethics."

I don't believe anyone *really* wins in life by doing what is wrong — not even when achieving right *ends* by wrong *means.* Opportunities abound to cheat one's way to *temporary victories* but, in the final judgment, the victors ultimately are losers, not winners.

Hopefully, then, *11 Words for Winning* says at least as much to you about *values* as it does about *success* by any measure.

The first three words are *The Accountability Factor.* Good, values-based personal _choices_ can override even the worst _circumstances_ and produce winning _outcomes_. And, ultimately, you and I and everyone *will* be held accountable for the _choices_ we make.

The second three words are *The Aspirations Factor* — but to _want_ what is *right*, choose a *right _way_* to get it, and do the _work_ by *right* standards, no matter the temptations to take "shortcuts."

The only place where success comes before work is in the dictionary.
Donald Kendall

I call the other five words *The Action Factor* with the MECCA acronymn representing five imperatives for success in anything. Doing what is *right* also should be implicit in all five — *motivation*, *education*, *concentration*, *communication*, and *achievement*.

Declaring Your Positive Values

Some years back, I felt a compelling need to identify my most important values, sort them out, and commit them to paper. But where to even begin?!?

I decided to start with the simple beauty of the *have-do-be* concept, all three slices of life being of importance to me. The end result hangs on the wall of my office (right under a copy of The 10 Commandments) as a declaration of *boundaries* within which to make my quest for certain success in an uncertain world.

If the *words* work for you, by all means copy and apply them. If not, but if the *concept* makes sense, use it with your own words.

Above all, I am a Human-*Being*.
As such, I choose to:
1. Believe in a Living, Loving God
2. Respect and Do Right by Others
3. Cherish Life
4. Set and Achieve Worthy Goals
5. Keep Growing and Going

My Most-Important Values for Relationships Are:
Love • Loyalty • Humility

But I also need to be a Human-*Doing*.
As such, I choose to:
1. Love What I Do
2. Work with Heart *and* Head
3. Deliver What I Promise — And More!
4. Be Valuable to Others
5. Maintain a Good Perspective on Life

My Most-Important Values for Work and Other Activities Are:
Integrity • Diligence • Common Sense

And, rich or poor, I am a Human-*Having*
As such, I choose to:
1. Meet or Exceed My Obligations
2. Manage Resources Carefully
3. Put Integrity Above Gain
4. Live *Beneath* My Means
5. Share With Others

My Most-Important Values for Material Wealth Are:
Gratitude • Frugality • Generosity

Keep Going and Growing in Faith

As I see it, the biggest reason so many people lack *values* in these times is that they lack *faith*.

They turn to lying, cheating, and stealing, because they lack faith in themselves and others that they can win in life *honestly*.

And they are quick to compromise moral and ethical values because they lack faith in a God who will help them win by doing what's right, and will hold them accountable for doing what's wrong.

They are quick to embrace *hope* as a way to win success and slow to embrace *faith* as a way to win success *and* conquer failure.

> Hope looks for unqualified success; but Faith counts certainly on failure, and takes honorable defeat to be a form of victory.
> Robert Louis Stevenson

We can learn so much from animals that I've come to believe that God put animals on earth to teach lessons to humans.

An impala, for example, can leap 30 feet through the air and reach a height of 10 feet, but won't jump over a wall three feet high. Why? Because an impala can't see over a three-foot wall and will never make *a leap of faith*.

Winning certain success in an uncertain world requires *many* leaps of faith, none of which (obviously) will be made without faith, no matter how great the skill in leaping.

Not long ago, a good friend faxed me the words of an anonymous poet whose definition of faith says it all:

> When you've come to the edge of all the light you know, and are about to step into the darkness, faith is knowing one of two things will happen: either there will be something solid to stand on, or you'll be taught how to fly.

May *11 Words for Winning* help you gain the faith to sprout wings and fly—all the way to *Certain Success in an Uncertain World*.

What *was* isn't.

What *is* won't be.

What *will be* is up to *you*!

A Daily Affirmation

Here's an affirmation to *start* your day and *make* your day, even when things go wrong. Cut it out of the book, copy it, hang it where you'll see it often. Use it every day.

Say these words out loud the moment you wake up. Say them *louder and louder* until you're on your feet, *raring to go*.

When something or someone starts to ruin your day, just smile and say: "AAAMEN!" *You'll* know what it means!

AAAMEN!

I'm **A**live!
I'm **A**wake!
I'm **A**lert!
I'm **M**otivated!
I'm **E**xcited!
and **N**othing

is going to keep me from having a GREAT DAY — because *this is a day the Lord has made* and I will rejoice and be glad in it! (Psalm 118:24)

A Daily Reminder

Here's a recap of the *11 Words for Winning* for you to clip and copy for your personal use.

As you plan each day, review the words carefully. Decide which words will be of greatest importance to fulfill the goals and tasks before you, ever mindful that each new day challenges you to make the best personal *choices*.

---

11 Words For Winning

The Accountability Factor:

Life is a series of personal
1. **Choices** made under the
2. **Circumstances** that surround you leading to
3. **Outcomes** in keeping with the will of God.

The Aspirations Factor:

To make the best choices and get the best outcomes, know exactly what you
4. **Want** out of life, find the best
5. **Way** to get it, and be willing to do the
6. **Work** and do it well.

The Action Factor:

To do the work well, harness the power of
7. **Motivation** to mobilize your *will* to win,
8. **Education** to develop your *skill* to win,
9. **Concentration** to focus on your *way* to win,
10. **Communication** to earn the *right* to win, and
11. **Achievement** to win *certain success*.

About the Author

As a motivational speaker, seminar leader and writer, Tom Ruddell helps people discover true success and make the most out of their lives.

He is the first to insist that life is anything but dull, having been a newspaper editor, radio newscaster, corporate executive, Army National Guard lieutenant colonel, head of a worldwide professional association, and founder of six organizations,

Tom also is the creator of a landmark assessment program for companies and non-profit groups called *The Organizational CATscan®.*

Having caught the entrepreneurial spirit, Tom and Nancy, his wife of more than 36 years, live joyfully job-free in southeast Alabama.

Programs Available

Keynote Presentations

Let Tom Ruddell enrich your event with a lively keynote address or mini-seminar tailoring the *11 Words for Winning* to your audience. Tom uses plenty of audience participation, humor, and hard-hitting realities to provide a fresh perspective on *Finding Certain Success in an Uncertain World.*

e-mail tomruddell@aol.com   or call (334) 673-1644

Seminars and Courses

Qualified trainer-facilitators and teachers are licensed by Capstar Corporation to present the half-day to three-day *11 Words for Winning* seminar using a comprehensive facilitator's manual and Capstar-provided workbooks.

These materials also adapt well for college and high-school-level courses on motivation, goal-setting, and life-skills as well as religion-based training.

Write to Capstar Corporation, P.O. Box 9415, Dothan, AL 33604-1415

Materials Available

Order additional copies of *11 Words for Winning* and associated materials from your favorite book store or Internet provider. Or, to order directly from Capstar, copy and fill out this page.

Your Name _____

Title _____ Phone (____)_____

Organization _____

Address _____

City _____ State _____ ZIP _____

11 Words for Winning (Hard Cover) (20 oz.)
 1 or 2 copies @ $21.95 (Can.$29.95) $_____
 3-9 copies @ $20.00 (Can.$27.00) $_____
 10 or more copies @ $18.00 (Can.$24.50) $_____

11 Words for Winning (Soft Cover) (17 oz.)
 1 or 2 copies @ $14.95 (Can.$19.95) $_____
 3-9 copies @ $12.00 (Can.$16.25) $_____
 10 or more copies @ $10.00 (Can.$13.50) $_____

11 Words for Winning Personal Planner (8.0 oz.)
7-hole punched to fit Day-Timer, Franklin-Covey, and other popular mid-size planners. Includes tabbed divider with road map from Chapter 6, dots, star, wallet cards, and 50 double-sided sheets to set up and track the planning process in Chapter 9.
 1-4 copies @ $13.95 (Can.$18.75) $_____
 5 or more copies @ $12.00 (Can.$16.25) $_____

The MECCA Matrix Self-Assessment & Progress Chart (4.0 oz.)
Colorful rendition of the matrix in Chapter 8 includes red, yellow, and green dots that serve like traffic lights in illustrating strengths, weaknesses, and development needs along with progress toward maximizing the 5 imperatives and 25 personal attributes.
 1-4 copies @ $5.95 (Can.$8.00) $_____
 5 or more copies @ $4.50 (Can.$6.00) $_____

11 Words for Winning Bible References
More than 200 verses from Hebrew Scripture and The New Testament put the *11 Words for Winning* into a biblical context. Ideal for adapting the book and other materials for Christian-based training. Soft cover, approx. 60 pages, available after Aug. 1, 1999.

* Shipping & Handling
Please add $3 (Can.$4) to order of any size for book-rate postal delivery in North America. For other destinations and/or for faster delivery, note weights, add correct amount and specify mode:
_____

Sub-Total $_____

AL orders add sales tax $_____

Shipping & handling* $_____

Total Enclosed $_____

Please make your check payable to Capstar & mail to Capstar Corp., P.O. Box 9415, Dothan, AL 33604-1415